Security Beyond the S

Across the globe, from mega-cities to isolated resource enclaves, the provision and governance of security takes place within assemblages that are de-territorialized in terms of actors, technologies, norms and discourses. They are embedded in a complex transnational architecture, defying conventional distinctions between public and private, global and local. Drawing on theories of globalization and late modernity, along with insights from criminology, political science and sociology, *Security Beyond the State* maps the emergence of the global private security sector and develops a novel analytical framework for understanding these global security assemblages. Through in-depth examinations of four African countries – Kenya, Nigeria, Sierra Leone and South Africa – it demonstrates how global security assemblages effect the distribution of social power, the dynamics of state stability, and the operations of the international political economy, with significant implications for who gets secured and how in a global era.

RITA ABRAHAMSEN is Associate Professor in the School of International Development and Global Studies at the University of Ottawa. She has lectured and published widely on African politics, and is currently joint-editor of the journal *African Affairs*. She is the author of *Disciplining Democracy: Development Discourse and Good Governance in Africa* (2000).

MICHAEL C. WILLIAMS is Professor in the Graduate School of Public and International Affairs at the University of Ottawa. He is a widely recognised scholar of international relations theory and security studies and the author of *The Realist Tradition and the Limits of International Relations* (Cambridge, 2005) and *Culture and Security: Symbolic Power and the Politics of International Security* (2007).

Security Beyond the State

Private Security in International Politics

RITA ABRAHAMSEN

MICHAEL C. WILLIAMS

CAMBRIDGE
UNIVERSITY PRESS

CAMBRIDGE UNIVERSITY PRESS
Cambridge, New York, Melbourne, Madrid, Cape Town, Singapore,
São Paulo, Delhi, Dubai, Tokyo, Mexico City

Cambridge University Press
The Edinburgh Building, Cambridge CB2 8RU, UK

Published in the United States of America by Cambridge University Press,
New York

www.cambridge.org
Information on this title: www.cambridge.org/9780521154253

First published 2011

Printed in the United Kingdom at the University Press, Cambridge

A catalogue record for this publication is available from the British Library

Library of Congress Cataloguing in Publication data
Abrahamsen, Rita, 1966–
    Security beyond the state : private security in international politics /
    Rita Abrahamsen, Michael C. Williams.
        p. cm.
    Includes bibliographical references and index.
    ISBN 978-0-521-76471-1 (hardback) – ISBN 978-0-521-15425-3 (paperback)
    1. Security, International   2. Private security services.   I. Williams,
    Michael C. (Michael Charles), 1960–   II. Title.
    JZ6005.A27 2011
    363.28′9–dc22
    2010035501

ISBN 978-0-521-76471-1 Hardback
ISBN 978-0-521-15425-3 Paperback

Contents

Figures

Preface

The research for this book was made possible through a generous grant from the Economic and Social Science Research Council (ESRC), Grant Number RES-223–25–0074. We are particularly grateful to the ESRC for its support. Special thanks are also due to Stewart Croft as the Director of the New Security Challenges Programme for his continued encouragement and upbeat enthusiasm for the project. The ESRC grant facilitated an intensive two-year period of fieldwork and travel. On our return to Aberystwyth, the Department of International Politics always provided an inspiring and collegial work environment. The Department was our intellectual home for a decade and occupies a special place in our hearts. To our friends, colleagues and students from Aberystwyth: we are forever grateful for your support, your constructive criticism and challenges – and for all the good times along the way!

We also owe thanks to other institutions. The Department of Political Studies at the University of Cape Town kindly accepted us as Visiting Fellows during one of our stays in Cape Town and provided a welcoming and conducive base from which to conduct our research. Very special thanks are due to Neil Walker and the Department of Law at the European University Institute (EUI) in Florence for hosting us during the winter and spring of 2007 and for allowing us the privilege of working in the tranquil and productive surroundings of the EUI. The final stages of the project were completed as Visiting Fellows at the School of Politics and International Studies at the University of Queensland in Brisbane. We could hardly have wished for a more convivial setting in which to finalize the manuscript, and we are very grateful to the School for providing such an enjoyable and intellectually stimulating environment. For the past year, the University of Ottawa has been a welcoming and exciting new institution in which to bring the project to completion. We are very grateful to our colleagues for making it so.

When we started this research, it is fair to say that we did not know quite what to expect. The sheer lack of secondary material and resources meant that much would depend on the ability to conduct primary research and on access to people and places. Many predicted that we would be met with closed doors, with standardized PR statements and with attempts to control information. Our experience has been very different. From company headquarters to local operations in Africa, all the major private security companies (PSCs) and resource companies have granted us access and interviews. The same applies to dozens of national and local security companies in Africa, who generously shared their knowledge and experience with us. In the course of the project we have conducted well over 100 formal interviews, in London; Washington, DC; Brussels; Madrid; South Africa; Nigeria; Sierra Leone; Kenya and Uganda. Others shared their insights and viewpoints with us in more informal settings and casual conversations, on security patrols, at checkpoints and in city streets and bars. There are simply too many names to mention. Others prefer to remain anonymous. Thanks are due to all. We are especially grateful to the people who facilitated our visits to the more inaccessible research sites in Nigeria and Sierra Leone.

In developing our analysis, we have benefited from the comments and insights of numerous audiences and individuals. We have presented the research, at various stages of completion, at countless venues and workshops. Throughout we have learnt from reactions and criticisms and would like to express our gratitude to everyone who arranged or attended these discussions. As newcomers to the discipline of criminology, we also learnt a great deal by participating in the ESRC network 'The Changing Political Economy of Security' organized by Ian Loader and Sarah Percy, where we encountered many of the criminologists whose work has both inspired and enabled us to conduct our own analysis. Finally, thanks to Adam Sandor for compiling the index with great skill and efficiency.

Introduction

'When you think of private security and international politics, what is the first image that springs to mind?' Over the past few years, we have asked this question dozens of times to groups and audiences in numerous countries and contexts. The answers have been remarkably uniform, usually revolving around burly men in combat fatigues, wrap-around sunglasses and automatic weapons. This is no great surprise: the return of mercenary activities in Angola and Sierra Leone in the immediate aftermath of the Cold War and the extensive involvement of private contractors in both Iraq and Afghanistan have justifiably placed corporate soldiers and private military companies (PMCs) at the centre of much public debate and scholarly enquiry.

Yet the growth and impact of private security extends far beyond the spectacular activities of corporate soldiers and the increased involvement of private companies in warfare and military affairs. In almost every society across the globe, private security has become a pervasive part of everyday life, and in many countries private security personnel now outnumber their public counterparts by a considerable margin. Recent decades have also seen the emergence of private security companies (PSCs) that operate on a global scale. The world's largest PSC, Group4Securicor (G4S), is present in over 110 countries, and, with 585,000 employees, it is the biggest employer on the London Stock Exchange. Engaged in the seemingly mundane protection of life and assets – the guarding of workplaces, shopping malls and universities, the monitoring of alarms and closed-circuit televisions (CCTVs), the provision of risk assessment and management – this aspect of security privatization has become so integrated into our daily activities of work and leisure as to go mostly unnoticed. Perhaps for this reason, it is also the untold story of security privatization in international politics.

In shifting the focus away from the battlefields and the spectacular exploits of the private military towards the phenomenal growth and globalization of commercial private security, this book seeks not only

1

to broaden the debate about security privatization in international politics, but also to show that the full significance and impact of contemporary processes of privatization cannot be grasped through a focus on the military sector alone. The routine, commonplace activities of commercial private security belie its importance to contemporary social order, and its expansion is crucial to an understanding of world politics and the shifting politics of protection across the globe. There are indications that these developments are gradually becoming more recognized by policy-makers and in public debate. In his capacity as acting president of the European Union (EU), for example, French President Nicolas Sarkozy observed that 'examining the role of private security in overall security in Europe is a way of looking after the everyday security of European citizens' since 'private security firms are being called upon more and more to assist states in providing this protection.'[1] Similarly, the *New York Times*, in the wake of the attacks on three Mumbai hotels in November 2008, made a direct link between private security and protection against terrorist violence, highlighting the increasing importance of private security in the country. 'In much of India', it informed its readers, 'the first line of defense against crime stands just over five and half feet tall, earns less than $100 a month and is armed with little more than a shiny belt buckle.'[2]

This book traces the phenomenal growth of commercial security globally and examines in detail its operations and impacts in specific settings. This is not simply an empirical enterprise – however important that is. It is also a theoretical and political argument about contemporary politics and world order. By widening the empirical lens to include non-militarized forms of private security we seek not only to capture the full scope of security privatization, but also to situate these developments analytically within broader transformations in social forces both within and between states. In particular, we anchor security privatization within the continually expanding contemporary security agenda and place social theories of globalization and

---

[1] 'Preface from Nicolas Sarkozy, President of the French Republic', in Confederation of European Security Services (CoESS) and Institut National de Haute Étude de Sécurité, *Private Security and Its Role in European Security*, White Paper, December 2008, p. 5.

[2] Heather Timmons, 'Security Guards Become the Front Lines in India', *New York Times*, 3 March 2009, p. A1.

neo-liberalism, commodification, risk and moralization at the centre of our analysis.

This perspective shifts our understanding of private security in international politics in numerous ways. While debates about the private military, especially in the early days, often centred on the challenges such actors pose to prevailing structures of authority, legitimacy and global governance, we show how the growth and globalization of private security is embedded in and inseparable from transformations in national and global governance. Rather than private security eroding the power of the state, or threatening its power and authority, its proliferation is linked to changes inside the state, and its power stems not primarily from the barrel of the gun but from its embeddedness in contemporary structures of governance and its links to public forms of power and authority. These transformations have led to the emergence of what we call *global security assemblages*: new security structures and practices that are simultaneously public and private, global and local. Within these assemblages, state power is certainly reconfigured, but it is not necessarily weakened. Instead, the very distinctions between the public and the private, the global and the local are rearticulated and reworked, giving rise to new practices and forms of power that cannot be neatly contained within the geographical boundaries of the nation-state. Within this new geography of security, various security actors interact in a field of tension, structured by the opposition between the public and the private and their different forms of material and symbolic power.

Global security assemblages connect security practices in different parts of the world in complex relations, exercising important impacts on security in specific sites. Our analysis takes Africa as its focus – a continent that is perhaps more than any other identified in both popular and scholarly imagination with the activities of private security. From early colonial times, Africa has been the playground of private military forces, while in the 1990s the continent provided the theatre of war for Executive Outcomes' (EO's) private soldiers. To date, however, the phenomenal recent growth of non-military private security in Africa has gone relatively unnoticed, as has its connections to global transformations and discourses. Yet the continent provides a prime site for investigating the global dynamics of security privatization, and, perhaps precisely because of its relative weakness within the international system, Africa offers a particularly intriguing opportunity to study the impact of private security on public–private, global–local relations. As a number of analysts have stressed, despite its apparent marginalization by globalization, contemporary Africa is marked by the emergence of new 'transboundary formations' – spaces that defy the neatly defined geographical boundaries of nation-states and that cannot be classified as either local, national or international.[3] By focusing on resource extraction in Nigeria and Sierra Leone, and on urban security in South Africa and Kenya, we show how security provision and governance occur within diverse global assemblages, stretched across territorial boundaries and involving multiple actors, values and discourses. These assemblages have important impacts on the operations of global capital, on the exercise of state power and on who is made secure, insecure, and how. The politics of protection in these specific settings thus reveals not only the extent of global security privatization but also the emergence of new geographies of security and power, with crucial implications for Africa and beyond.

Situating the study of private security

Writing about security in the post-9/11 era of general unease and heightened security concerns is, as Ian Loader and Neil Walker have noted, fraught with difficulties, potential pitfalls and opportunities for misunderstanding.[4] The rhetoric and imperatives of security are seemingly omnipresent in today's society, a fact that is far from always reassuring.[5] Writing about *private* security is perhaps even more difficult and prone to misapprehension. The very idea of private violence stands in a tension-filled relationship to both traditional theoretical conceptions of the state and to deeply held convictions about the proper responsibilities of modern governments, the rights of citizens and principles of democracy. Since the history of state formation is commonly told as the story of the centralization of legitimate violence in the hands of the uniformed agents of the state, its re-emergence

---

[3] See Thomas Callaghy, Ronald Kassimir and Robert Latham (eds.), *Intervention and Transnationalism in Africa: Global-Local Networks of Power*, Cambridge: Cambridge University Press, 2001.

[4] Ian Loader and Neil Walker, *Civilizing Security: Policing and Political Community in a Global Era*, Cambridge: Cambridge University Press, 2007.

[5] Mark Neocleous, *Critique of Security*, Edinburgh: Edinburgh University Press, 2008.

in the hands of private actors almost inevitably conjures images of a return to a pre-modern, darker age: to a neo-medieval condition of fragmented and competing sovereigns and loyalties, or perhaps to the private force of the financial and industrial 'robber barons' of the nineteenth and early twentieth centuries, with their gangs of armed Pinkertons. For the more futuristically oriented, it evokes fears of the post-modern fortified city, a *Blade Runner* world where the rich barricade themselves behind higher and higher security walls and from the designer fortresses that have become their homes observe the outside as an increasingly dangerous space inhabited not so much by fellow humans as by potential intruders, thieves and killers.[6] Internationally, the phenomenal growth of private military actors raises a different spectre – one of shady mercenary activities in far-flung places or, in more sophisticated assessments, of privatized 'corporate warriors' removed from democratic oversight and accountability, allowing the pursuit of corrupt public interests through violent, private means, while intensifying the destabilization and exploitation of already fragile and poor states.[7]

Providing a critical appraisal of the impacts of private security thus inevitably enmeshes us in wider moral and political debates and controversies. Private security inescapably generates strong feelings, and there is little doubt that the effects and implications of the privatization of force need sustained political analysis. The possible abuses that follow from the ability of private actors to wield force, to influence political agendas, to accumulate knowledge and transfer competences away from the public domain and to move decision making outside democratically accountable forums to private offices are key challenges of our times. It is all the more serious then, that there is a relative dearth of empirical investigations of security privatization, especially outside the industrialized world and in the non-military

---

[6] For a striking example, see Mike Davis's well-known treatment of Los Angeles in *City of Quartz*, London: Verso, 1990; and for one of the most nuanced and insightful studies in this area, Teresa Caldeira, *City of Walls: Crime, Segregation and Citizenship in São Paulo*, Berkeley, Calif.: University of California Press, 2001.

[7] For particularly useful treatments, see Deborah Avant, *The Market for Force*, Cambridge: Cambridge University Press, 2005; Abdel-Fatau Musah and J. Kayode Fayemi (eds.), *Mercenaries: An African Security Dilemma*, London: Pluto, 2000; and Peter W. Singer, *Corporate Warriors: The Rise of the Privatized Military*, Ithaca, NY: Cornell University Press, 2003.

sphere. As a consequence, the field has been wide open to speculative
and impressionistic generalizations. Captured in a seemingly endless
repetition of recycled, second-hand evidence from a limited number
of cases and with conclusions that often reflect a priori reasoning
rather than sustained empirical research and theoretical reflection,
the impact of commercial security, especially in the developing world,
has frequently been subject to a peculiar combination of caricature
and disregard. This has, in turn, impeded critical appraisal, both theoretically and politically, with preconceived notions of good and bad
clouding a comprehensive engagement with the social world. In this
book, we adopt a less explicitly normative starting point, focusing
instead on power and transformations in contemporary social and
political forces. In doing so, we seek both to elucidate the implications
of security privatization for the issues of equality, accountability and
violence and to demonstrate how the current empowerment of private
actors is deeply enmeshed in broader political processes. Coming to
terms with these processes, we argue, is an indispensable element in
any cogent political and normative appraisal of private security and
its global impacts.

   A key starting point for such an analysis is the historically constituted division between the public and the private, and the way this
has been reflected in the study of international politics and security. As Patricia Owens has recently commented, 'IR [International
Relations] has not been very good on the history and theory of the
public-private distinction or at conceptualizing how force is constituted transnationally.'[8] Part of the reason for this lies in the fact
that distinctions between public and private and inside and outside
are both submerged within and foundational to the discipline of
International Relations and the study of security, in much the same
way as the relationship between the public, the private and security
can be seen as constitutive elements of both modern sovereignty and
the international system.

   In very broad terms, the evolution of modern sovereignty was
defined by an increasingly clear distinction between private and

[8] Patricia Owens, 'Distinctions, Distinctions: Public and Private Force',
   International Affairs 85 (5) (2008): 977–90; p. 988. Throughout this book,
   we follow the convention of using 'International Relations' when referring to
   the field of study and 'international relations' when referring to the domain of
   international affairs.

public violence. As part of this process, the private right to wield force and settle grievances through violence was gradually delegitimized and instead monopolized in the hands of public authorities. The very constitution of a 'private' sphere was thus in important ways made possible by the removal of the control of violence and coercion – what we today call 'security' – from private hands into the 'public' or political domain. While there is little doubt that historically the state's monopoly of violence has always been, in Janice Thomson's formulation, the exception rather than the norm, it remains the case that the public nature of protection – of equality before the law and equal protection by officers of the law – is (in theory) among the most important constitutive principles of the modern state and conceptions of sovereignty, and one of the key markers and tests of legitimacy in modern politics.[9] The division between the inside and the outside, or the domestic and the international, emerged alongside these historical processes and embodied a range of liberal democratic values ranging from the general exclusion of the military from domestic politics, to the traditional distinctions between justice within and beyond state boundaries.

It is no exaggeration to say that, generally speaking, the study of security has reflected (and helped reproduce) these boundaries, with the 'inside' the domain of criminology and criminal justice studies and the 'outside' the sphere of war appropriated by International Relations and its sub-field of security studies.[10] In turn, these divisions have not only come to guide analyses and perceptions of what is important and what is not, but also to reify the public and the private, the internal and the external as natural and fixed categories rather than historically and politically constituted ones. That said, it is crucial to recognize that while constructed, these distinctions are far from being simply a set of abstract theoretical devices or disciplinary divides. Notions of public and private, inside and outside are embedded in many of the most powerful institutional and conceptual expressions of modern sovereignty, as well as in deeply held political values. The public–private–security relationship is part of powerful

---

[9] Janice Thomson, *Mercenaries, Pirates and Sovereigns: State Building and Extraterritorial Violence in Early Modern Europe*, Princeton, NJ: Princeton University Press, 1994.

[10] The classic treatment here is R. B. J. Walker's *Inside/Outside: International Relations as Political Theory*, Cambridge: Cambridge University Press, 1992.

institutions and practices – it has concrete effects through its role
in structuring understandings of (and controversies over) the place
of private security and actions that follow from them. Frequently
expressed concerns about the erosion of previous boundaries between
the public and private force, as well as between internal and external security agencies, such as the increasing role of the police in
international issues and the military in domestic security, illustrate
both the deeply political nature of these divisions and their practical
importance. Moreover, as we show in this book, the designations of
public and private, global and local, also constitute important forms
of power that actors employ in their struggles for influence within
security assemblages, and as such cannot be simply abandoned as
irrelevant or anachronistic.

Understanding contemporary private security and its globalization
thus requires not only an appreciation that these boundaries are historically constituted, but also a rather more difficult engagement with
the ways that they are embodied in modern political institutions and
practices. As Owens nicely puts it, this is 'a joint task for historical
sociology and international political theory'.[11] Sociologically, we need
to capture not only the historical relationship between public and private force, but also the new social forces and rearticulations of the
public and private that are part of the striking resurgence of private
security. Theoretically, we need to explore how specific articulations
of the public–private–security relationship are constitutive features
of modern liberal politics and the international system, and how they
too are being influenced, challenged and rearticulated through contemporary processes of security privatization.

This means that we need to think of security within categories that
can retain the continuing salience of the public–private and national–
international divides, while at the same time locating them within
wider social transformations in order to see how their shifting con-
figurations reflect and influence how power is organized and legitimated in different historical periods and political settings. A logical
place to begin this enquiry is with the state itself. The idea of the state
as defined by its monopoly of legitimate violence remains central to
political analysis, and nowhere is this more clearly illustrated than in
studies of private security, where Max Weber's famous definition of

[11] Owens, 'Distinctions, Distinctions', p. 988.

the state in these terms rarely fails to make an appearance.[12] Essential and illuminating as this may be as a starting point for analysis, too narrow a vision of the state's monopoly on violence risks becoming a hindrance, leaving only the options of seeing private security as a straightforward erosion of the state or as delegation by a state whose monopoly and power remain essentially unaltered. As the best analyses of private security have argued, and as we try to demonstrate in the following chapters, the transformations involved are more complex than can be captured in these alternatives and hence require correspondingly multi-layered concepts.

Pierre Bourdieu's variation on Weber's famous formula is helpful in this regard. For Bourdieu, the difficulty with many contemporary appeals to Weber's vision of the state is that unlike Weber himself they too often present the monopoly of legitimate violence as equivalent with or reducible to physical coercion. By contrast, Bourdieu argues that while this form of coercion was essential to state formation, it was only one aspect of a process of concentration that included symbolic and cultural power. Framing this point within the analytic categories of capital and field, he thus argues:

The state is the *culmination of a process of concentration of different species of capital*: capital of physical force or instruments of coercion (army, police), economic capital, cultural or (better) informational capital, and symbolic capital. It is this concentration as such which constitutes the state as the holder of a sort of meta-capital granting power over other species of capital and over their holders ... It follows that the construction of the state proceeds apace with the construction of *a field of power*, defined as the space of play within which the holders of capital (of different species) struggle *in particular* for power over the state ...[13]

If we take this as a starting point, the question becomes not whether the state is gaining or losing sovereignty via private security actors, but how its place and relationship to other actors in a field of power is shifting and how, in the process, state power itself is reconfigured.

---

[12] H. H. Gerth and C. Wright Mills (eds.), *From Max Weber: Essays in Sociology*, Oxford: Oxford University Press, 1958.

[13] Pierre Bourdieu, 'Rethinking the State: Genesis and Structure of the Bureaucratic Field', in George Steinmetz (ed.), *State/Culture: State Formation after the Cultural Turn*, Ithaca, NY: Cornell University Press, (1999): 53–75; pp. 57–8.

Historically, it is clear that the public–private distinction has always reflected particular relations of power at particular moments in time and that 'private' force has long played significant roles in public security. The use of a wide variety of private force for the task of 'public' policing was, for instance, widespread in Europe until the latter decades of the nineteenth century. The same was true in the United States of America (USA), where the activities of one of the most famous – and in some eyes infamous – commercial private security firms, Pinkerton's, provided investigative, coercive and arrest capacities on railways across the country. For a time, the company even policed substantial parts of the city of Chicago, and its often violent role in the suppression of labour disputes in the early part of the twentieth century continues to colour perceptions of the politics of private security today.[14]

The use of private force was also central to imperial expansions and serves to illustrate how different public–private articulations have long been part of global power structures. In the colonies, private force was perhaps even more prevalent than in the metropoles, and the connections between private and public force equally complex. Policing was a central aspect of strategies of imperial domination, but it often bore little resemblance to the idealized public monopoly of legitimized violence associated with the modern state. In fact, imperial rule in Africa and Asia generally relied extensively on private forces, as well as on a range of indigenous structures, chiefs and more or less invented 'traditional' rulers for various policing and security tasks. The British South Africa Company of Cecil Rhodes, for example, had its own paramilitary, mounted infantry force, while later during the colonial period commercial companies such as the Sierra Leone Selection Trust, a subsidiary of De Beers, employed a private police force of thirty-five armed men to protect its diamond concession in the Kono area. Similarly, the first recognizable police force in Kenya was private, in the sense that it was set up by the East Africa Trading

---

[14] On Pinkerton's, see Frank Morn, *The Eye that Never Sleeps: A History of the Pinkerton's National Detective Agency*, Bloomington, Ind.: University of Indiana Press, 1982. For the history of private security, see Les Johnston, *The Rebirth of Private Policing*, London and New York: Routledge, 1992. On the emergence of the police, see Lucia Zedner, 'Policing before and after the Police: The Historical Antecedents of Contemporary Crime Control', *British Journal of Criminology*, 46 (1) (2006): 78–96.

Company (later the Imperial East Africa Trading Company) in 1896. The company had an armed security force, recruited predominantly among the Indian police and watchmen, and the force was governed by Indian police statutes.[15]

Militarily, too, private violence often played crucial roles in the emerging world system. Privateering or piracy was an integral element of early modern commercial, as well as military, competition.[16] The imperial commercial activities of the Chartered Companies involved the use of extensive private force throughout the seventeenth and eighteenth centuries; by 1782, for example, the English East India Company's armed force outnumbered that of the British Army at the time, consisting of over 100,000 British, German, Swiss and Indian soldiers. The expanding European empires relied substantially (and in some cases primarily) on forces that were neither 'national' nor 'public' in the sense that we understand these terms today, with a variety of local forces or 'indigenous mercenaries' central to the wielding of force and the maintenance of imperial authority.[17] As Tarak Barkawi has shown, the mobilization of foreign imperial soldiers, especially from the nineteenth century onwards, enabled European powers to project their military power across the globe. Thus, state formation and the concomitant centralization of force in many imperial European states was achieved in the context of a wider international organization of force that was not only imperial but also quasi-private in character.[18] Indeed, as a number of analysts have recently stressed, appreciating the role of this 'foreign' and often 'private' force in the evolution of European states puts the colonial world at the centre of

---

[15] Anthony Clayton and David Killingray, *Khaki and Blue: Military and Police in British Colonial Africa*, Athens, OH: Ohio University Press, 1989; see also David Anderson and David Killingray, *Policing the Empire: Government, Authority, and Control, 1830–1940*, Manchester: Manchester University Press, 1991.

[16] William H. McNeil, *The Pursuit of Power: Technology, Armed Force and Society since A.D. 1000*, Chicago, Ill.: University of Chicago Press, 1982; Thomson, *Mercenaries, Pirates and Sovereigns*.

[17] See G. J. Bryant, 'Indigenous Mercenaries in the Service of European Imperialists: The Case of the Sepoys in the Early British Indian Army, 1750–1800', *War in History*, 7 (1) (2000): 2–28; Victor Kiernan, *Colonial Empires and Armies, 1815–1960*, Stroud: Sutton, 1998.

[18] Tarak Barkawi, *Globalization and War*, Oxford: Rowman & Littlefield, 2006.

the evolution of modern states and the interstate system rather than at its margins.[19]

For the purpose of our analysis, three broad, methodological points emerge from this brief discussion of the historically constructed and political character of both the domestic–international and public–private distinctions. First, the significance and impact of security privatization cannot be captured through the lens of a public–private opposition but requires instead the recognition of how these distinctions are being reconfigured into networks and practices indicative of new relations of power. Since security privatization crosses the domestic–global divide, it demands a political sociology that cuts across boundaries but which at the same time remains cognizant of the important constitutive features of the divisions between the national and the international. Thus, in much the same way that Robert Cox once suggested that in order to grasp the emerging structure of world politics, studies of international relations needed to move beyond their concentration on a system of states to look at the broader relationship between 'social forces, states and world orders', the study of private security requires a focus on the reconfiguration of the relationship between the public and the private, the global and the local.[20] Our approach in this book seeks to show how global security privatization reflects transformations in both the developed and developing worlds, and the connections between them. By locating our empirical investigation in advanced industrialized countries and on the African continent, we seek to break with the conventional inside–outside distinction and move instead towards seeing the global as 'one analytical field', connected by a multitude of mutually constitutive relationships.[21]

Second, the study of contemporary global private security calls for a more interdisciplinary approach. The present-day globalization of private security activities cuts across conventional disciplinary

[19] See Tarak Barkawi and Mark Laffey, 'The Postcolonial Moment in Security Studies', *Review of International Studies*, 32 (2) (2006): 329–252; Barkawi, *Globalization and War*; Owens, 'Distinctions, Distinctions'.

[20] Robert Cox, 'Social Forces, States and World Orders: Beyond International Relations Theory', *Millennium*, 10 (2) (1981): 126–55.

[21] Laura Ann Stoler and Fredrick Cooper, 'Between Metropole and Colony: Rethinking a Research Agenda', in Fredrick Cooper and Laura Ann Stoler (eds.), *Tensions of Empire: Colonial Cultures in a Bourgeois World*, Berkeley, Calif.: University of California Press, 1997, pp. 1–57.

boundaries of criminology and International Relations and demands that we confront the complex questions of bringing these usually disparate fields of enquiry into closer connection. As John Braithwaite has commented with reference to criminology, 'the intellectual tools of the discipline are of diminishing relevance to the social world that is now emerging.'[22] The same can be said for International Relations and political studies approaches that take a strict divide between inside and outside as their starting points. Instead, new perspectives and methodologies are needed to capture the reconfigured security field within global security assemblages.

Finally, methodologically, adopting a less state-centric perspective allows us to see how transformations in security governance in the North have been essential in creating the conditions for the emergence of private security firms with expansive global capacities. Neo-liberal economic policies and ideologies have been key aspects facilitating the expansion of security services in both national and global markets, and the same forces have also informed and spurred the transformation of developing societies and states in ways that make them more open to, and in need of, private security provision. In developing this global analysis, we are acutely aware of the dangers of generalizing about private security. As we will show, its spread, dynamics and implications vary widely. Yet we do believe that grasping the specific articulations of contemporary security privatization requires locating it within wider dynamics and shifts in social forces. These dynamics and forces are not identical: the factors driving security privatization in the USA or Western Europe clearly differ in many ways from those operating in Kenya or Sierra Leone, but they are not wholly disconnected. In short, grasping the emergence of global security assemblages requires analyses that are simultaneously global and local and that treat public and private as relational, not opposed, categories.[23] Our analysis is thus at once a call for broad-based theorization and specific empirical exploration.

Accordingly, this book investigates private security at the point where the global is inserted and translated into the local. Our

---

[22] John Braithwaite, 'The New Regulatory State and the Transformation of Criminology', *British Journal of Criminology*, 40 (2) (2000): 222–38; p. 222.
[23] Barkawi and Laffey, 'The Postcolonial Moment', p. 349.

analysis is based on research in Kenya, Nigeria, Sierra Leone and South Africa, drawing on over 100 formal interviews and even more numerous informal conversations. In each country, we interviewed representatives of the main global and local PSCs, the public police, government officials and private security clients. We also spent time at the specific locations discussed in Chapters 4 and 5, enabling us to observe at close hand the interactions between private security agents and state security actors, as well as the relationship between private security and the local population. This research was supplemented by interviews in the United Kingdom (UK), the USA, Belgium and Spain, with chief executive officers (CEOs) and directors at PSC headquarters, representatives from a range of regulatory authorities, industry associations, government ministries, development organizations and major oil companies. As will become clear from our theoretical and empirical discussion, the private security sector is not only vast but also immensely varied. Hence, while we are all too aware that our findings are inevitably specific, we hope that our theoretical approach offers a wider framework of analysis for understanding the broader dynamics of contemporary global private security.

An overview of the book

In Chapter 1, we begin by detailing the untold story of security privatization in international politics. We argue that the tendency to treat security privatization as synonymous with the private military – what we term the mercenary misconception – has led to both an empirical neglect of the expansion of commercial private security and to analytical and political assumptions that prevent a full appreciation of the sources and implications of contemporary privatization. We discuss three dimensions of the mercenary misconception. First, the causal explanation centred on the end of the Cold War and military rationalization, which cannot alone account for the rise of commercial PSCs. Second, the tendency in literature on non-state actors in global governance to treat private security as illicit, illegal and immoral, which results in a specific blindness towards the activities of PSCs and their connections to wider structures of global governance. Third, we question Africa's prominent yet radically underinvestigated status in many accounts of security privatization, suggesting that against the background of a 'dangerous' Africa where private security is portrayed as rampant, the norm of the Western state's monopoly of violence is reconfirmed, even as that norm is being reconfigured in the West itself. We conclude the chapter by providing an overview of the key companies and market dynamics, stressing the centrality of commercial private security in securing what Zygmunt Bauman has termed 'liquid modernity' – the flows of deterritorialized elites and the boundaries of the excluded.

Chapter 2 situates the expansion of private security within today's pervasive security agenda and the broader transformations in governance associated with late modernity. Drawing on a range of treatments in criminology and sociology, we show how the rise of private security reflects shifts in social forces that long pre-date the end of the Cold War. In particular, we focus on the rise of neo-liberalism in the 1970s and 1980s, the evolution of new attitudes towards crime, punishment and responsibility, and the increasing commodification of security and emergence of risk mentalities. Domestically, these developments have led to a substantial pluralization of security actors and the proliferation of national and international market opportunities that have in turn been key drivers of the transnationalization of PSCs. The net result is that across the globe a host of different actors, including PSCs, are being enlisted in various forms of security or policing partnerships, marking a shift from police to policing, so that it no longer makes sense to think about the public police as the sole provider of security. This perspective shows that rather than representing a threat to, or diminishment of, state power and authority, security privatization is part of a reconfiguration of the public–private distinction and a restructuring of the state. Despite numerous sophisticated treatments of these developments in criminology, their global ramifications have yet to be fully elaborated, in large part because criminological analyses remain overwhelmingly tied to the territorial state. Thus, after discussing attempts to analyse security governance within states, we turn in Chapter 3 to the task of developing an analytical framework for understanding the security field in what we term global security assemblages.

The first element of our analysis in Chapter 3 draws on recent theories of globalization, assessing the relationship between the restructuring of the national state and global transformations. From this perspective, globalization should not be understood as a process whereby global forces erode state power from the outside; instead, changes within the nation-state are crucial to the development of global structures and relations. Specifically, we argue that security privatization is part of a wider process that Saskia Sassen has characterized as the partial 'disassembly' of the state and the concomitant emergence of global assemblages that link national and global structures and give rise to new security institutions and practices that simultaneously cross the national and global, the public and private.[24] The second part of the chapter seeks to outline a conception of power that can capture the relations and practices of actors within global security assemblages. To this end, we turn to the sociology of Pierre Bourdieu and explore how his concept of fields of practice helps reveal the different forms of power available to actors within new transnational security fields. Thus, while the terminology of global security assemblages captures the 'unbundling' of territory and authority, the Bourdieuian perspective allows us to retain an appreciation of the continued power, both materially and symbolically, of state security and its varied relations to private actors. At the same time, it allows us to connect the local and the global and to overcome the neglect of power that plagues many discussions of global governance.

While Chapter 3 is predominantly conceptual, Chapters 4 and 5 turn to investigate specific global security assemblages. Globalization is not a uniform process, and, by the same token, the transformations that have occurred in the security field differ across time and place. As such, our approach calls for grounded theory and an appreciation of how the global is produced in actions that are by definition localized.[25] Africa provides an excellent place to examine these dynamics, given its prominent status in the literature on military privatization, the pervasiveness of commercial private security on the continent and also the salience of global actors in the continent's new forms of deterritorialized governance. Chapter 4 explores the role and influence of private security in the traditionally controversial settings of resource enclaves. While this issue has received considerable attention in its connections to the so-called neo-mercenary activities of companies such as EO in Angola and Sierra Leone throughout the late 1990s, we

---

[24] Saskia Sassen, *Territory, Authority, Rights: From Medieval to Global Assemblages*, Princeton, NJ: Princeton University Press, 2006.

[25] See Marilyn Strathern, *Shifting Contexts: Transformations in Anthropological Knowledge*, London and New York: Routledge, 1995.

argue that in many contemporary enclaves PSCs draw their power not primarily from the barrel of the gun, but from transformations in global governance and their interactions with public security structures. Looking at the role of private security in the oil industry in Nigeria and in diamond and rutile mining in post-conflict Sierra Leone, we analyse the role and impact of private security actors within these global security assemblages. We show that although resource extraction is located in spatial enclaves in both countries, these enclaves are institutionally and normatively embedded within broader structures of global governance and public authority, with significant implications for the politics of protection and for state sovereignty.

In Chapter 5 we turn to the role of private security in the provision of everyday security in urban settings, an issue that is gaining increasing importance as we enter the 'urban century' when for the first time in history the majority of the world's population live in urban areas. As a wide range of analyses have argued, cities are prime sites for the breakdown of global and local distinctions, and new forms of public–private relations are emerging in the field of urban security governance. Focusing on two highly insecure African cities – Cape Town and Nairobi – we discuss the very different impacts and dynamics of private security within urban global security assemblages. In Cape Town, the emergence of a commercialized and formalized public–private policing partnership has led to an arrangement whereby the world's largest PSC – G4S – plays a prominent role in policing the public space of the city and where relatively tightly integrated public–private, global–local security structures have an important impact on political power and state legitimacy. In Nairobi, a highly insecure urban environment is marked by intense competition between the public and the private security sectors, as well as within the private sector itself. In both cases, the politics of protection cannot be contained within the boundaries of the nation-state, and private global actors are deeply implicated in struggles over economic development, social exclusion, elite privilege and human security – thus revealing the intricate political economy of privatized security.

The final chapter seeks to grapple with a number of the theoretical and political challenges presented by global security privatization. Describing global security assemblages as *boundary fields* that lie between the commonplace distinctions of public and private, global and local, we discuss some of the implications of global security privatization for security governance, the state and the possibilities and conditions for political struggles. Private security, we suggest, is not only crucial to an understanding of global security governance but also provides a particularly useful window for understanding the complex contemporary relationship between productive and coercive (or governmental and sovereign) power. While global security assemblages can be seen to represent a normative narrowing, privileging particular security logics and limiting the possibilities for political debate, the very nature of their global reach also provide a domain of action where claims can be made about rights, community and politics.

1 | *The untold story: the globalization of private security*

Spurred by the apparent return of mercenary activities in Africa at the end of the Cold War, and given further impetus and urgency by the substantial involvement of private military contractors in Afghanistan and Iraq, the privatization of security has become one of the most controversial issues in contemporary international politics. Once obscure companies such as Blackwater, Triple Canopy and Erinys have joined with tales of 'neo-mercenaries' such as EO in Sierra Leone and Simon Mann's attempted coup in Equatorial Guinea to become the focus of widespread journalistic coverage, popular books, TV dramas, Hollywood films and increasingly sophisticated scholarly analysis.[1]

Yet the privatization of security and its consequences go well beyond the activities of mercenaries and the corporate military. Away from the battlefields, in the day-to-day activities of ordinary life, private security has also become ubiquitous. Less spectacular than the 'return of the dogs of war', commercial private security activities, ranging from manned guarding and alarm installation to risk analysis and surveillance, have expanded at a phenomenal rate. Worldwide, the commercial private security market is valued at over $139 billion, and its growth is forecast to continue at an annual rate of 8 per cent to reach a value of $230 billion in 2015.[2] Indeed, what was once

---

[1] In an ever-expanding list, see Stephen Armstrong, *War PLC: The Rise of the New Corporate Mercenary*, London: Faber and Faber, 2008; Madelaine Drohan, *Making a Killing: How and Why Corporations Use Armed Force to Do Business*, Toronto: Random House, 2003; Adam Roberts, *The Wonga Coup: Guns, Thugs, and a Ruthless Determination to Create Mayhem in an Oil-Rich Corner of Africa*, Washington, DC: Public Affairs Publishers, 2007. Amongst a spate of memoirs, see James Ashcroft, *Making a Killing*, London: Virgin Books, 2007; and Bob Shepherd, *The Circuit: An Ex-SAS Soldier's True Account of One of the Most Powerful and Secretive Industries Spawned by the War on Terror*, Basingstoke: Macmillan, 2008; For television dramas, the BBC's *Coup!*, and for films, *Blood Diamonds*. We discuss the extensive scholarly literature in subsequent sections.

[2] Securitas, *Annual Report 2007*, Stockholm: Securitas, 2007, p. 13.

described by two prominent criminologists as a 'quiet revolution' in security provision has become global in scope.[3]

A whirlwind tour of the globe demonstrates the point: in the UK, private security personnel now outnumber the public police by a ratio of nearly two to one, and between 1951 and 2001 total employment in the sector increased from 66,950 to 161,013.[4] In the USA, the ratio of private security personnel to public police is almost three to one. As the largest private security market in the world, the USA has between 1.5 million and 2 million private security personnel, while in Japan the sector has grown from employing 41,146 guards in 1972 to 459,305 in 2003, generating revenues of $30.6 billion.[5]

In Russia, the formal private security sector exploded following its legalization in 1992: within a year, there were 4,000 PSCs, and by 1999 the figure stood at 6,775, not including 4,612 in-house security operations. The number of personnel licensed to carry firearms had risen to 196,266, and the sector as a whole was estimated to exceed 850,000 employees.[6] In Bulgaria, as many as 9 per cent of all employed males are estimated to be engaged in private security activities, with the industry's 130,000 personnel standing in sharp contrast to the country's 28,000 police officers.[7] The expanding economies of Asia echo this trend: in India, the private security sector employs about 5.5 million people, 1.3 million more than the country's combined police and armed forces. The Indian sector has an estimated value of $2 billion, it is the country's largest corporate tax payer and is expected to

---

[3] Clifford Shearing and Philip C. Stenning, 'Modern Private Security: Its Growth and Implications', in Michael Tonry and Norval Morris (eds.), *Crime and Justice: An Annual Review of Research*, Chicago, Ill.: Chicago University Press, 1981, pp. 193–245.

[4] Francesco Mancini, *In Good Company: The Role of Business in Security Sector Reform*, London: Demos, 2006; Trevor Jones and Tim Newburn, 'The United Kingdom', in Trevor Jones and Tim Newburn (eds.), *Plural Policing: A Comparative Perspective*, London and New York: Routledge, (2006): 34–54, pp. 41–2.

[5] Mancini, *In Good Company*; Peter K. Manning, 'The United States of America', in Jones and Newburn, *Plural Policing*, pp. 98–125, p. 103; Naoko Yoshida and Frank Leishman, 'Japan', in Jones and Newburn, *Plural Policing*, pp. 222–38, pp. 226–7.

[6] Vadim Volkov, *Violent Entrepreneurs: The Use of Force in the Making of Russian Capitalism*, Ithaca, NY: Cornell University Press, 2002.

[7] Philip Gounev, 'Bulgaria's Private Security Industry', in Alan Bryden and Marina Caparini (eds.), *Private Actors in Security Governance*, Berlin: Lit Verlag, 2006, pp. 109–28.

grow at approximately 25 per cent a year, while in Asia's other economic giant, China, the number of guards is expected to grow from 3 to 5 million in the next five years.[8]

In most Latin American countries too, private security officers outnumber public police, especially in the continent's mega-cities. Overall, there are approximately 1.6 million registered private security employees on the continent, with probably a further 2 million working informally or illegally.[9] In Mexico, there are as many as 7,000 PSCs employing 200,000 guards, with about half of these working the streets of the capital, Mexico City. In Brazil, the Federal Police estimated the sector to be worth $4.5 billion in 1998, including approximately 1,200 companies employing 400,000 registered agents. A study conducted at the end of 2001 concluded that in the state of São Paulo alone, there were 1,300 legal companies, employing 330,000 guards with 255,000 firearms; in addition, there were an estimated 5,000 unregistered, illegal PSCs, employing approximately 600,000 guards.[10] On the African continent, South Africa is home to the largest private security market in the world measured as a percentage of GDP, with over 6,000 companies employing 375,000 active officers.[11] In other countries, exact statistics are hard to come by, but in Nigeria there are between 1,500 and 2,000 PSCs, and in Kenya some 2,000 companies employ approximately 48,000 people. In Uganda, the number of private guards equals that of police officers, and in many other African countries private security is one of few sectors of employment growth and expansion.[12] Tellingly in this

[8] Timmons, 'Security Guards Become the Front Lines in India'; Jody Ray Bennett, 'India's Private Security Metamorphosis', *ISN Security Watch*, 27 November 2009; Ann Petrie, 'Top Security', *Business Voice*, April 2008, pp. 34–8. On China, see People's Daily Online (2006) 'China to Beef Up Security Guard Services for Beijing Olympics', 20 September, available at http://english.peopledaily.com.cn (accessed 24 June 2010) and (2006) 'Security Service Market Ready to Open to Private, Foreign Investors', 21 September, available online at http://english.peopledaily.com.cn (accessed 24 June 2010).

[9] Mark Ungar, 'The Privatization of Citizen Security in Latin America: From Elite Guards to Neighbourhood Vigilantes', *Social Justice*, 34 (3/4) (2007): 20–39.

[10] Jennifer Wood and Nancy Cardia, 'Brazil', in Jones and Newburn, *Plural Policing*, pp. 139–68.

[11] Private Security Industry Regulatory Authority (PSIRA), *Annual Report 2008/2009*, Pretoria: PSIRA, 2009, p. 29.

[12] Patrick Keku and Tunde Akinbade, *Industrial Security in Nigeria*, Lagos: Authorhouse, 2003; Francis Wairagu, Jan Kamenju and

regard, G4S is, according to some estimates, the continent's largest single private employer, with a total payroll of 106,605 people across twenty-nine African countries.

As the criminologist Ian Loader has pointed out, the process of privatization marks a significant shift in security provision in modern societies. In his words:

We are living in the midst of a potentially far-reaching transformation in the means by which order and security are maintained in liberal democratic societies, one that is giving rise to the fragmentation and diversification of policing provision, and ushering in a plethora of agencies and agents, each with particular kinds of responsibility for the delivery of policing and security services and technologies. What we might call a shift from police to policing has seen the sovereign state – hitherto considered focal to both provision and accountability in this field – reconfigured as but one node of a broader, more diverse 'network of power'.[13]

Loader's astute observations are essential to thinking about the shifting nature of contemporary security. But, as the brief survey above shows, the process he describes goes well beyond liberal democratic societies: it is a global phenomenon, and the 'networks of power' are often transnational.

This is the untold story of security privatization in international politics. Despite the attention private security has received in recent years, the growth and globalization of commercial security has been strikingly absent from most discussions, banished to the sidelines by an overwhelming concern with private military violence and corporate soldiers.[14] To be clear: our argument is not that the focus on

Mwachofi Singo, *Private Security in Kenya*, Nairobi: Security Research and Information Centre, 2004; on Nigeria and Sierra Leone, see Rita Abrahamsen and Michael C. Williams, *The Globalisation of Private Security: Country Report – Nigeria*, Aberystwyth: University of Wales, Aberystwyth, 2005; and *The Globalisation of Private Security: Country Report – Sierra Leone*, Aberystwyth: University of Wales, Aberystwyth, 2004.

[13] Ian Loader, 'Plural Policing and Democratic Governance', *Social and Legal Studies*, 9 (3) (2000): 323–45, p. 323.   ·

[14] In an extensive and increasingly sophisticated literature on this topic, see Avant, *The Market for Force*; David Isenberg, *Shadow Force: Private Security Contractors in Iraq*, New York: Praeger, 2008; Christopher Kinsey, *Corporate Soldiers and International Security*, London and New York: Routledge, 2006; Anna Leander, 'The Power to Construct

military privatization is wrong, or that it is unimportant – far from it. The difficulty is that the understandable concern with these developments has led to a neglect of the breadth of security privatization and, perhaps more importantly, to a general disregard of how its growth and globalization is linked to broader transformations in national and global governance. At this point in time, it is paramount to expand the debate and to build on the important insights raised by the literature on the private military to capture the full picture and importance of security privatization. Thus, while debates over the privatized military, especially in Africa, have often centred on the challenges such actors pose to prevailing structures of authority, legitimacy and global governance, the argument of this book, by contrast, is that the growth and globalization of private security is embedded in, and inseparable from, transformations in governance.

In this chapter we develop this argument through a discussion of what we term the 'mercenary misconception'– the tendency to equate private security in general with the private military and thus obscure its commercial, non-military dimensions from view.[15] This does not imply a critique of specific authors but rather acts as a vehicle for highlighting what can be considered a series of unintended consequences of the focus on private military actors. We examine three dimensions of the mercenary misconception. First, the causal explanation focused primarily on the end of the Cold War and military rationalization, which cannot alone account for the rise of commercial PSCs. Second, the tendency in the literature on non-state actors in global governance to treat private security as illicit, illegal and immoral, which again does not capture the vast majority of activities undertaken by PSCs.

International Security: On the Significance of Private Military Companies', *Millennium: Journal of International Studies*, 33 (3) (2005): 803–26; Musah and Fayemi, *Mercenaries*; Sarah Percy, *Mercenaries: History of a Norm in International Relations*, Oxford: Oxford University Press, 2007a; Singer, *Corporate Warriors*; David Shearer, *Private Armies and Military Intervention*, Oxford: Oxford University Press, 1998.

[15] We are aware that the very term 'mercenary' strikes at the heart of debates over whether contemporary PMCs fit this description. Without wanting to enter into these complex controversies, our simpler point is that their very existence marks off the privatized military from the wider sphere of commercial security companies, where such issues are rarely raised. For a revealing discussion of the former issue, see Sarah Percy, 'Mercenaries: Strong Norm, Weak Law', *International Organization*, 61 (2) (2007): 367–97.

Third, we draw attention to the implications of the mercenary misconception for understandings of Africa and question the continent's
prominent, yet radically underinvestigated status in the literature on
private military activities. We conclude the chapter by providing an
overview of the key companies and market dynamics, emphasizing the
centrality of commercial private security in securing what Zygmunt
Bauman has termed 'liquid modernity': the flows of the deterritorialized elite and the boundaries of the excluded.[16]

The mercenary misconception and the illegal, illicit and invisible

There is little doubt that the increased role of private military actors
poses a series of important challenges for contemporary politics,
including questions of reliability, accountability, democratic control, legitimacy and responsibility.[17] According to many reports, the
ratio of private contractors to US servicemen and women during the
recent conflict in Iraq was approximately 1:10, compared to 1:100
in the first Gulf War, making PMCs the second largest component
of the 'Coalition of the Willing'.[18] Private military contractors have
also come to play an increasing role as part of peacekeeping operations, and as international development assistance has become more
and more concerned with security, they have been incorporated into
a host of reform and training initiatives. Accordingly, companies
such as Military Professional Resources Incorporated (MPRI), Pacific
Architects and Engineers (PAE), Dyncorp and ArmorGroup provide
military advice and training to a number of poor countries, often as
part of broader security sector reform programmes funded at least in
part by development budgets.[19]

---

[16] Zygmunt Bauman, *Liquid Modernity*, Cambridge: Polity Press, 2000.
[17] See the contributions to 'The Mercenary Debate: Three Views', *The American Interest*, May/June 2009, pp. 32–48, particularly that by Deborah Avant; and Paul Verkuil, *Outsourcing Sovereignty*, Cambridge: Cambridge University Press, 2006.
[18] Steven Evans, 'Private Wars Need New Laws', *BBC News*, 10 May 2004; Avant, *Market for Force*.
[19] Kwesi Aning, Thomas Jaye and Samuel Ayobi, 'The Role of Private Military Companies in US–African Policy', *Review of African Political Economy*, 35 (118) (2008): 613–228; Sean McFate, 'Outsourcing the Making of Militaries: Dyncorp International as Sovereign Agent', *Review of African*

Most accounts of the emergence of private security actors in the twentieth century start with the end of the Cold War.[20] Here, the military downsizing that resulted from the end of superpower rivalries is seen as providing both 'push' and 'pull' factors: on the one hand, demobilized military personnel and decommissioned equipment provided a ready supply of capacity; on the other, demand increased as both the West and the East became more and more reluctant to intervene in unstable parts of the globe and abandoned former Cold War allies or clients to their own devices. In the case of Africa, the site of some of the most spectacular private military activities, the end of apartheid and the restructuring of the South African security apparatus provided an added 'push' factor as previously combat-active soldiers from the South African Defence Forces became the main recruitment pool for the PMCs of the 1990s, while higher-ranking officers formed the management of companies such as EO.[21] Often highly trained and with combat experience, South Africans continue to make up a substantial contingent of private security personnel across the globe, including the war in Iraq, despite the South African government's attempt to regulate such activity through the Regulation of Foreign Military Assistance Act passed in 1998.[22]

Although recent analyses have stressed that military privatization cannot be understood in isolation from the shifts and pressures arising

Political Economy, 35 (118) (2008): 645–54. On the use of private security providers in humanitarian operations, see Abby Stoddard, Adele Harmer, and Victoria Didomenico, *Private Security Contracting in Humanitarian Operations*, London: Overseas Development Institute, 2009.

[20] Avant, *Market for Force*; Robert Mandel, *Armies without States: The Privatization of Security*, Boulder, Col.: Lynne Reinner, 2002; Greg Mills and John J. Stremlau (eds.), *The Privatization of Security in Africa*, Pretoria: South African Institute of International Affairs, 1999; Singer, *Corporate Warriors*.

[21] Peter Lock, 'Africa, Military Downsizing and Growth in the Security Industry', in Jakkie Cilliers and Peggy Mason (eds.), *Peace, Profit or Plunder? The Privatisation of Security in War-Torn African Societies*, Pretoria, Institute of Security Studies, 1999, pp. 11–36; Musah and Fayemi, *Mercenaries*.

[22] See Mark Malan and Jakkie Cilliers, *Mercenaries and Mischief: The Regulation of Foreign Military Assistance Bill*, Pretoria: Institute for Security Studies, 1997; Raenette Taljaard, 'Implementing South Africa's Regulation of Foreign Military Assistance Act', in Alan Bryden and Marina Caparini (eds.), *Private Actors and Security Governance*, Berlin: Lit Verlag, 2007, pp. 167–86.

from broader political and economic processes,[23] the end of the Cold War continues to act as the master narrative in most discussions. As a result, security privatization appears linked primarily to the end of bipolarity and military institutions and dynamics, but separate from larger social forces and the economic and political transformations in global and local governance that have underpinned the growth and globalization of commercial security. This is not to say that the end of the Cold War is unimportant, and thus to substitute one explanation for another – indeed, the dawn of unipolarity accelerated the advance of neo-liberal policies and made them almost impossible to resist, especially for African countries. It also facilitated, in important respects, a settlement in South Africa that preserved enough of the old security apparatus for that country to become a leader in the private security industry. In this sense, geopolitics interlace with broader socio-economic transformations, underscoring the need for an explanation of the global rise of private security to incorporate a wider set of factors than those commonly addressed in the early International Relations literature on military privatization.

Identifying these wider shifts and their connections to private actors has of course been the focus of inquiries into the role of non-state actors in global governance. Parting company with the traditional state-centrism of International Relations, this literature points to the manner in which the authority of private actors, be it in public welfare, environmental protection, trade regulation or the fight against poverty, is giving rise to new structures of global governance and novel relations and networks of power, thereby reconfiguring traditional conceptions of statehood and sovereignty.[24] In many ways, this

---

[23] For example, Avant, *Market for Force*, conclusion; Anna Leander and Rens Van Munster, 'Private Security Contractors in the Debate about Darfur: Reflecting and Reinforcing Neo-Liberal Governmentality', *International Relations*, 21 (2) (2007): 201–16.

[24] In a large literature, see, for example, A. Claire Cutler, *Private Power and Global Authority*, Cambridge: Cambridge University Press, 2003; A. Claire Cutler, Virginia Haufler and Tony Porter (eds.), *Private Authority and International Affairs*, Albany, NY: State University of New York Press, 1999; Edgar Grande and Louis W. Pauly (eds.), *Complex Sovereignty*, Toronto: University of Toronto Press, 2006; Richard Higgott, Geoffrey Underhill and Andreas Bieler (eds.), *Non-State Actors and Authority in the Global System*, London and New York: Routledge, 2000; Karsten Ronit and Volker Schneider (eds.), *Private Organizations in Global Politics*, London and New York: Routledge, 2000; Robert Falkner, 'Private Environmental

appears as an ideal vantage point from which to examine global private security, but private security actors are rarely included in these discussions, and, when they are, they often appear primarily as actors standing in opposition to the state and its continuing monopoly of legitimate violence in the security sphere.[25]

In large part, this tendency arises from the association of security privatization with privatized military force, and with mercenaries in particular. In their path-breaking and insightful discussion of non-state actors in global governance, for example, Rodney Hall and Thomas Biersteker argue that while private security actors certainly exercise authority, it should be viewed as 'illicit' authority, discussed and classified alongside mafias and transnational organized crime. Distinguishing between power and authority on the grounds that the latter is recognized and legitimated through norm-based consent, and defining private security as 'private authority associated with organized violence', they argue that 'the form of private authority exercised by mafias and mercenaries' is '"illicit" authority because the activities of these groups violate domestic and international legal norms. However, these groups often enjoy a legitimate social recognition to the extent that they step into a power vacuum left by a weak state and provide public goods that the state fails to provide.'[26] As such, private security actors are cast as illustrations of the pathological aspects of private actors and governance networks and as relatively marginal and illegitimate actors in global governance.

Hall and Biersteker's classification of private security actors as exercising 'illicit' authority draws primarily on a contribution to

---

Governance and International Relations: Exploring the Links', *Global Environmental Politics*, 3 (2) (2003), 72–87.

[25] The absence is both long-standing and revealing. In one of the earliest and most influential treatments, Susan Strange argued that we are witnessing a 'retreat of the state' in finance and production, but not in security – though she was willing to ask whether the latter would also eventually follow suit; see Susan Strange, *The Retreat of the State*, Cambridge: Cambridge University Press, 1996.

[26] Rodney Bruce Hall and Thomas Biersteker, 'The Emergence of Private Authority in the International System', in Rodney Bruce Hall and Thomas Biersteker (eds.), *The Emergence of Private Authority in Global Governance*, Cambridge: Cambridge University Press, 2002, pp. 1–21; p. 16.

the same collection, which discusses the privatization of security in
Africa under the arresting title 'The Return of the Dogs of War?' and
focuses on the privatization of warfare.[27] Nevertheless, a familiar
slippage from the privatized military to *private security* in general
is clearly observable, for example in general references to 'corporate mercenaries and "private" policing'.[28] The result is that private
security in all its forms, not merely the likes of EO, are classified as
actors that can only exercise illicit authority and that can only be
controlled through successful state-building or 'external intervention
and/or policing by transnational public authorities'.[29]

In the immediate aftermath of EO's exploits in Africa, these were
important and understandable concerns. They remain so, but at the
same time it is crucial to recognize that today many of the activities
of private actors in security do not involve mercenaries (or mafias)
in warfare but take place in the very different domain of day-to-day
security provision in non-conflict situations. Moreover, the external policing envisioned to remedy the situation would today most
likely be at least in part outsourced from public authorities to PSCs.
The classification of private security as illicit cannot capture these
contemporary forms and aspects of privatization, as well as many
of the key processes and dynamics fostering the growth of private
security worldwide, since it tends to suggest that private security
actors are intrinsically in conflict with state authority and recognized legal norms. But far from existing in the illicit shadows of
authority, PSCs – whether in the military or the non-military sector – are often directly interlaced with contemporary structures of
authority and legitimacy, both public and private. In fact, as we
discuss in greater detail in Chapter 2, the privatization of security
frequently occurs at the instigation of the state, as part of policies of
outsourcing, cost recovery and efficiency. Thus, far from standing
in inevitable opposition to state authority, or pointing to the necessary erosion of state power and sovereignty,[30] security privatization

---

27 Bernadette Mutheun and Ian Taylor, 'Return of the Dogs of War? The
    Privatisation of Security in Africa', in Hall and Bierstecker, *The Emergence
    of Private Authority*, pp. 183–99.
28 Hall and Bierstecker, 'The Emergence of Private Authority', p. 17.
29 Hall and Bierstecker, 'Private Authority as Global Governance', in Hall and
    Bierstecker, *The Emergence of Private Authority*, pp. 203–22; p. 217.
30 For a reading along these lines, see Sabelo J. Ndlovu-Gatsheni, 'Weak States
    and the Growth of the Private Security Sector in Africa: Whither the African

illustrates instead the emerging imbrication of private and public actors in new security governance structures. In short, in the same way that the causal force assigned to the end of the Cold War fails to capture the relationship between security privatization and broader social and political dynamics, a blanket classification of all non-state security actors as illicit also obscures our understanding of their relationship to contemporary global governance.

A similar view of private security as illicit and marginal colours one of the few analyses of the growing importance of public–private partnerships in International Relations.[31] Given that the expansion of the private security sector is closely linked to shifting relations between the public and the private, it would seem a likely candidate for inclusion in discussions of public–private partnerships. But, yet again, the tendency to regard security privatization as inherently illicit, and to associate it with 'mercenaries' and the privatized military, leads Tanja Börzel and Thomas Risse to treat security privatization explicitly as both marginal and as *outside* the broader legitimated processes of public–private partnerships. In their words:

In rare circumstances, core state functions, such as the monopoly on the legitimate use of force, are delegated to private actors. Many weak Third World governments are no longer able to provide national security for their citizens and have started to contract out military security to private firms such as Executive Outcomes, a modern-day mercenary group. The privatization of security and defence policy, however, appears to be rare and is usually closely scrutinized by other states, including Western powers.[32]

Leaving aside the sweeping over-generalizations and inaccuracies about the impact of security privatization in the developing world, this type of analysis serves to reinforce the invisibility of security privatization. As the brief world tour at the start of this chapter

State', in Sabelo Gumedze (ed.), *Private Security in Africa*, Pretoria: Institute of Security Studies, 2007, pp. 17–38; Michelle Small, *Privatisation of Security and Military Functions and the Demise of the Modern Nation-State in Africa*, London: ACCORD, 2006.

[31] Tanja A. Börzel and Thomas Risse, 'Public-Private Partnerships: Effective and Legitimate Tools of Transnational Governance', in Grande and Pauly, *Complex Sovereignty*, pp. 195–216.

[32] Börzel and Risse, 'Public-Private Partnerships', p. 202.

demonstrates, security privatization is neither rare, nor limited to 'weak Third World governments', where in any case it is only very infrequently outsourced in this fashion – and certainly not to EO, which has been defunct for over a decade. Security privatization and public–private partnerships in the security field are ubiquitous in the modern world – so much so that, far from being 'closely scrutinized' by either Western governments or scholars, they are taken for granted and actively encouraged by many governments and is part of widely adopted policing strategies. The current penchant for so-called community policing, for example, incorporates public–private partnerships of various sorts as part of its key tenets, whereas 'new public management' strategies actively encourage similar initiatives.[33] The former, it is worth noting, is now actively exported to the developing world as part of various development efforts and security sector reform programmes.[34] The notion that the security field is unaffected by the trend towards public–private partnerships is thus not only wrong, but also prevents us from seeing how this field provides ample opportunities for analysing how power and authority are being reconfigured precisely through such technologies of governance.

Lest we be misunderstood, it bears repeating that numerous important insights have emerged from these and many other discussions of military privatization. Moreover, some of the reflections on the relationship between private security and authority inevitably reflect their location in a period when the re-emergence of mercenaries was very much on the public agenda. But, at the same time, there is little doubt that over the years a trend towards conflating military privatization with security privatization per se has emerged, and questions of its origin and legitimacy have overwhelmingly been cast within these parameters. Thus, at this moment in time, much is to be gained from complimenting this existing research with a broader empirical focus and an analytical engagement with social theories of globalization and transformation.

---

[33] Frank Leishman, Barry Loveday and Stephen P. Savage (eds.), *Core Issues in Policing*, Harlow: Pearson, 2000.
[34] See Mike Brogden and Preeti Nijhar, *Community Policing: National and International Models and Approaches*, London: Willan, 2005; and Bill Dixon, 'Globalizing the Local: A Genealogy of Sector Policing in South Africa', *International Relations*, 21 (2007): 163–82.

Africa and the mercenary in the mirror

As is clear from the discussion above, the South, and in particular Africa, plays a prominent part in the literature on security privatization, and the mercenary misconception is particularly powerful in the African context. There are, of course, good reasons for this. Historically, African countries have been the playing fields of the modern mercenary: in the Congo, from 1960 to 1968, French, South African, Rhodesian, Spanish, Italian, British and Belgian mercenaries fought on both sides, while in the Nigerian Civil War, Americans, Germans, Frenchmen, Britons, Egyptians, South Africans and Rhodesians enlisted their services with both the Federal Government and the Biafran separatists.[35] In the brutal Angolan Civil War, as many as 1,000 mercenaries – American, British, Dutch, German, Portuguese and Belgians, to mention a few – were central to the conflict.[36]

When in June 1976 Angola executed three Britons and one American citizen for mercenarism and other crimes, it seemed to mark a decline (but by no means the complete disappearance) of mercenary activities on the continent. Until, that is, the emergence of EO and Sandline International. The operations of these companies in the late 1980s and early 1990s seemed to presage a new lease of life for the private soldier and the 'dogs of war', with African countries, and the developing world more generally, once again becoming their primary arenas. While eager to differentiate their operations from legendary and notorious mercenaries such as Bob Denard and 'Mad' Mike Hoare, the highly publicized military campaigns undertaken by these companies posed serious and far-reaching political challenges, and popular as well as scholarly interest in their operations is easy to understand.[37]

---

[35] S. J. G. Clark, *The Congo Mercenary*, Johannesburg: South African Institute of International Affairs, University of Witswatersrand, 1968; Anthony Mockler, *The Mercenaries*, New York: Macmillan, 1969; John de St Jorre, *The Nigerian Civil War*, London: Hodder & Stoughton, 1972.

[36] Wilfred Burchett and Derek Roebuck, *The Whores of War: Mercenaries Today*, New York: Penguin Books, 1977.

[37] See Guy Arnold, *Mercenaries: The Scourge of the Third World*, Basingstoke: Palgrave Macmillan, 1999; Cilliers and Mason, *Peace, Profit, or Plunder?*; Herbert M. Howe, *Ambiguous Order: Military Forces in African States*, Boulder, Col.: Lynne Rienner Publishers, 2001; Musah and Fayemi,

Today, however, both the prevalence and acceptability of these types of private military operations have declined. It is worth remembering, for instance, that despite its continuing prominence in contemporary discussions, EO's most notorious activities are now well over a decade in the past, and the company itself ceased operations on 1 January 1999.[38] To be sure, the mercenary continues to be part of the private security landscape, but his importance has arguably been exaggerated vis-à-vis other processes of security privatization and the activities of today's PMCs often bear relatively little resemblance to the combat roles so widely associated with events in Angola and Sierra Leone in the last decade of the twentieth century. Instead, present-day PMCs operating in Africa and other developing countries are often contracted by Western donor governments to provide training for local soldiers and police forces, logistical support for peacekeeping operations and a variety of other relief or development-related activities. This is not to say that private armies have gone away, or that the possibility of their intervention in African and other poor countries has disappeared – suffice to mention the botched military coup spearheaded by Simon Mann in Equatorial Guinea in 2004.[39] Nor is it to say that vigilance and critical attention are not needed in respect of the privatized military, or that their new 'corporate' image should automatically bestow legitimacy on their activities. But, in retrospect, the spectacular interventions of EO and Sandline International may well appear more the product of specific historical juncture than an emerging political

---

Mercenaries; Mills and Stremlau, *The Privatization of Security*; Shearer, *Private Armies and Military Intervention*.

[38] Peter Singer argues that EO did not so much close, as globalize, and that its operations continued through numerous 'spin-offs'. While some of the companies Singer mentions have since closed, new ones have emerged, and it undoubtedly remains the case that networks for mercenary recruitment continue to exist. However, Singer's comment that were EO still around and wanted to hire 3,000 men, the town of Pomfret in South Africa would be a ghost town, says less about mercenarism and recruitment networks as such than about the exclusion and radical abandonment of the black Angolan soldiers who fought for the apartheid army. It was, for example, from this town that most of the participants in the failed coup in Equatorial Guinea were hired. Singer, *Corporate Warriors*, p. 118.

[39] For an account, see Roberts, *The Wonga Coup*.

trend, and they differ in numerous ways from the operations of most contemporary PMCs.[40]

There is, then, ample justification for the prominence and concern given to the activities of private security in the South, but the status of Africa in this literature nevertheless merits a degree of suspicion, and it is sometimes difficult to escape the impression that this interest risks contributing to distortive and often sensationalist visions of security situations and the role of private security in these areas. In Africa in particular, a tendency towards sweeping generalization and a failure to distinguish between private military activities and those of PSCs means that discussions seem inevitably to invoke the images of mercenaries, of fragile or failing states, or of resource enclaves defended by private armies armed to the teeth. At the same time, the relative absence of primary research and in-depth analysis means that a handful of examples tend to be recirculated. Prime among these are the interventions of EO, which then become generalized almost beyond recognition until they become synonymous with private security in Africa and developing countries. The slippage from mercenaries and militias to *private security* risks creating an image of private security in Africa and the developing world more generally as inevitably military, violent and uncontrollable.

One result is the creation of an image of private security on the rampage in Africa and in other developing areas. For instance, in his otherwise insightful and well-informed study of the rise of the corporate military, Peter Singer asserts that 'private security is rampant' in Africa.[41] If this is taken to mean simply that security privatization is pervasive on the continent, it is, as we will demonstrate in later chapters, absolutely correct. Given, however, that the focus of Singer's book is on the privatized *military*, such a claim gives the misleading impression that PMCs are running amok all over Africa – an impression heightened by the choice of the word 'rampant', implying a process that is out of control, unchecked, raging, even epidemic.[42]

[40] See Aning *et al.*, 'The Role of Private Military Companies in US–African Policy'; McFate, 'Outsourcing the Making of Militaries'.

[41] Singer, *Corporate Warriors*, p. 11.

[42] While Singer's analysis is focused on the 'corporate soldier', that is, on the military sphere, and a large part of his argument concerning Africa hinges on a discussion of the specific activities of EO, his presentation of private security as 'rampant' has in turn been generalized and reproduced in numerous subsequent accounts by other authors.

Although, as we noted earlier, there is no disputing the existence and impact of private military force in Africa both past and present, many of the more extensive operations of private security on the continent fit uneasily into this category. In Nigeria, the continent's most populous country, for example, foreign participation in the private security sector is restricted by the state, and even in the resource enclaves of the oil-rich Niger Delta the sector is, by law, unarmed. Similarly, in one of the largest and most insecure of Africa's cities, Nairobi, private security is ubiquitous, but it is again by law forbidden from carrying firearms.[43] Thus, while private security is certainly pervasive in Africa at the beginning of the twenty-first century, to identify this with the activities of the private military and the combat-active soldier is not only empirically questionable, but also risks presenting a deeply misleading picture and reinforcing images of Africa as a place of chaos and ungovernability, of 'lesser breeds without the law', as Rudyard Kipling would have put it.[44]

The developing world also occupies a telling place in discussions of security privatization that focus on its local or domestic impacts, where the retreat of the rich to their fortified private security enclaves is often starkly exhibited in rapidly expanding cities.[45] Here, the spatial proximity between the super-rich and the marginalized multitudes gives private security an air of social irresponsibility and political abandonment and also raises important conceptual and theoretical questions concerning its impact in settings where states are no longer able or willing to exercise the range of powers and functions commonly associated with the Weberian state. But in these discussions too, it is often

---

[43] Aspects of the private security sector in Nigeria and Kenya are analysed in Chapters 4 and 5 respectively.

[44] Rudyard Kipling, 'Recessional', in *The Complete Verse*, London: Kyle Cathie Limited, 1990. First published 1897.

[45] See Caldeira, *City of Walls*; Eric Denis, 'Cairo as Neo-Liberal Capital? From Walled City to Gated Community', in Diane Singerman and Paul Amar (eds.), *Cairo Cosmopolitan: Politics, Culture and Urban Spaces in the New Middle East*, Cairo: American University of Cairo Press, 2006, pp. 47–71; on urban segregation in the rich world, see the well-known study by Mike Davis, *City of Quartz*, London: Verso, 1992, as well as Evan Mckenzie, *Privatopia*, New Haven, Conn.: Yale University Press, 1994; Thomas Agnotti, 'A Metropolis of Enclaves: Image and Reality in Urban North America', *Urbana*, 22 (1997): 13–24; and Setha Low, *Behind the Gates: Life, Security, and the Pursuit of Happiness in Fortress America*, London and New York: Routledge, 2003.

possible to discern patterns where casual references to poor countries, built on remarkably little empirical evidence, are employed to support particular narratives where the failed (often African) state stands as the furthest expression of a broader social alienation and communal disintegration caused by security privatization. It should, for instance, give us at least some pause when a well-researched book of detailed local case studies on gated communities in the USA suddenly and seamlessly turns to a brief two-paragraph discussion of Nairobi as an exemplification of extreme fear and urban security enclavism.[46] The claim about the security situation in Nairobi is not incorrect: it is certainly a dangerous city where security is extensively privatized.[47] But these dynamics – and the role of private security within them – call for serious analysis rather than serving as a supposedly cautionary anecdote for a very different society halfway around the world.

In many cases, such discussions posit (or warn of) a downward spiral of social fragmentation, where due to the privatization of security 'society fractures into a world of markets and tribes' as the rich opt out of public provision and the state in turn abdicates its responsibilities.[48] This kind of statement seems so intuitively plausible, and its normative and political consequences so obviously undesirable, that the so-called failed or failing states of the developing world are almost irresistibly attractive as illustrations of the furthest development of security privatization. These are important and difficult issues, but at the same time their very (often a priori) plausibility should be treated with care. There is indeed something strange as well as disturbing about the status of the developing world in general, and Africa in

[46] To wit: 'The fear in Nairobi is palpable. Visiting an old friend from graduate school, I am dismayed to see a rape gate and padlock in front of her bedroom door, as well as gates at the entrance to her house, and a guarded entrance to her land. She lives on the edge of Nairobi, locked and barricaded inside.' Low, *Behind the Gates*, p. 113.

[47] The organization UN-HABITAT rates Nairobi as one of the world's most dangerous capitals: see Aki Stavrou, *Crime in Nairobi: Results of a Citywide Victim Survey*, Nairobi: UN-HABITAT, 2002.

[48] Loader and Walker, *Civilizing Security*, p. 210; see also the publication *Human Security for an Urban Century*, p. 26, co-sponsored by the Canadian Department of Foreign Affairs and International Trade (DFAIT) and the Canadian Consortium on Human Security. Available online at www.interpeace.org/pdfs/Publications_(PDF)/Current_Reports/Human-Security-for-an-Urban-Century.pdf (accessed 24 June 2010). It is not always clear here whether private security is a cause or an indicator of this fragmentation.

particular, in many discussions of security privatization. Too often, as
we have seen, speculation, assertion and abstract theorizing replaces
first-hand evidence, and in a process that Edward Said would surely
have recognized, single case studies or texts become transformed by
repeated citation into generalized truths about security privatization
in the developing world as a whole.[49] Thus, African cities are presented as exemplifying the same dynamics as those in Brazil, or Sierra
Leone's experiences in the 1990s become a template for the continent
as a whole.[50] In the process, many of the normal rules of social science seem almost to be suspended. This lack of primary research and
extensive fieldwork on private security outside Europe, North America
and Australia recalls one of Achille Mbembe's characterizations of
much academic discussion on Africa: 'instead of patient, careful, in-
depth research', he observes, 'there are off-the-cuff representations
possessed and accumulated without anyone's knowing how, notions
that everyone uses but of origins quite unknown – in Kant's well-
known formulation, "groundless assertions, against which others
equally specious can always be set".'[51] This is undoubtedly much too
harsh a condemnation of the research cited above. Yet it remains the
case that in more general discussions and popular imaginations of
private security the simultaneous presence *and* absence of Africa is
salient: the continent is present as a general trope of the failure of
public provision and the dangers of private actors, but absent as a specific investigation of its social reality, extent and consequences. The
question thus arises as to the function of the South or Africa in analysis of security privatization: does it go beyond its ability to elucidate
empirical and theoretical questions, to become a kind of 'unspoken

---

[49] Edward Said, *Orientalism*, New York: Vintage, 1978. For a discussion
   of Orientalism and criminology, see Maureen Cain, 'Orientalism,
   Occidentalism and the Sociology of Crime', *British Journal of Criminology*,
   40 (2) (2000): 139–60.

[50] One of the few detailed empirical studies, Caldeira's analysis of São Paulo
   in *City of Walls* is cited in a remarkable number of discussions of security
   privatization, her impressive text occupying a similar position to that of
   EO in the literature on private military companies – though it is by no
   means clear that many of those who cite her have reviewed her subtle and
   contextualized arguments very carefully.

[51] Achille Mbembe, *On the Postcolony*, Berkeley, Calif.: University of
   California Press, 2001, pp. 7–8.

other' – the unarticulated background that allows certain arguments about the West and about private security more generally?

Historically, of course, non-Western cultures, and Africa in particular, have often existed as the 'other' through which the West constructs its own civilization, enlightenment and progress.[52] Again, in the words of Achille Mbembe, 'Africa as an idea, a concept, has historically served, and continues to serve, as a polemical argument for the West's desperate desire to assert its difference from the rest of the world.'[53] Africa and other areas of the developing world thus frequently appear in discussion in terms of its absences, its lacks and incompleteness, as failed or weak states, as underdeveloped or transitional. In the case of security and private security, Africa figures for its radical insecurity, its lack of order, its ungoverned private security actors and its ungoverned spaces that are now even cast as geopolitical threats in a world of networked terrorism. In this way, Mbembe argues, narratives about Africa are 'always pretext for a comment about something else, some other place, some other people. More precisely, Africa is the meditation that enables the West to accede to its own subconscious and give public account of its subjectivity.'[54] This observation is pertinent to our discussion: in analysis of private security there is at least the possibility that the predominance of a few doomsday scenarios and examples – be they of mercenaries, of private armies or of walled cities and neo-medieval societies – serve as a reminder of what *could* happen. In other words, against the background of a dangerous Africa where private security is portrayed as rampant, the norm of the Western state's monopoly of violence is reconfirmed – even as that norm is being reconfigured in the West itself.

These are tricky questions, and we do not discount the concerns raised by much writing on private security in relation to Africa and developing countries, nor do we dismiss the sociological claims they advance. To be clear, our argument is not that 'all is well in Africa' and with private security – far from it.[55] Yet, the ease with which

---

[52] See, for example, Valentin Y. Mudimbe, *The Invention of Africa: Gnosis, Philosophy and the Order of Knowledge*, Bloomington, Ind.: Indiana University Press, 1988.

[53] Mbembe, *On the Postcolony*, p. 2.

[54] *Ibid.*, p. 3.

[55] We are also conscious that to raise these criticisms runs the risk of sounding like uncritical supporters of the private security industry or appearing

powerful claims about the necessary links between sovereignty and security are juxtaposed to images of privatization and fragmentation and reasserted so as to make the conclusions (analytic, ethical and political) about political instability and possible state collapse seem almost obvious must be resisted. Security privatization in Africa and elsewhere in the developing world is just as complex as in the West. It demands to be studied on its own terms. Indeed, Africa, with its prominent, yet radically underinvestigated status in the literature, is an excellent place to explore the place and politics of private security in contemporary global governance.

Filling in the blanks: the story of security privatization

Given the relative lack of attention that global commercial security has received, particularly in the field of International Relations, a brief survey of its main contours is in order. Perhaps the best place to start is with the vexed issue of definitions. As we all know, definitions are inevitably political; yet social and political analysis requires some degree of specificity in order to be meaningful. In discussing private security the question of definitions looms large, and any attempt at boundary-drawing is fraught with difficulties and subject to possible abuse. This should not, however, serve as an excuse to abandon all attempts at specification, as little is gained by broad-brush analyses that treat all forms of security privatization as the same.

In particular, a complete conflation of private security and private military activities is as unhelpful as it is inaccurate. It is nevertheless common, perhaps because the very existence of private security seems to offend deeply held sensibilities to such an extent that some commentators are prone to dismiss it out of hand as immoral and undesirable. Thus, Abdul-Fatau Musah declares that 'What is known today as "private security" is in effect the logical transformation of traditional mercenary activities into a variety of new forms.'[56] At other times, the conflation seems to arise largely from a lack of awareness about the

---

  sociologically naive or politically reactionary concerning its impacts and
  implications.
[56] Abdel-Fatau Musah, 'Privatization of Security, Arms Proliferation and
  the Process of State Collapse in Africa', *Development and Change*, 33 (5)
  (2002): 911–33; p. 913. The same formulation is repeated in Wairagu *et al.*,
  Private Security in Kenya, p. 17.

range and depth of private security activities, or – in International
Relations in particular – perhaps from the assumption that only international military activities are the relevant concerns of the field, with
the remainder left to law or criminology.

In one of the most systematic attempts to draw a distinction between
the private security and private military sectors, Simon Chesterman
and Chia Lenhardt argue that the term 'private military company'
should denote 'firms providing services outside their home states with
the potential for use of lethal force, as well as training of and advice
to militaries that substantially affects their war-fighting abilities'.
This definition, they continue,

> includes firms engaging in those offensive and defensive operations in low-
> intensity conflicts where there is no clear front line. Semantically, the term
> 'military' better captures the nature of these services as it points to the
> qualitative differences between firms operating in conflict zones in a mili-
> tary environment and 'security firms' that primarily guard premises in a
> stable environment.[57]

There is a good deal of sense in this distinction, and for the purpose
of our discussion the term 'private security company' refers to companies whose main business is in the 'protection of life and assets',
as opposed to support for military activities. But it must be acknowledged that even this broad definition does not fully suffice. While
activities such as guarding, alarm monitoring and cash transportation are key services of the commercial private security industry, there
is no clear dividing line between PMCs and PSCs. Many companies
have contracts in both areas, and PSCs might thus also be involved
in more military-related activities, and vice versa.[58] It would also be
mistaken to assume that the distinction between PMCs and PSCs

---

[57] Simon Chesterman and Chia Lenhardt, *From Mercenaries to Market: The
Rise and Regulation of Private Military Companies*, Oxford: Oxford
University Press, 2007, p. 3. For a sophisticated six-fold categorization
of the sector as a whole, see Les Johnston, 'Glocal Heroes: Transnational
Commercial Security Companies in the 21st Century', paper presented at the
workshop on 'The New Economy of Security', Merton College, Oxford, 3–4
July 2008.

[58] For these reasons, Avant suggests that a focus on types of contracts rather
than firms provides a better basis for categorization. Avant, *The Market for
Force*.

means that the latter do not have the capacity to wield lethal force. This varies not only from company to company but also from country to country. Thus, Group4Securicor officers in Sweden and South Africa are often, but not always, armed, whereas the same company's guards are issued only with batons and whistles in Sierra Leone and Nigeria. However, as we demonstrate in later chapters, even in the highly unstable environments of these two West African countries, PSCs exert a powerful influence on the security field and on the exercise of lethal force, notwithstanding their unarmed status.

Private security actors themselves have clear, if varied, stakes in how their activities are labelled, with all seeking to distance themselves from the tarnished image of the mercenary and others clearly preferring the increased political legitimacy that flows from the designation PSC as opposed to the military image associated with the PMC. For other companies, the process works the other way around, with contracts and recognition more likely to result from being seen as a designated military provider. Definitions then, are not only inevitably political, they also emerge from and reflect concrete practices and are part of struggles between actors in specific security fields, an argument we develop in subsequent chapters.

As the opening paragraphs of this chapter briefly detailed, the non-military dimensions of private security have become ubiquitous features of modern life. The industry's near-universal growth has been accompanied by the development of a global security market, valued at $139 billion.[59] Of this, guarding is by far the largest component, accounting for 47 per cent, with the other main sub-markets being alarms (approximately 30 per cent) and cash-handling services (9 per cent). Geographically, North America and Europe unsurprisingly account for the largest percentage of the global market (70 per cent), but, while annual growth rates here are around 8 per cent, many developing countries are experiencing double-digit growth. As a result, by 2015 it is estimated that so-called 'emerging markets' will account for 35 per cent of a total market forecast to be worth some $230 billion, while Latin America and Asia alone are expected to account for 37 per cent the guarding market, up from 25 per cent today.[60] Given

[59] Securitas, *Annual Report 2007*, p. 13.
[60] *Ibid.*, p. 13.

these spectacular growth forecasts, the main PSCs are increasingly targeting these areas as offering lucrative opportunities.

While the majority of security companies in any one location are likely to be small to medium-sized businesses providing basic manned guarding, the development of a global market has been accompanied by the emergence of powerful global PSCs. The sector has undergone a remarkable process of mergers and acquisitions, resulting in an overall decrease in the number of larger security companies. In 1990, the four largest security companies in Europe had a combined market share of 15 per cent. Today, the three largest companies have 35 per cent. In the USA, the five largest companies accounted for 33 per cent of the total market in 1990, whereas today their market share is 50 per cent.[61] At the same time, the sector has become increasingly specialized. Whereas in the past many PSCs were part of general service companies, the largest companies today market themselves as highly specialized, knowledge-intensive and expertise-oriented providers of 'integrated security solutions' ranging from basic manned guarding, electronic alarms, surveillance, close protection services and assets in transit to satellite tracking and risk assessment.[62] By virtue of their reach, resources and revenues, these transnational companies constitute an increasingly significant presence in international politics and security.

The evolution of the world's three leading security companies illustrates these developments with particular clarity.[63] G4S has achieved its status as the world's largest PSC through a combination of strong organic growth and a series of mergers and acquisitions. Today, the company is present in more than 110 countries and has over 585,000 employees (see Figure 1.1). Its annual turnover grew from £4.5 billion in 2007 to £5.9 billion in 2008 – nearly double what it was in 2004.[64]

[61] Securitas, *Annual Report 2007*, p. 12.
[62] Prosegur, for example, previously ran a temporary employment company, Umano, which was later sold as part of a move to concentrate on security. Similarly, Securicor was at one point part of a much larger general property servicing concern.
[63] The company histories that follow draw on extensive interviews at company headquarters, as well as information from company websites and public statements.
[64] David Fickling, 'G4S Leapfrogs Rival on Revenue', *Financial Times*, 10 March 2009; G4S, *Annual Report and Accounts, 2008: Securing Your*

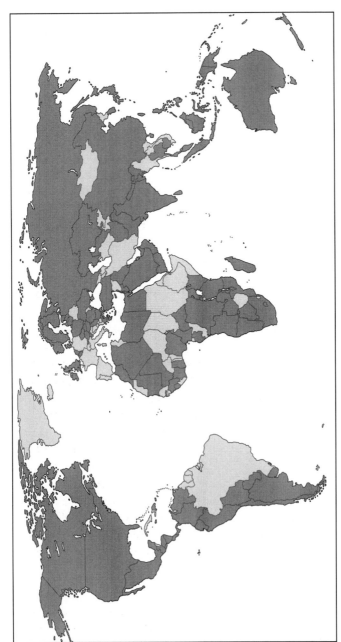

Figure 1.1 Group4Securicor: countries of operations – 'Securing Your World'.

This contemporary security giant has grown from a family-owned business started in Denmark in 1901, when Philip Sørensen and Marius Hogrefe established the guarding company Kjøbenhavn Frediksberg Nattevagt (Night Watch). In the 1930s, the company established a subsidiary in Sweden, and in 1950 the second generation of the Sørensen family expanded into the UK. From the mid-1960s onwards, the UK-part of the business traded under the name Group4 (Total Security) and was managed by Jørgen Philip-Sørensen, one of the two grandsons of the company's founder who together took over the business in 1974. In 1981, the family concern was split, with Jørgen Philip-Sørensen becoming responsible for the European activities within the Group4 division and his brother Sven Philip-Sørensen acquiring the Swedish activities under the name of Securitas AB. From the late 1980s onwards, Group4 started a period of outward expansion, moving into the Indian market in 1989, and then subsequently Hungary, Belgium, Turkey, the United Arab Emirates, Austria, Canada, Ukraine and Bangladesh, to mention but a few.

In 2000, Group4 merged with the Danish company Falck to form what was then the second-largest security services operator in the world. Falck had a history stretching back nearly as far as Group4 and had grown from its Copenhagen origins as an ambulance and fire service to span several European markets. The new Group4Falck grew at a startling pace: almost immediately it acquired several security businesses in Europe, including in Germany, the Czech Republic and Norway. In 2001, it strengthened its position in the rapidly expanding South African market through the acquisition of two companies, Callguard Security Services and Federal Protection Services.

In 2002, the company acquired the second-largest US-based PSC, the Wackenhut Corporation. The takeover marked Group4Falck's entrance into the $14 billion guarding market in the USA, which was becoming ever-more lucrative as a result of intensified security concerns. Wackenhut had enjoyed a close relationship with the US Government, holding a contract for the protection of US embassies worldwide, and its revenues from global business grew nearly 12 per cent in 2001 to reach $1.2 billion. With the acquisition of Wackenhut,

---

World, London: G4S, 2008. While the company has for some time been the largest PSC in terms of employees, it only surpassed its rival Securitas in total turnover in the first quarter of 2009.

Group4Falck expanded its number of employees from 148,000 to 205,000, increased its countries of operation from approximately fifty to more than eighty, and reached an annual turnover of $3.7 billion.

In the summer of 2004, Group4Falck merged with the UK-based firm Securicor, to form Group4Securicor. Securicor had itself undertaken an aggressive strategy of global expansion: it was present in fifty-four countries and employed approximately 125,000 people – a huge transformation from its 1935 London beginnings, when as Night Watch Services it employed fifteen uniformed watchmen on bicycles armed with truncheons, torches and whistles. By 2004, Securicor had pre-tax profits in the region of £50 million and an annual growth rate of 5 per cent, with particularly strong performances in cash services. The company also had a solid foothold in Africa. Its first operations on the continent date from the 1960s, when operations began in Kenya, Malawi and Zambia. In 2000, through its acquisition of the South African firm Gray Security, its African reach expanded to some twenty countries and over 40,000 employees. Securicor had had less luck with its American acquisition; shortly after its purchase of the firm Argenbreit, the subsidiary ran afoul of US authorities for poor standards, resulting in a fine of $1.5 million and the loss of several key contracts. The liabilities arising from this situation, along with the restrictions on private airport security following the attacks on 11 September 2001, were a major reason for Securicor's merger with Group4Falck.[65]

Under the slogan 'Creating a Global Leader in Security Services', G4S has become the world's largest security company. Listed on the London and Copenhagen Stock Exchanges, it ranks as one of the 100 largest corporations in the UK by market capitalization and is also the biggest employer on the London Stock Exchange. The company employs over 106,500 people in Africa alone and is, according to some accounts, the continent's largest private employer.[66] There are no signs that the company's appetite for global expansion is decreasing: on the

---

[65] As part of the merger, the rescue and safety divisions associated with Falck were separated out. Falck A/S is now listed on the Copenhagen Stock Exchange. Global Solutions, a division of Group4Falck responsible for many public–private partnerships, prisons and detention centres was divested, but in 2008 G4S reacquired the company for £176.1 million.

[66] UNI Global Union, 'G4S and UNI Sign Global Agreement', 16 December 2008.

contrary, G4S acquired the UK-based company ArmorGroup as well as the US-based mine-clearance company Ronco, and in 2008 the Chief Executive stated that he was '"happy to spend £150 million [$300 million]" on acquisitions this year, mainly in the developing world'.[67] This focus is hardly surprising, since the company's fastest growing division (Latin America, Africa and the Middle East) 'now accounts for almost a fifth of company revenue, just less than is made by the North American security business', while 'profit margins in these developing markets are 25 per cent higher than in the company's Europe division'.[68]

While G4S has combined growth in the commercial security field with a degree of expansion into more military-oriented and high-risk services and operations, its close rival Securitas has deliberately maintained its focus on guarding and everyday forms of non-conflict security provision. Otherwise, the story is strikingly similar in terms of continual growth, acquisitions and specialization. Intriguingly, the two competitors originate from the same family company, Kjøbenhavn Frediksberg Nattevagt and had a shared history until 1981, when Sven Philip-Sørensen took over the Swedish branch, Securitas AB. Two years later, the company was sold out of the Philip-Sørensen family, and, in 1989, the company began its rapid international expansion, first into Norway, Denmark, Portugal and Hungary. This strategy continued after Securitas was listed on the Stockholm Stock Exchange in 1991, with acquisitions that awarded it firm footholds in France, Switzerland, Austria, Germany and Spain.

In 1997, Thomas Berglund, CEO of Securitas at the time, was quoted as saying that 'the size of the market is no restriction ... the amount we can grow ... is more a question of our own energies'.[69] Two years later, the company moved into the North American

[67] Stanley Pignal, 'G4S Hungry for More Buys', *Financial Times*, 13 May 2008, p. 19. Such acquisitions again illustrate the difficulty of drawing a clear PMC/PSC divide, since Armorgroup has long operated in military environments, including in Iraq. This said, these moves into the more militarized side of security reflect a clear strategic decision by G4S, a strategy quite different from many (indeed most) of its major competitors – including its major rival, Securitas.

[68] John O'Doherty, 'G4S Hopes to Push the Boat Out More', *Financial Times*, 28 August 2008.

[69] Quoted in Les Johnston, 'Transnational Private Policing', in J. W. E. Sheptycki (ed.), *Issues in Transnational Policing*, London and New York: Routledge, 2006, pp. 21–42; p. 37.

market, acquiring Pinkerton, the largest security company in the USA, and then, the following year, the second largest company, Burns Security, as well as a series of regional PSCs. At this point, Securitas became the largest private security provider in North America, with a 20 per cent market share. Since then, growth by acquisitions has continued. With a succession of takeovers in Columbia, Argentina, Uruguay, Mexico and Peru, Securitas now has almost 20,000 guards in Latin America. The company continues to seek opportunities for further global expansion, including those opened up by the 'huge economic welfare revolution in Asia and other markets undergoing rapid economic expansion'.[70] In line with this strategy, Securitas in 2007 acquired a controlling share in the leading Indian security company Walsons, which employs 12,000 guards. The company has also allocated resources to start operations in China, the Middle East and most countries in Eastern Europe and pursued a particularly aggressive acquisition strategy in 2009, buying fifteen companies and adding 14,000 employees to its payroll. The year also marked Securitas' entry into several new countries, including Vietnam, Morocco and South Africa – the company's first foray in sub-Saharan Africa. All told, Securitas has implemented more than sixty acquisitions over the past two decades and now has 12 per cent of the global outsourced security market. The company's total sales in 2009 amounted to 62.667 million Swedish kroner, approximately $8.4 billion.[71] Securitas now operates in forty countries and employs 240,000 people worldwide (see Figure 1.2).

Securitas is organized into four main divisions that usefully illustrate the diversity of PSC activities. Security Services North America and Security Services Europe both provide specialized guarding services in their respective geographical areas, while the European division also includes Aviation security in nine European countries. The Mobile and Monitoring Division sells mobile security services and beat patrols to small and medium-sized businesses that do not need a full-time security service, as well as a range of electronic-alarm surveillance services to both homes and businesses. Under the Alert

[70] Securitas, *Annual Report 2006*, Stockholm: Securitas, 2006.
[71] Securitas, *Securitas AB Full Year Report, January–December* 2009, Press Release – 4 February 2010; see also Securitas, *Annual Report 2008*, Stockholm: Securitas, 2008, p. 3 and p. 6.

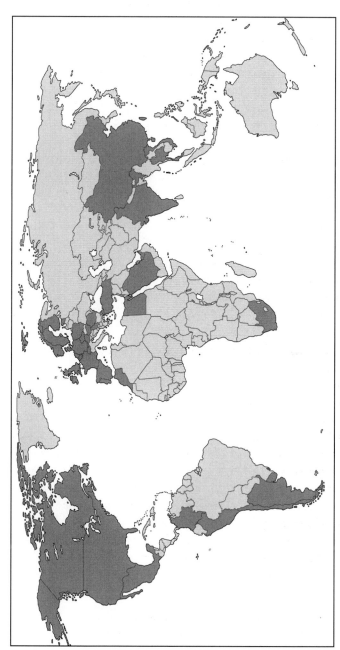

Figure 1.2 Securitas: countries of operations – 'A Knowledge Leader in Security'.

Services brand, Securitas markets an integrated global positioning system (GPS) track-and-trace service that covers a large part of the EU area. The final division is Loomis, the cash-handling service dealing primarily with banks and retail businesses in Europe and the USA. Despite poor performance in recent years, Loomis has a 20 per cent share of the cash-handling market. Securitas' main strategy for the coming years is an increasing specialization of these services, as well as expanding its global reach. As the current President and CEO Alf Göransson observes, 'Many people I have met tell me that business is local. I disagree – relationships are certainly local, but knowledge is global. Securitas will organize itself accordingly.'[72]

A Spanish company, Prosegur, ranks as the third-largest PSC in the world. Employing 80,000 people in thirteen countries, it was founded in 1976 by the Argentinean Herberto Gut, just at the end of the Franco era when the Spanish economy was liberalizing and the demand for commercial security was increasing. The company has since expanded rapidly, and, in 1987, with profits of €6 million, Prosegur became the first Spanish security company to float on the Madrid Stock Exchange. In 1995, Prosegur successfully expanded into Central and South America, a move which was followed by a second round of expansion in 2001. The company currently has operations in Argentina, Brazil, Chile, Colombia, Mexico, Paraguay, Peru and Uruguay and is a market leader in many Latin American countries where it has a linguistic and cultural advantage. In Europe, it has significant market shares in Spain, France, Portugal, Italy and Romania.[73] The process of growth by acquisitions continues.

It is also important to mention that the alarm market includes the security giants ADT and Chubb, in addition to the companies above. Both these companies are part of large transnational corporations. In July 2003, Chubb became part of United Technologies, a $31 billion, New York Stock Exchange-listed global corporation headquartered

---

[72] Securitas, *Annual Report 2007*, p. 7.

[73] Prosegur's move into Romania is particularly interesting; the aim is not simply to capture a share of this emerging market, but also to train and import cheap Romanian security workers to Spain to remedy the more or less permanent shortage of available guards. Romanian labour will not have access to Spain until two years after accession to the EU, but Prosegur has already begun a training programme in anticipation that when immigration is made legal, a pool of guards will be available.

in Hartford, Connecticut. Chubb itself has annual revenues of $1.5 billion. Similarly, ADT Security Systems was bought by Tyco International in 1998 and is now part of a Fire and Security Services company that operates in 100 countries, employs 267,000 people, serves 7.8 million customers around the world and responds to nearly 34 million alarm signals every year. The electronic security market is predicted to continue to be one of the highest-growth areas of the sector, allowing cost savings (and hence increased profits) by replacing a large labour force with technologies such as perimeter alarms and rapid-response systems, thereby also minimizing the 'human factor' through centralized monitoring and surveillance systems. Such developments depend, however, on both infrastructural elements (reliable electricity, communications and transportation systems, for example), as well as effective coordination with public authorities – all of which vary greatly, especially in the developing world.

As this brief overview demonstrates, private security may have a long history, but, at the same time, the contemporary sector has departed in important ways from the nightwatchman or 'gate swinger' of yesteryear. While basic manned guarding remains the mainstay of the sector, and accounts for about 47 per cent of the global market, these services are supported by increasingly sophisticated technological solutions. As such there has been a growing differentiation in the sector, with many countries having a large number of PSCs offering low-tech manned guarding and a few, large companies offering a broader range of high-tech 'integrated security solutions'. At the top of this hierarchy sit the global companies described above, which, by virtue of their resources and the seemingly insatiable demand for security in the modern world, have been able to continually expand their market reach.

Securing liquid modernity

The social theorist Zygmunt Bauman has described the contemporary era as one of 'liquid modernity', a world increasingly formed by flows rather than rigid demarcations.[74] A similar metaphor is used by Arjun Appadurai, who presents a globe not delineated so much by territorial

---

[74] Zygmunt Bauman, *Globalization: The Human Consequences*, Cambridge: Polity, 1998, and *Liquid Modernity*.

boundaries as by a set of 'scapes' across and through which flows of people, capital, communication and information circulate in ever-increasing volumes and velocities.[75] But these flows are far from equal or egalitarian, and one of Bauman's most arresting images is that of a world increasingly filled with 'tourists and vagabonds'.[76] Tourists, he argues, are the increasingly mobile inhabitants of a networked world. Working in different cities or countries, holidaying or even owning property abroad, ceaselessly on the move whether for work or for pleasure, the tourists comprise one side of late modernity's transformative flows. Their opposite, or alter ego, are the vagabonds, those who seek to move due to dire necessity or in search of opportunity. As Bauman puts it, the 'tourists move because they find the world within their (global) reach irresistibly *attractive* – the vagabonds move because they find the world within their (local) reach unbearably *inhospitable*.'[77] In the globalized world, the ex-territoriality of the elite is matched by the forced territoriality of the rest, as global flows are controlled and managed by the simultaneous erection of new fences and new boundaries.[78] Private security is an increasingly integral part of this world, deeply embedded in its mundane as well as its more dramatic dimensions.

To begin at the more mundane end of the spectrum, consider one of the lowliest conduits in the flow of capital: the cash dispenser or ATM (automatic teller machine). While in studies of the global economy the phrase 'flows of capital' is perhaps most readily associated with the electronic circulation of vast sums through the world's financial markets, it is worth recalling the centrality of ATMs to daily economic activity. No longer tied to banking hours or to domestic branches of a specific bank, a visit to the ATM is one of those daily tasks that rarely merits a second thought. It is also an aspect of modern life that has spurred the growth of PSCs. In many countries, cash processing and management for the banking and retail sectors has been almost entirely outsourced to the private security sector. For example, Securitas handles 40 per cent of all cash deposits made in the UK, storing, sorting and circulating money for commercial banks as well as for

---

[75] Arjun Appadurai, *Modernity at Large*, Minneapolis, Minn.: University of Minnesota Press, 1996.
[76] Baumann, *Globalization*, pp. 77–102.
[77] *Ibid.*, pp. 92–3.
[78] *Ibid.*, p. 23.

the Bank of England. Similarly, G4S's UK operations handle over £25 billion a year, while the company's global operations transport more than £300 billion. In Spain, Prosegur transports 75 per cent of all the cash moved between the country's banks and ATMs.[79] The transport and processing of cash is also a service that global private security firms seek to export to new markets around the world and one that they continue to see as an area of significant growth – especially in developing countries where financial systems are often unreliable or inefficient and where wages are often paid in cash on site.

Private security companies have acquired increasing levels of technological capacities for the protection of 'assets in transit', and satellite tracking, communications and centralized control systems now often provide real-time management of assets-in-transit services and emergency responses from the companies and the police if necessary. For example, all Prosegur's assets-in-transit vehicles in South America are tracked by satellite and monitored from a central control room in Madrid, where the operators can demobilize the engine and keep the doors locked in the event of a robbery. Such protective technologies are not for show. On 21 February 2006, the largest-ever cash robbery in the UK took place from a Securitas depot in Kent, with thieves making off with over £53 million.[80] While the Depression-era bank-robber Willie Sutton once famously quipped that he robbed banks because that was where the money was, his primary target today would in all likelihood have been a private security firm.

Private security services are also important to the expansion of global capital and have become embedded in the day-to-day activities of global business. For many transnational corporations, the availability of private security services is often seen as a requirement for entry into new or emerging markets. As Nick Buckles, CEO of G4S

---

[79] The total amount of cash in circulation continues to increase: in Europe by about 7 per cent annually since the introduction of the euro and in the USA by an average of about 4 per cent in the past decade. Securitas, *Annual Report, 2006*.

[80] BBC News, 'What Happened at the Securitas Depot?' 28 January 2008. Available onlineat http://news.bbc.co.uk/2/hi/uk_news/4741734.stm. Such events are not infrequent; in Taiwan, the country's largest-ever theft took place from a G4S armoured car in 2006, prompting the national police agency to fine the firm $1 million Taiwan dollars ($30,000) and to undertake an intensive investigation of the sector's adequacy. Jimmy Chuang, 'Police Agency Blames Security Company for Heist', *Taipei Times*, 5 January 2007, p. 2.

puts it: 'These countries are high-risk from a security perspective, and security is at the core of our customer's operations.'[81] Thus, PSCs frequently grow and expand with their clients; as the telecommunications firms, banks and resource extraction companies that make up their client list venture into other countries and continents, they consult about risks and the possibilities for effective protection and frequently take their private security services with them. As such, there is a clear trend towards what the industry terms global or international accounts, where transnational corporations use the same security company for their operations worldwide. General Motors, for example, in 2001 signed a contract with Group4Falck (as it was then named) to protect all its sites throughout the European region, which was then defined as from the 'Atlantic to the Urals'.[82] G4S has also become the global provider for Chevron; Securitas protects the internet provider Cisco throughout its facilities in the USA, Canada and Latin America; and Prosegur has a similar arrangement with a major Spanish bank and a clothing manufacturer. In effect, private security has become a key element in the flow and expansion of multinational capital, and, while this is of course not a new phenomenon, increasing risk awareness has led more and more companies to expand with the help and protection of external private security.

Private security is equally entwined in the global flow of humans. For the 'tourists' of liquid modernity, the goods and services of private security providers ensure their passage from airports, to downtown business districts, shopping malls, hotels and increasingly 'exotic' holiday destinations. Enter an airport and the likelihood is that your bags will be security checked by a private company rather than a state official. Even as the US Government has taken airport security back into public hands following the events of 11 September 2001, airport security continues to be in part provided by private firms, and the role of private actors in aviation security has escalated as security regulations are continually tightened to address perceived new risks.[83] Enter a shopping precinct, and the uniformed guards and undercover detectives of PSCs are again likely to greatly outnumber the public police. Downtown business districts with their own security services

---

[81] Quoted in O'Doherty, 'G4S Hopes'.
[82] *Group4Falck Magazine*, 2003, p. 7.
[83] See the extended discussion in Verkuil, *Outsourcing Sovereignty*, pp. 57–77.

have proliferated, as in New York's MetroTech scheme, Toronto's Chinatown and Cape Town's Central Business District, while shopping malls have long relied on the private sector for the protection of their 'mass private property', thus allowing both businesses and shoppers to profit or indulge in a more care- and crime-free environment. Macy's, the Manhattan department store, has a security system employing 'one hundred officers, four German shepherds, hundreds of cameras, and a closed circuit television centre reminiscent of a spaceship control room'.[84] Enter a hotel or tourist resort almost anywhere in the world and its perimeters may well be patrolled and surveilled by private security guards and CCTV. Tourism is the world's fastest-growing industry, and, as tour operators and hotel owners know all too well, globetrotting travellers expect First World security as they explore newly 'discovered' destinations. The services of the private security sector thus follow in the footsteps of the tourists who, whether on business or pleasure, whether decrying or luxuriating in the opportunities provided by the political economy of distant locales, in all likelihood seldom reflect on how private security is crucial to their passage through modernity.

For Bauman's vagabonds, or migrants as they have come to be called in many countries, private security is encountered in different settings and in different ways. The globalized world is geared for the tourists' dreams and desires. The vagabonds are its unavoidable side effect. Vagabonds lack the wherewithal to flow freely through the globalized world; they travel surreptitiously and dangerously and often figure high on the security agenda of others. In the same way as private security plays a key role in securing the safe passage of the tourists, it ensures that the free flow of vagabonds is restrained and contained at the appropriate points.[85]

Across the developed world, PSCs are engaged in running detention centres for migrants, refugees and asylum-seekers and escorting

---

[84] Andrea Elliot, 'Stores Fight Shoplifting with Private Security', *New York Times*, 17 June 2003. The company also operates holding cells in its stores that in 2003 processed 12,000 people in its 105 locations, only 56 per cent of whom were referred to the police.

[85] See Didier Bigo, 'Globalised (In)security: The Field and the Ban-Opticon', in Didier Bigo and Anastassia Tsoukala (eds.), *Terror, Insecurity and Liberty: Illiberal Practices of Liberal Regimes after 9/11*, London: Routledge, 2008, pp. 5–49.

them 'home' when their applications have been declined. In the UK, G4S runs most of the short-term holding facilities for the government's Immigration and Nationality Directorate, being present at the ports where immigrants are held while awaiting decisions or action on their right to enter and remain in the country. G4S also operates immigration reporting centres, including implementation and administration of client processes. Private providers such as G4S, Global Solutions Limited (GSL, now part of G4S), Serco and Kalyx also run the unusually frankly named immigration removal centres on behalf of the UK Immigration Service. At one of these centres near Heathrow, more than 40,000 detainees have passed through the doors since it opened in 2004.[86] G4S is the main provider of escorted and non-escorted repatriations services, and, as its website records in the language of efficiency, 'we have successfully cooperated with other European states to share chartered flights to specific destinations, coordinating action to make best use of resources.'[87]

In Australia, where the law requires that all foreigners arriving without a visa must be detained, the Government in 2003 outsourced the operation of all detention centres and immigration reception and processing centres to GSL.[88] In April 2009, the country's detention facilities held 575 people, a significant decrease from 2004–5 when they detained 7,490, some for several years.[89] GSL insists that for the employees of its detention centre on Christmas Island in the Indian

---

[86] See Secro's website: www.serco.co.uk.

[87] G4S, www.g4s.com (accessed 10 April 2009).

[88] GSL was then a division of Group4Falck, specializing in public–private partnerships contracts. It was sold as part of the merger between Group4Falck and Securicor in 2005, and then reacquired by G4S in 2008. GSL until recently operated three immigration and detention facilities in the UK: Yarl's Wood Removal Centre in Bedfordshire, Tinsley House Removal Centre at Gatwick Airport, and Oakington Reception Centre in Cambridgeshire, with a total capacity of nearly 1,000 people. The contract for the first facility passed to Serco in 2007.

[89] Government of Australia, 'Fact Sheet 82: Immigration and Detention' (Sydney: Department of Immigration and Citizenship, 2007). Available online at www.immi.gov.au/media/fact-sheets/82_detention.htm (accessed 3 March 2007); 'Immigration Detention Statistic Summary', Community and Detention Services Division, Department of Immigration and Citizenship, 17 April 2009. Available online at www.immi.gov.au/managing-australias-borders/detention/_pdf/immigration-detention-statistics-20090417.pdf (accessed 9 May 2009).

Ocean, 'living and working on this exotic tropical island is a place that rests firmly in dreams', unwittingly underscoring the division between tourists and vagabonds.[90] In the USA, detention has increased following a new policy requiring that all detained non-Mexican illegal immigrants are held in custody until their cases are determined. The result has been a dramatic increase in the number of detained illegal immigrants, from 19,718 a day in 2005 to 26,500 in 2007, and predicted to reach 32,000. Many are held in private prisons, and the *New York Times* reports increasing concerns over numerous deaths and attempts to cover up ill-treatment of migrants in these facilities.[91]

Imprisonment is another key form of exclusion in liquid modernity, and privately run prisons and prisoner-management services have become a globally traded commodity with some companies operating across jurisdictions. Kalyx, for example, is part of the global services company Sodexho Alliance. It operates four prisons in the UK and provides services to correction departments in eight countries on three continents. Serco, another international services company, runs one prison in Australia, and four private prisons and two young-offender institutions in the UK. G4S has retained only one UK prison, although it manages seven juvenile facilities in the USA and supplies staff to six prisons in the Netherlands. The company's GSL division operates three prisons in the UK, two in Australia and one in South Africa. The latter – the Mangaung Correctional Centre – was the first private prison on the African continent and houses 3,000 maximum-security prisoners. South Africa's only other private prison – the Kutamana Sinthumale Correctional Centre in Limpopo – is also run by an international company, the Geo Group, which was formerly part of Wackenhut.[92] The Geo Group also runs six prisons in

---

[90] See GSL's website: www.gslglobal.com.

[91] Spencer S. Hsu and Sylvia Moreno, 'US: Border Policy's Success Strains Resources: Tent City in Texas among Immigrant Holding Sites Drawing Criticism', *Washington Post*, 2 February 2007; Nina Bernstein, 'Officials Obscured Truth of Migrant Deaths in Jail: Evidence of Mistreatment Was Routinely Covered Up, Documents Show', *New York Times*, 10 January 2010. For an earlier study of policing the US–Mexican border, see Peter Andreas, *Border Games: Policing the US–Mexican Border*, Ithaca, NY: Cornell University Press, 2000.

[92] On private prisons in Africa, see Andrew Coyle, 'Prison Privatization in the African Context', *Review of African Political Economy*, 35 (118) (2008): 660–5.

Australia, as well as being one of the biggest companies in the prison and immigration detention sector in the USA. In the USA itself, the largest company is the Corrections Corporation of America (CCA), which operates sixty-five facilities, with approximately 72,500 prisoners in nineteen states, thereby controlling more than 50 per cent of the private US prison market. In fact, CCA is the fifth largest correctional system in the USA, surpassed only by the Federal Government and three states.[93]

Conclusion

Largely unrecognized, the commercial private security sector has come to occupy a prominent place in modern societies and has increasingly significant impacts and implications at the global level. Capturing these emerging structures and their dynamics presents considerable challenges to some of the most fundamental divides in modern politics and social science – the division between the domestic and the international, between the public and the private and between security inside and outside the state. Indeed, grasping the development of security structures beyond the state requires a wider empirical gaze, and a different set of theoretical tools than commonly found in studies of private security. It also demands that we question long-standing disciplinary divides – including those between International Relations, criminology and political sociology – as well as powerful and deeply entrenched assumptions about the nature of politics.

In the next chapter, we draw upon a range of perspectives from each of these fields and seek to show that in its broader dimensions private security should not be seen as standing outside structures of national and transnational governance but as arising from shifts *within* those structures. Far from representing an automatic erosion or threat to the state, or an illicit strata operating in the shadows of global governance, contemporary security privatization is better understood as part of broader transformations in governance – a reconfiguration

---

[93] See www. correctionscorp. com, and the analysis in Loic Wacquant, 'The Great Penal Leap Backwards: Incarceration in America from Nixon to Clinton', in John Pratt, David Brown, Simon Hallsworthy, Mark Brown and Wayne Morrison (eds.), *The New Punitiveness*: Trends, Theories Perspectives, London: Willan, 2005), pp. 3–26.

of both public and private power rather than a simple privatization of previously public functions. Indeed, in security, as in many other spheres, the public–private distinction, as well as the global–local division, is increasingly unhelpful as a means of grasping contemporary international politics.

2 | Late modernity and the rise of private security

Security has become a – if not the – dominant discourse of modern life; as Michael Dillon observes, it 'saturates the language of modern politics. Our political vocabularies reek of it and our political imagination is confined by it.'[1] Law and order issues, once the terrain of the political right, have become the rallying cry of virtually all political parties, and security is increasingly the lens through which political issues are filtered, be they international migration, health, environmental degradation or development aid.[2] In the wake of the attacks of 11 September 2001, these dynamics have intensified yet further, and the urgent need for security, the containment of danger and the identification and management of any kind of risk have become a pervasive rhetoric. In this sense, Ulrich Beck's description (though perhaps not his diagnosis) of late modernity as 'risk society' appears ever-more accurate: risks, in Beck's terminology, are open to social definition and construction. They are also insatiable, infinite, 'a bottomless barrel of demands'.[3]

---

[1] Michael Dillon, *The Politics of Security*, London and New York: Routledge, 1996, p. 12.

[2] See, for example, Rita Abrahamsen, 'Blair's Africa: The Politics of Securitization and Fear', *Alternatives*, 30 (1) (2005): 55–80; Mark Duffield, *Global Governance and the New Wars*, London: Zed Books, 2001; Mark Duffield, *Development, Security and Unending War: Governing the World of Peoples*, Cambridge: Polity, 2007; Elspeth Guild and Joanne Van Selm (eds.), *International Migration and Security: Opportunities and Challenges*, London and New York: Routledge, 2005; Jef Huysmans, *The Politics of Insecurity*, London and New York: Routledge, 2006; Neocleous, *Critique of Security*.

[3] Ulrich Beck, *Risk Society: Towards a New Modernity*, London: Sage, 1992, p. 23. For an insightful analysis in the UK context, see Ian Loader, 'Private Security and the Demand for Protection in Contemporary Britain', *Policing and Society*, 7 (3) (1997): 143–62; and in a rapidly expanding literature on risk in International Relations, Mikkel Rasmussen, *The Risk Society at War*, Cambridge: Cambridge University Press, 2005.

Any understanding of the role and expansion of private security in contemporary international politics needs to be set against this backdrop of an expanding security agenda. The growth and globalization of private security reflects significant shifts in social and political life, and in economic structures. These transformations are located at the local and national levels, but they are connected to global dynamics and discourses in myriad ways and have combined to give rise to transnational security actors and structures. The task of this chapter is to situate the growth of private security within this broader context and the related reconfiguration of the relationship between public and private power and authority.

To develop our argument, we turn to studies in the fields of criminology and sociology. Although little known in International Relations, these analyses provide some of the most sophisticated theoretical and empirical treatments of security privatization. Following their lead, we examine how security privatization and its globalization is linked to three interrelated aspects of late modernity: neo-liberalism and responsibilization, new attitudes towards crime and punishment, and, finally, commodification and the increasing salience of risk in perceptions and practices of security. To date, the global ramifications of this more 'pluralized' or 'hybrid' security field have received little attention, as the extensive and incisive studies by criminologists remain overwhelmingly focused on the national level.[4] Thus, after discussing attempts to analyse security governance within states, we turn in Chapter 3 to the development of an analytical framework for understanding the security field in what we term global security assemblages.

Neo-liberalism and the responsible security consumer

It is impossible to understand the growth and pervasiveness of private security without consideration of the contemporary dominance

---

[4] Trevor Jones and Tim Newburn, *Private Security and Public Policing*, Oxford: Clarendon Press, 1998; Loader, 'Plural Policing and Democratic Governance'; Les Johnston and Clifford Shearing, *Governing Security*, London and New York: Routledge, 2005. On the global dimensions: Les Johnston, 'Transnational Private Policing', as well as Les Johnston, 'Transnational Security Governance', in Jennifer Wood and Benoît Dupont (eds.), *Democracy, Society and the Governance of Security*, Cambridge: Cambridge University Press, 2006, pp. 33–51.

of neo-liberal modes of governance.[5] As numerous analyses have stressed, since the late 1970s, privatization, outsourcing and public–private partnerships have become commonplace, as governments have sought to streamline 'bloated' bureaucracies and tighten welfare budgets.[6] In almost any area previously dominated by public provision – from health care to education – a host of different actors and institutions are now involved. The result has been a general move away from the vertically integrated, hierarchical and state-centred structures of service provision characteristic of the welfare state, towards more diverse, horizontally linked complexes of actors.[7] As its advocates argue, neo-liberalism promotes a form of networked governance and involves a shift towards

a new model of government in which executives' core responsibilities no longer centre on managing people and programs, but on organizing resources, often belonging to others ... Government agencies, bureaus, divisions, and offices are becoming less important as direct service providers, but more important as generators of public value within the web of multiorganizational, multigovernmental, and multisectoral relationships that increasingly constitute modern government.[8]

---

[5] These connections are explored in Johnston and Shearing, *Governing Security*; David Garland, *The Culture of Control*, Oxford: Oxford University Press, 2001; Pat O'Malley, 'Risk, Power and Crime Prevention', *Economy and Society*, 21 (3) (1992): 252–75; and Lorraine Mazerolle and Janet Ransley, *Third Party Policing*, Cambridge: Cambridge University Press, 2005, pp. 1–22.

[6] See John D. Donahue, *The Privatization Decision: Public Ends, Private Means*, New York: Basic Books, 1989; Andrew Gamble, *The Free Economy and the Strong State: The Politics of Thatcherism*, Basingstoke: Macmillan, 1988. On the impact of neo-liberalism in development policy and developing countries, see John Toye, *Dilemmas of Development: Reflections on the Counter-Revolution in Development Theory and Policy*, Oxford: Blackwell, 1987; and Giovanni Andrea Cornia, Richard Jolly and Francis Stewart (eds.), *Adjustment with a Human Face*, Oxford: Clarendon Press, 1987.

[7] See Donahue, *The Privatization Decision*; Stephen Goldsmith and William D. Eggers, *Governing by Network: The New Shape of the Public Sector*, Washington, DC: Brookings Institution Press, 2004; Donald F. Kettl, *Sharing Power: Public Governance and Private Markets*, Washington, DC: Brookings Institution Press, 1993; Donald F. Kettl, *The Global Public Management Revolution: A Report on the Transformation of Governance*, Washington, DC: Brookings Institution Press, 2000; John M. Kamensy and Thomas J. Burlin, *Collaboration: Using Networks and Partnerships*, Lanham, Md.: Rowman & Littlefield, 2004.

[8] Goldsmith and Eggers, *Governing by Network*, p. 8.

In a metaphor often cited by criminologists, the role of the state has shifted from 'rowing' towards 'steering'.[9]

While the security sector may initially have been more resistant to the neo-liberal ethos than other public sectors, it has in no way been immune to these pressures, and in recent years the delivery and governance of security has been significantly transformed. The police in many countries have had to adapt to the demands of the 'new managerialism' and strategies of new public management for cost efficiency, results and effectiveness.[10] Public–private policing partnerships have proliferated, and the widespread adoption of community policing is in large part a response to such pressures. 'Post-Keynesian policing', as Pat O'Malley and Darren Palmer describe it, has moved away from imageries of public dependency on police expertise towards 'a more contractual neo-liberal imagery, with quite different implications for the government of crime and disorder. In this emergent discourse, the community appears as a network of agentive, expert and independent actors who enter *partnerships* with police'.[11] Similarly, a key tenet of community policing is the mobilization of private actors in policing. The strategy was clearly articulated in the British Government's 2001 statement on *Criminal Justice: The Way Ahead*:

There has always been a wide range of people contributing to community safety in various forms. These include park keepers (some with constabulary powers), security guards in shopping centres, car park attendants, neighbourhood wardens, night club bouncers and the private security industry. The issue for policing is how these various activities can be coordinated to make the most effective contribution to making safer communities.[12]

The fact that a strikingly similar formulation can be found in a 1998 South African White Paper on Safety and Security points to

---

[9] David Osborne and Ted Gaebler, *Reinventing Government*, New York: Addison-Wesley, 1992.

[10] See, for example, Leishman *et al.*, *Core Issues in Policing*.

[11] Pat O'Malley and Darren Palmer, 'Post-Keynesian Policing', *Economy and Society*, 25 (2) (1996): 137–55, 138.

[12] Quoted in Johnston and Shearing, *Governing Security*; see also the British Crime and Disorder Act 1998.

the increasing globalization of neo-liberal models of policing.[13] Community policing, with its emphasis on partnerships and community engagement, has been promoted and often implemented throughout the world as the most efficient form of policing.[14] Similarly, a widespread outsourcing of security functions and services previously regarded as the proper domain of the state, such as prisons, prisoner transport and airport security, to mention a few, has occurred across the globe and not only in 'advanced' liberal democracies of the North.[15] In South Africa, for example, the Government has outsourced the protection of all the country's police stations to PSCs, and, as we saw in Chapter 1, private corporations have established important positions in correctional services.[16] The growth of private security is thus connected to the proliferation of market opportunities and the availability of substantial longer-term contracts created at the national level by privatization and government outsourcing.[17] This is particularly the case with the major security companies, which have significant contracts with governments and, to a lesser but increasing degree, have also established relationships with ministries of foreign affairs and development agencies.[18]

One powerful interpretation of the connections between neo-liberalism and security privatization stresses the fiscal crisis of the

---

[13] Government of South Africa, Department of Safety and Security, *White Paper on Safety and Security: In the Service of Safety, 1999–2004*, Pretoria: Department of Safety and Security, 1998. The South African experience is discussed in more detail in Chapter 5.

[14] See Brogden and Nijhar, *Community Policing*; Mutuma Ruteere and Marie-Emmanuelle Pommerolle, 'Democratizing Security or Decentralizing Repression? The Ambiguities of Community Policing in Kenya', *African Affairs*, 102 (409) (2003): 587–604; Dixon, 'Globalising the Local'.

[15] O'Malley and Palmer, 'Post-Keynesian Policing'; David Shichor, *Punishment for Profit: Private Prisons/Public Concerns*, Thousand Oaks, Calif.: Sage, 1995; Michael J. Quinlan, Charles W. Thomas and Sherril Gautreaux, 'The Privatization of Correctional Facilities', in Deborah Ballati (ed.), *Privatizing Governmental Functions*, New York: Law Journal Press, 2001.

[16] Coyle, 'Prison Privatization in the African Context'. See also Chidi Amuta, 'Nigeria: A Case for Private Prisons', *This Day*, 19 February 2009.

[17] Mark Button, *Private Policing*, London: Willan, 2002; Garland, *Culture of Control*; Johnston, *Rebirth of Private Security*; Alison Wakefield, *Selling Security: The Private Policing of Public Space*, London: Willan, 2003.

[18] The major private prisons companies, as well as the main military 'logistical support' companies such as Brown and Root, rely heavily on government contracts.

Keynesian state that gathered force in the late 1970s.[19] According to this argument, as the state's capacity to fund public services decreased (whether through economic necessity, political design or both), the private sector expanded to fill the various 'gaps' that ensued – including in the area of security. There is much to this argument, but there are also a number of areas where a purely economic focus, particularly on the fiscal crisis of the state, falls short. First and most importantly, while it is certainly the case that under neo-liberal policies many areas of public spending have decreased, it is difficult to make this case for the security sector. Indeed, in many countries in the North, spending on public security (both military and policing) has increased at the same time as the private security sector has grown. The idea of a gap filled by private security cannot therefore be supported by reference to a universal retrenchment of public capacities. Second, the policies of outsourcing did not represent a simple retreat of the state from security provision but rather were part of a crucial relocation of its place within such provision. A more complex process than mere fiscal restraint has been under way – one involving both the commodification of security and attempts by the state to make social actors of all kinds – individuals, corporations, communities – responsible for a greater involvement in their own security. The increased role of private security, in other words, is part of a general intensification of security activity across societies – a process abetted by the state and, in many countries, drawing power from an increasing demand for security from other sectors of society.

In sub-Saharan Africa and other parts of the global South, the undoubted insights of the 'fiscal restraint' thesis require even further modification. While military spending has remained more or less constant in Africa during the period from 1988 to 2006, there is nevertheless a clear case of the retreat of the state from public security

---

[19] See Steven Spitzer and Andrew Scull, 'Privatization and Capitalist Development: The Case of the Private Police', *Social Problems*, 25 (1) (1977): 18–29; Nigel South, 'Private Security, the Division of Policing Labor and the Commercial Compromise of the State', *Research in Law, Deviance and Social Control*, 6 (1984): 171–98; and Nigel South, *Policing for Profit*, London: Sage, 1988. For a wider perspective, see O'Malley and Palmer, 'Post-Keynesian Policing'; and, for an overview, Jones and Newburn, *Private Security and Public Policing*.

provision.[20] The neo-liberal order, reinforced by the structural adjustment programmes of the International Monetary Fund (IMF) and the World Bank, has had particularly harsh consequences, and, although the impacts vary, almost all countries have experienced a drastic reduction in state expenditure on social welfare, education and capital investment. While the new aid modality of post-conditionality and poverty reduction may have gone some way towards reversing this trend, the consequences for security are still apparent. Many police forces have become badly under-resourced and underpaid (and sometimes not paid at all and certainly not on time), leading to a lack of efficiency and intensifying the temptation towards petty corruption and predatory activities. In this sense, the fiscal constraint perspective holds considerable insights when applied to the African context, and there is little doubt that the expansion of private security coincided to a large extent with the rise to prominence of neo-liberal economic policies. On the other hand, this connection should not be viewed too mechanically, or in a purely functional sense where the private inevitably fills the vacuum left by the public. On closer inspection, the situation is somewhat more complex, and the fiscal crisis argument needs to be tempered by political, sociological and historical factors.

Key among these is the preoccupation of many African security forces with a narrowly defined regime security. As Alice Hills argues, policing in Africa has generally been preoccupied with 'the enforcement of order on behalf of a regime' rather than with crime prevention and public protection.[21] This concern with regime survival finds its historical roots in the colonial origins of the state and its police forces and has been further reinforced by the lack of popular legitimacy of many governments. As the period of neo-liberal restructuring alienated ever-larger sections of the population, the need for regime security intensified. During this period then, the state was not only weakened in terms of its (economic) ability to provide for its citizens, it was also to a certain extent privatized by political elites concerned primarily with their own survival.[22] There are, of course, important

---

[20] Military spending in North Africa has increased in the same period; for valuable data, see *The Military Expenditure Yearbook* published by the Stockholm International Peace Research Institute.

[21] Alice Hills, *Policing Africa: Internal Security and the Limits of Liberalization*, Boulder, Col.: Lynne Rienner, 2000, p. 162.

[22] See Mbembe, *On the Postcolony*, pp. 66–101 especially.

variations, and while all policing and law enforcement is inherently political and defends a particular socio-economic order, the direct ability of political leaders to influence police operations significantly diminishes the public accountability and democratic control of many African police forces. This tendency towards the privatization of public violence, although by no means uniform, needs to be factored into any explanation of why people turn to non-state solutions for their everyday protection. Given that the military in many African countries is also frequently used for internal security purposes, any automatic assumption that there has been a decline in the *ability* of the state to provide security needs to be treated with caution. It may be the case in some countries, but not in others. Indeed, the state's coercive apparatus may well have retained its powers, while its priorities shifted.[23] The behaviour of the Kenyan Police in the post-election violence of 2007–8 is a case in point and shows how an ostensibly public police force often acts for private political purposes.

In Africa as in the North, therefore, the relationship between security and neo-liberalism involves much more than economic reform, and the move towards neo-liberal governance does not necessarily entail a diminishment in the power of the state, the simple transfer of previously public functions to private actors, or the mere pluralization of centres of power. Instead, these developments indicate important changes in the relationship between security and the sovereign state, and structures of political power and authority. At the core of the neo-liberal move is a transformation in the technologies and modes of power. As Mitchell Dean points out, while neo-liberalism holds that to govern less is to govern better, and while neo-liberal forms of governance entail an increasing fragmentation and pluralization of decision-making centres away from the state towards individuals, civil society, and a plethora of quasi-autonomous non-governmental organizations (NGOs) and institutions, such strategies of decentralization are simultaneously accompanied by a vast array of new mechanisms and techniques of auditing, accounting, monitoring and

[23] Hamilton Sipho Simelane's analysis of the emergence of private security in Swaziland is a useful illustration here, showing the interaction of economic decline, political concerns with regime survival, and citizens' subsequent turn to private security. Simelane, 'Security for All? Politics, Economy and the Growth of Private Security in Swaziland', *Review of African Political Economy*, 35 (118) (2008): 599–612.

evaluation that link these disparate entities to political strategies at the state level.[24] In the words of Nikolas Rose, neo-liberalism is a form of rule that governs through 'the instrumentalization of a regulated autonomy'.[25]

These shifts render many conventional readings of the relationship between power, governance and privatization inadequate. In fact, as Nikolas Rose and Peter Miller have suggested,

the political vocabulary structured by opposition between state and civil society, public and private, government and market, coercion and consent, sovereignty and autonomy and the like, does not adequately characterize the diverse ways in which rule is exercised in advanced liberal democracies ... individuals are not merely subjects of power but play a part in its operations.[26]

Seen in this way, governance is no longer merely about decision making, or, in the case of security, about direct social control, coercion and discipline; it is also about the production and constitution of social subjects through systems of knowledge and discursive practices. In Foucault's well-known formulation, the subject is not only power's intended target but also its effect, and the modern state is increasingly focused on the 'conduct of conduct', enlisting the powers of private actors in strategies of rule at a distance.[27] In this context, David Garland has characterized private actors as a 'third sector' of security provision, operating alongside the policing and punitive

---

[24] Mitchell Dean, *Governmentality: Power and Rule in Modern Society*, London: Sage, 1999. See also Michael Power, *The Audit Society: Rituals of Verification*, Oxford: Oxford University Press, 1997; Nikolas Rose, 'Governing "Advanced" Liberal Democracies', in Andrew Barry, Thomas Osborne and Nikolas Rose (eds.), *Foucault and Political Reason*, London: UCL Press, 1996, and Nikolas Rose and Peter Miller, 'Political Power beyond the State: Problematics of Government', *British Journal of Sociology*, 43 (2) (1992): 173–205.

[25] Rose, 'Governing "Advanced" Liberal Democracies', p. 57.

[26] Rose and Miller, 'Political Power beyond the State', p. 174. As we argue later in this chapter, the precise ways that neo-liberal structures of rule apply outside advanced liberal states (and between these states and the developing world) is a complex issue. We also return to this question in Chapter 6.

[27] Michel Foucault, *The Order of Things: An Archeology of the Human Sciences*, New York: Pantheon, 1970, and 'Governmentality', in *The Foucault Effect: Studies in Governmentality*, edited by Graham Burchell, Colin Gordon and Peter Miller, University of Chicago Press, 1991, pp.87–104.

institutions of the state. The result is a more governmental approach to security:

> Instead of addressing crime in a direct fashion by means of the police, the courts and the prisons, this approach promotes a new kind of indirect action, in which state agencies activate action by non-state organizations and actors. The intended result is an enhanced network of more or less directed, more or less informal crime control, complementing and extending the formal controls of the criminal justice state. Instead of imagining that they can monopolize crime control, or exercising their sovereign powers in complete disregard of the powers of other actors, state agencies now adopt a strategic relation to other forces of social control. They seek to build broader alliances, enlisting the 'governmental' powers of private actors, and shaping them to the ends of crime control.[28]

This more devolved approach to security has implications for the self-perceptions of individuals and the social and institutional pressures to which they are subjected, and one result is a growing 'responsibilization' whereby individuals, communities, businesses and other actors come to accept substantial responsibility for their own safety and security. Within this more individualized and market-oriented view, consumers of security – be they homeowners, parents, travellers, women, business owners and every conceivable population 'at risk' – are provided with advice on how to minimize their chance of 'victimization'.[29] Thus, responsible individual and corporate behaviour entails installing burglar alarms and surveillance systems, engaging the services of a security company, participating in neighbourhood watches, and other forms of non- or quasi- state-related security behaviour. The rational consumer of market-provided security services becomes the norm of responsible action undertaken by security-conscious individuals. Choice becomes transformed into an imperative, as the decision to participate in these opportunities becomes a mark of responsible behaviour: individuals and communities are imagined as getting the degree of security against crime that they deserve – whether by making their own

---

[28] Garland, *Culture of Control*, p. 124; Jonathan Simon, *Governing through Crime*, Oxford: Oxford University Press, 2006.
[29] Parents, for instance, are now given the opportunity to use surveillance systems such as Nanny-Buster or Nanny Watch. For an example in London, see www.ableinvestigationsuk.com; in the USA, nanny-cam systems have been reported on media outlets including CNN and Fox News.

arrangements, through their ability to pay for enhanced protection, or both.[30] Those who participate in community policing programmes, purchase security-enhancing commodities and learn crime-prevention skills and habits will be protected from crime by market and quasi-market processes as well as by the police. By contrast, those who relinquish their responsibility and rely totally on the social and the state will face heightened levels of risk and potential victimization. Contemporary security policies thus encourage prudent, rational and knowledgeable individuals who accept responsibility for their own security. Inevitably, this expands the market opportunities for PSCs, both domestically and globally.[31]

This understanding of power as productive, as constitutive of social subjects and as operating through diverse and dispersed social practices has important implications for understanding security and security privatization. It draws attention to the emerging imbrication of private security actors with public structures, problematizes the idea of strictly hierarchical conceptions of sovereignty and political authority and demands a view of power that moves beyond coercive or compulsory power alone. In fact, one of its most significant consequences is to point to the ways in which different forms of power – including the compulsory power traditionally associated with the

---

[30] As Richard Ericson and Kevin Haggerty note, neighbourhood watches and the like can be seen as means to security but they are also policies in which 'the idea is to make a community by creating a communality of fear. In risk society negativity and fear must be kept alive in order to mobilize the population and sustain reflexivity'. *Policing the Risk Society*, Oxford: Oxford University Press, 1997, p. 157.

[31] The gated community provides one illustration of these processes. Such arrangements have become commonplace across the globe. As one study observes, 'the number of people estimated to be living in gated communities in the USA increased from four million in 1988, to eight million in 1997 and to sixteen million in 1998. By 1997, it was estimated that there were in excess of twenty thousand gated communities with more than three million housing units'. Despite some regional variation, the pattern is pervasive: 'in areas such as Tampa, Florida, gated communities account for four out of five home sales of $300,000 or more'. While gated communities on Long Island, New York, were rare in the 1980s, 'by the 1990s almost every condominium development of more than fifty units had a guardhouse'. Low, *Behind the Gates*, p. 15. Low's study provides a valuable account of the multiple reasons – including a desire for community, exclusivity (and social exclusion), enhanced facilities, and residential maintenance – that people have for moving to gated communities in the USA; there is more to this than just fear, though security undoubtedly seems central.

police and other public security institutions – is being reconfigured within contemporary security arrangements, an issue we turn to in more detail in Chapter 3.

A key analytical issue raised by viewing these processes at a transnational level, however, is the varying capacities of states to actually 'govern' or 'steer' within such devolved networks. While the numerous processes associated with neo-liberal governance have resulted in a pluralization of actors involved in security delivery and governance, this development cannot be read as a simple extension of state power. Even in the most powerful states, with efficient and well-functioning bureaucracies, private actors once empowered are often able to set agendas and to influence them and act according to their own interests. Moreover, private security initiatives have emerged not only at the instigation or encouragement of the state but also in situations where the state has, or is perceived to have, a reduced capacity to provide protection. In sum, although the neo-liberal approach leads to a proliferation of security actors, and these actors do not exist in separation from the state, we cannot assume a priori that the state is in a position of controlling and directing them. This is particularly the case in many poor countries, where economic liberalization (often in the form of structural adjustment programmes) has resulted in declining public expenditure and a loss of vital state capacities for governance. Similar initiatives may not have similar results; and global effects may be produced without being planned in any direct sense as the practices, preferences and values of various non-state actors are shaped by and interact with neo-liberal government. As such, the transformations associated with the neo-liberal approach to security do not simply replace public levers of power with private ones. Instead, as we will discuss in the next chapter, they reconfigure the relations of power operating in a given field of practice.

Security, crime and punishment in risk society

Neo-liberal transformations in public policy have been accompanied by changes in the socially dominant attitudes, norms and practices underpinning the provision of security. In particular, two seemingly divergent and yet paradoxically related developments in attitudes towards crime and punishment are crucial. On the one hand, crime and the provision of security has been depoliticized and transformed from a problem to be solved by the welfare interventions of the state into technical problems to be managed through security logics. Social responsibility and direct state intervention have thus been supplemented and to some degree supplanted by techniques of crime control based on efficiency, surveillance and spatial design. On the other hand, there has been an intensified politicization of crime and security, as concerns over crime and security have heightened and responses hardened at the level of both political rhetoric and concrete policy. The consequence of both these developments has been an increase in the role played by private security across contemporary societies.

The broad context for these shifts in attitudes and policies can be traced to the early 1970s and the beginning of what Garland has termed the 'crisis of penal modernism': a widespread scepticism towards rehabilitative approaches to criminality, accompanied by the rise of more punitive approaches stressing the importance of incarceration and the tightening of parole provisions.[32] Whereas previous 'welfarist' understandings stressed the social origins of crime, the past three decades have seen an increasing ascription of criminal behaviour to individual characteristics. The explanatory categories of deprivation, inequality and deviance have been eclipsed by the ascendance of 'economic' explanations that stress rational calculation and opportunity structures as key variables of criminal behaviour. As a result, the idea that the state itself can solve the problem of crime has been eroded, and instead strategies for countering crime have been individualized and justice has in important respects been configured as the strict application of the law separated from social policy. In the perhaps extreme but telling words of one of the most vocal advocates of this position: 'A lawful system has only a minor interest in the reasons why someone commits the crime. The criminal justice system is

---

[32] Garland, *Culture of Control*. Interestingly, both Garland and Loïc Wacquant attribute this decline in part to the influence of 'critical' criminological and sociological approaches and movements (such as those associated with Foucault) that attacked the disciplinary and normalizing effects of rehabilitative parole, probation and prison policies. There are intriguing, if not always comforting, implications concerning the unintended consequences of 'critical' thinking across the social sciences in this observation. See Loïc Wacquant, 'Penal Truth Comes to Europe: Think Tanks and the "Washington Consensus" on Crime and Punishment', in George Gilligan and John Pratt (eds.), *Crime, Truth and Justice: Official Inquiry, Discourse, Knowledge*, London: Willan Publishing, 2004, pp. 161–80.

there to punish the guilty, exonerate the innocent, and serve the interests of the law-abiding.'[33] While less well documented, similar shifts in policy and attitudes have also taken place in developing countries, in part through the globalization of public policy.[34]

By viewing crime as to some degree a consequence of opportunistic rational action, contemporary security policy downgrades responses rooted in public welfare and reform interventions tied to the political rights and purview of public agents and facilitates a specific form of depoliticization that stresses technical, managerial and technological responses. It focuses on designing-in security: on prevention in the sense of spatial control, the monitoring and regulation of flows and access, the acquisition of information, its dissemination across a range of 'security' actors, the identification of risk behaviours and the development of risk profiles.[35] These techniques narrow the gap between public policing and the activities of private security providers, encouraging and legitimating an increased role for private companies and allowing the two sectors to be seen as complementary if not parallel endeavours. In some settings (particularly but by no means exclusively in the developing world) the private sector may even possess expertise and resources (in surveillance technologies and techniques, for example) that exceed those of the public police. In many urban areas, private resources are mobilized in integrated public–private structures. The Lower Manhattan Security Initiative, for example, is inspired by systems in London and proposes installing more than 100 license-plate readers in the area. According to one report, the resulting system 'will include not only license plate readers but also 3,000 public and private security cameras below Canal Street, as well

---

[33] Quoted in Wacquant, 'The Great Penal Leap Backward', p. 169.

[34] Dixon, 'Globalising the Local'; on the globalization of public policy more broadly, Diane Stone, 'Global Public Policy, Transnational Policy Communities, and Their Networks', *Policy Studies Journal*, 36 (1) (2008): 19–38.

[35] For an early treatment of surveillance, see Christopher Dandeker, *Surveillance, Power and Modernity*, Oxford: Polity Press, 1990. Interesting studies in a rapidly expanding literature include David Lyon (ed.), *Surveillance as Social Sorting*, London and New York: Routledge, 2002; Louise Amoore and Marieke de Goede, 'Governance, Risk and Dataveillance in the War on Terror', *Crime, Law and Social Change*, 43 (2) (2005): 149–73; Elia Zureik and Mark B. Salter (eds.), *Global Surveillance and Policing*, Cullompton: Willan, 2005.

as a centre staffed by the police and private security officers', where the 'police and corporate security agents will work together'.[36] In London, the integration of public policing and private surveillance was evident in the extensive use of CCTV footage in the wake of the 7 July 2007 bombings and in the investigation of a series of high-profile murders.

Alongside processes of depoliticization and rationalization, a second and in many ways seemingly contradictory trend has witnessed the increasing political moralization of criminality and a heightened concern with victimization. In this domain, the shift away from penal welfarism has been accompanied by a move towards treating crime as a question of individualized *moral* responsibility rather than as a consequence of social disadvantage or deprivation. This has further shifted the politics of security from a public welfare issue towards an intensely punitive populism. When placed in a moral register, the representation of criminals as rational actors not only enables their placement as calculating agents with a matrix of risk management but also allows them to be represented as wilfully recalcitrant individuals wholly responsible and morally culpable for their own actions and deserving retributive justice and/or requiring removal from society. Almost universally, the result has been a populist moral politics of crime, now cast in the language of security, that heightens awareness of (in)security and that has also had important impacts on the growth and roles of private security.[37]

In one sense, individual and community declarations of moral outrage have devalued the expert knowledge previously claimed by penal reformism and have made crime and responses to it part of more populist

---

[36] Cara Buckley, 'New York Plans Surveillance Veil for Downtown', *New York Times*, 9 July 2007, p. 3. There are already 4,200 public and private security cameras below 14th Street, a fivefold increase since 1998.

[37] This trend has been supplemented by an intensified focus on the moral and political status of the individual victim. As Garland puts it, in this view 'it is no longer sufficient to subsume the individual victim's experience in the notion of the public good: the public good must be individuated, broken into component parts. Specific victims are to have a voice – making victim statements, being consulted about punishment and decisions about punishment and decisions about release, being notified about the offender's subsequent movements. There is, in short, a new cultural theme, a new collective meaning of victimhood, and a reworked relationship between the individual victim, the symbolic victim, and the public instruments of crime control and criminal justice', *Culture of Control*, p. 12.

agendas.[38] The notion of victimization and the fear of becoming a victim have also come to play a key part in the politics of knowledge surrounding security. As Garland points out, 'Government sponsored research now regularly investigates the levels and character of this fear, categorizing and measuring the emotional reactions prompted by crime – concrete fears, inchoate fears, generalized insecurity, anger, resentment – and correlating these with actual patterns of risk and victimization.'[39] This process is by no means limited to rich industrialized countries. Across the developing world, victimization surveys are now regularly undertaken by numerous NGOs, institutes of security studies and perhaps most prominently by the United Nations Human Settlements Programme (UN-HABITAT).[40] In this way, risk society comes to developing countries in large part through global development actors. While the collection and publication of data about fear of crime, victims of crime and crime 'hotspots' may be valuable in terms of policy and planning, such knowledge simultaneously becomes an important element in debates over security – new structures of social knowledge that have effects on the politics of security.

These effects can be seen in the development of a new cultural theme in contemporary societies, one illustrated by public-opinion research that

finds that there is a settled assumption on the part of a large majority of the public in the US and the UK that crime rates are getting worse, whatever the actual patterns, and that there is little public confidence in the ability of the criminal justice system to do anything about this.[41]

The rhetoric of political actors and media representations of crime and insecurity have played an important role in these perceptions. In addition to the popularity of police dramas and 'reality' crime shows, violent crime has become increasingly prominent in the news media. According to one analysis of the USA,

---

[38] See David C. Anderson, *Crime and the Politics of Hysteria*, New York: Times Books, 1995; Hans Boutellier, *Crime and Morality*, Amsterdam: Kluwer Academic Publishers, 2000.

[39] Garland, *Culture of Control*, p. 12.

[40] See, for example, the initiatives taken under the Safer Cities Programme (www.unhabitat.org).

[41] Garland, *Culture of Control*, p. 10.

Between 1989 and 1993, the number of such reports on the nightly news
of the three major national networks (ABC, CBS, and NBC) quadrupled
to reach 1,632, or nearly five per evening, despite the drop in offending
rates ... Crime rates continued to decrease rapidly for six years; yet in 1999
the three leading news outlets still broadcast an astounding 1,613 crime
reports, keeping crime the first news topic (tied with the raging war in
Kosovo at 1,615)'.[42]

The most obvious results of this heightened sense of insecurity and political punitiveness have been an increase in police personnel dedicated
to crime-fighting, a stress on incarceration and a general stiffening of
punitive sentencing.[43] The rise in incarceration has been particularly
striking in the USA, leading one observer to claim that it is 'without
precedent in the history of democratic societies'.[44] In 1975, the US
prison and jail population counted 380,000. By 2007, it was 2.2 million.[45] While the proportion of the population in prison in the USA is
nearly seven times higher than in most of Western Europe, here too
incarceration has grown.[46] In England and Wales, the prison population has shot up from 45,000 to 80,000 since 1993, and there are now
more people in prison than at any time in history.[47] The Home Office
predicts a rise to 90,000 and possibly to 106,500 by 2013.[48]

The impact of these developments on private security has been two-
fold. First, the cultural themes of crime and victimization, along with
policies of responsibilization, have contributed to the perception that
individuals should (and must) contribute to their own security. The

---

[42] Wacquant, 'Penal Truth', p. 18; for an earlier treatment see Richard Sparks,
*Television and the Drama of Crime: Moral Tales and the Place of Crime in
Public Life*, Milton Keynes: Open University Press, 1992.
[43] On how this insecurity was mobilized politically in the USA, see Katherine
Beckett, *Making Crime Pay: Law and Order in Contemporary American
Politics*, Oxford: Oxford University Press, 1997.
[44] Wacquant, 'Great Penal Leap Backward', p. 5.
[45] Jason De Parle, 'The American Prison Nightmare', *New York Review of
Books*, 12 April 2007, pp. 33–6.
[46] For an analysis tracing the transmission of American ideas about crime and
imprisonment to Europe over recent decades, see Wacquant, 'Penal Truth'.
[47] De Parle, 'American Prison Nightmare'; National Offender Management
Service, 'Prison Population and Accommodation Briefing for 15 June 2007'
(www.hmprisonservice.gov.uk).
[48] Nisha De Silva, Paul Cowell, Terence Chow and Paul Worthington, 'Prison
Population Projection, 2006–2013: England and Wales', *Home Office
Statistical Bulletin*, July 2006.

growth in private security services, from alarms to gated communities, has been a consequence. Second, private prisons and prisoner-management services have expanded rapidly, responding to a lack of public prison capacity and financing.[49] In the USA, 6.5 per cent of federal and state prisoners are now in private facilities; the figures are 9 per cent in the UK and 18 per cent in Australia.[50] Private security providers also play a key role in the electronic monitoring of offenders, or so-called electronic tagging. In the UK, G4S's Justice Service unit receives approximately £36 million a year from the Government for offender monitoring and tagging. The company also monitors offenders in the USA and Israel, and on a daily basis monitors more than 35,000 people. In Scotland, electronic monitoring has been outsourced to the private firm Serco, which monitors curfews and offender movements.

The creation of an extensive private security and prison industry with close links to criminal justice systems and the massive expansion of the state's concern with crime has led some analysts to draw explicitly upon analogies from the world of international security, with Garland proposing that what has emerged is a new 'penal-industrial complex'.[51] Others have suggested that as the national and international aspects of crime and insecurity are increasingly interacting, we have witnessed the 'rise of the American crimefare state'.[52] What is clear, from the point of view of our argument, is that the rise of private security actors is closely connected to these social and political shifts in contemporary modern societies. Indeed, transformations in the politics of security at the level of public policy and popular

---

[49] As Wacquant notes, this expansion had important links to wider financial developments: 'with 26 federal prisons and 96 state penitentiaries under construction in 1996, the financing of carceral building had become one of the most profitable sectors in the bonds market. This was not lost on the big Wall Street brokerage firms, such as Goldman Sachs, Smith Barney Shearson, Prudential-Bache, and Merrill Lynch, who sunk two to three billion dollars into it during the 1990s'. 'Penal Truth', p. 10.

[50] Johnston, 'Transnational Security Governance', p. 38.

[51] David Garland, 'Limits of the Sovereign State: Strategies of Crime Contol in Contemporary Society', *British Journal of Criminology*, 36 (4) (1996): 445–71; p. 463; see also Steven Donziger, *The Real War on Crime*, New York: Basic Books, 1996, pp. 63–8.

[52] Peter Andreas and Richard Price, 'From War Fighting to Crime Fighting: Transforming the American National Security State', *International*

discourse in the North and in many developing countries have played
an important role in the increased acceptance and legitimacy of
security privatization, its incorporation into everyday practices and
the commercial opportunities behind the emergence of today's global
security companies.

Commodification and risk

The processes described above are closely connected to the increasing
commodification of security, whereby security becomes a service to
be bought and sold in the marketplace and a commodity capable of
being globally exported as a set of technical capabilities and skills.
In consequence, security ceases in part – but in an important part –
to be a quintessentially social and public concern. As a technique
partially severed from local conceptions of justice, security becomes
distinguishable in principle from the sensitive political issues of security that governments have usually reserved for themselves under the
claim of state sovereignty.[53] While security remains the prerogative
of the state in many areas of policing, the capacity to cast it as a
politically neutral service legitimately provided by the private sector
allows private firms to draw upon logics of free trade to facilitate
their entry into new markets, even where these are resisted by the
host state.[54] The World Trade Organization (WTO) includes private
security in the General Agreement on Trade in Services and thus
encourages member countries to allow free and fair competition in
security services. Indeed, China's decision to open its security market
to foreign investment in advance of the 2008 Olympic Games was
partly in response to WTO requirements. The EU has also sought

Studies Review, 3 (3) (2001): 31–52; and Peter Andreas and Ethan
Nadelmann, *Policing the Globe*, Oxford: Oxford University Press, 2006.
[53] It is less clear that this is the case with companies operating in the private
military sector, especially those involved in combat-active roles; for a
systematic discussion see Avant, *Market for Force*. In relation to PSCs, by
contrast, the treatment of both Securitas and Group4Falck as exemplary
models of 'service' companies in Waldemar Schmitt, Gordon Adler and
Els Van Weering, *Winning at Service*, New York: Wiley, 2003, and the
discussion in John Stees, *Outsourcing Security: A Guide for Contracting
Services*, Woburn, Mass.: Butterworth-Heinemann, 1998, are indicative of
the extent to which this view is accepted.
[54] For an illustration, see our discussion of South Africa in Chapter 3.

to promote free trade in security services across Europe as part of its Services Directive, although the Europe-wide security industry association Confederation of European Security Services (CoESS) has contested this, arguing that with over twenty different criminal justices systems a genuine internal market is impossible and that a lack of regulation in some member states will give companies originating there an unfair competitive advantage over those imposing more stringent rules. Nonetheless, the security sector's exclusion from the Services Directive is to be reviewed by the EU Commission at the end of 2010.[55]

At the level of daily life, a further sign of security's commodification can be found in its recent transformation from a utility to consumer luxury, or an object of desire.[56] As the style and architectural magazine *Wallpaper* recounts, 'the trend is moving towards making security more chic', and thankfully, 'deterring intruders is no longer an ugly business.'[57] From fencing to window screens, from steel doors to CCTV cameras, the market in 'good looking' security gadgetry is growing. What in other manufacturing industries has been dubbed the 'handbag effect' is thus entering the security market; the realization that design can elevate an everyday object from the category of commodity to the category of lifestyle component, and a pragmatic

[55] Similarly, government trade bodies across the globe frequently advertise their security markets: the Indian Embassy in Washington, DC, for example, eagerly promotes investment opportunities for US security companies on its website, while the Government of Israel in 2004 released a report on the possibilities for Israeli PSCs in India. Government of Israel (2004) *Economic Review of India: India Security Market*, available online at www.moital.gov.il/NR/exeres/DE1DDFE9–4B91–46AD-A20E-18C642166454.htm (accessed 24 June 2010). In January 2010, the UK's Department of Trade and Investment organized a security and fire trade mission to East Africa, stressing that 'most organisations within this region are looking to develop integrated, sophisticated, and pre-emptive security solutions and are constantly searching for professionalism, experience and expertise to deliver security solutions to protect and sustain their businesses, personnel and assets. In addition, the Kenyan and Tanzanian Governments would like to put in place the right policies to help mitigate geopolitical upheaval and counter fraud, corruption, terrorism and organised crime'. 'Security and Fire Trade Mission to East Africa', available online at https://uktradeinvest.gov.uk (accessed 15 January 2010).

[56] On the aesthetics of security, see Ian Loader, 'Consumer Culture and the Commodification of Policing and Security', *Sociology*, 33(3) (1999): 377–94; and Caldeira, *City of Walls*.

[57] *Wallpaper*, 'Nice to CCTV You!', May 2007, pp. 200–5.

investment is thereby rendered compatible with a style-driven consumer society. As keeping your home, your family and your possessions safe has become an integral part of modern life, it is no longer only about keeping safe but also about staying 'chic'; for the fashionably secure, greeting guests at the door now involves saying, 'Nice to CCTV you!', as *Wallpaper* coyly puts it.

Another aspect of the commodification of security is the growing prevalence of logics, technologies or mentalities of risk in the security field. Risk is, of course, far from a straightforward concept. In the broadest sense, it conveys the idea that individuals and organizations exist in ever-more-complex environments characterized by what Anthony Giddens usefully termed 'distanciation', where their security is increasingly affected by factors beyond their immediate knowledge and control, both spatially and temporally.[58] In such settings, face-to-face relationships are replaced by dependence on abstract systems and institutions, which, through their ability to span space and time beyond the capabilities of individuals or single organizations, provide actors with the means of collecting knowledge, exerting control and allowing effective agency. Risk, in this sense, is not simply a synonym for danger; it is a particular way of thinking about and responding to potential dangers.[59] Risk is preventative, not restorative; it is primarily actuarial and calculative and works by designing and controlling spaces, by the collection of statistics and the production of categories of danger, and through surveillance. In the words of Ericson and Haggerty:

Rationalities of risk are designed to reduce uncertainty to the point where the actor feels confident in taking action. Grounded in probabilistic thinking and predictions, they allow deselection of specific factors and thereby point to preferable courses of action. They are hyper-rational and deeply pragmatic, always scanning for technical solutions to problems that incapacitate action. They eschew causality in favour of laws of regularity that establish standards of objective fact and the basis of objective knowledge.[60]

[58] Anthony Giddens, *Consequences of Modernity*, Cambridge: Polity Press, 1990.
[59] The relevant literatures on risk across several fields are now enormous; for an important historical and philosophical treatment, see Ian Hacking, *The Taming of Chance*, Cambridge: Cambridge University Press, 1990; in sociology, Mary Douglas, *Risk and Blame*, London and New York: Routledge, 1994; in International Relations, Rasmussen, *The Risk Society at War*.
[60] Ericson and Haggerty, *Policing the Risk Society*, p. 87.

Whereas the public police have traditionally been primarily concerned with criminal justice and the punishment of past crimes, commercial security, as Les Johnston and Clifford Shearing observe, tends towards anticipatory strategies and risk management. In recent decades, however, risk-based technologies have become increasingly prominent in the security field as a whole, playing a key part in the practices of public security agents.[61] This in turn has facilitated and encouraged interaction between public and private security actors and has also contributed to the legitimation of the latter, allowing PSCs to exercise claims to expert authority in both the technical and managerial dimensions of security provision, as well as in broader forms of risk analysis and intelligence.[62] Security can thus be seen as operating increasingly within a web of what Ericson and Haggerty have usefully termed 'risk institutions'. In this view, policing is not only, or even primarily, about crime-fighting in a direct sense. It is about the management of risks – about the collection of data and the production of knowledge about risks, and the interaction between multiple risk agencies, including PSCs.

Importantly for our argument here, the techniques of risk are in principle applicable across social and geographical settings. Allowing, of course, for local modifications, at its core, risk-oriented thinking is neutral and universalizable, delinked from particular political strategies and welfarist understandings of crime and insecurity. Risk-based security techniques and technologies are thus another element underpinning the growth of the global private security market. Global corporations rely extensively on political risk analysis to safeguard their operations, and while some companies have in-house security divisions, many look to the services of a range of companies such as Control Risks, Kroll or the Eurasia Group, to provide comprehensive risk-management services and business intelligence

---

[61] Johnston and Shearing, *Governing Security*. Importantly, there is an increasing emphasis on 'intelligence-led policing', focused on generating and analysing information on crime patterns, known offenders, and crime 'hot spots'. In this way, the police become knowledge workers, generating and distributing authoritative information to other actors. See Ericson and Haggerty, *Policing the Risk Society*.

[62] For analyses of PMCs in this regard, see Leander, 'The Power to Construct'; and Leander and Van Munster, 'Private Security Contractors', as well as the special issue on risk technologies of *Security Dialogue*, 39 (2–3) (2008).

about international threats affecting their interests or compromising the safety of their operations and personnel. The lucrative nature of this part of the private security sector is attested by G4S's launch of its own separate political risk section as part of their Global Risks division, promising an 'integrated' security service to its customers. Indeed, the capacity to provide integrated risk analysis for agents who operate in multiple geographic settings is one of the selling points of transnational security firms, a capacity that in turn drives them to further global extension.

Perceiving security as a field of risk, and private security as a risk institution within it, draws attention to the important relationship between risk and trust. As individuals and organizations come to rely on distanced organizations and abstract systems to provide security against a range of putative risks, they need to trust organizations staffed by individuals they in all likelihood do not know personally and that deal with areas of activity and expertise that they as clients or consumers do not understand. In this setting, a reputation for expertise and trustworthiness becomes a key asset for PSCs to acquire, and a crucial marketing device when achieved.[63] As the CEO of G4S argues, 'Because of our international brand and expertise, a lot of multi-nationals are keen to use our services.'[64] Like the police, private security firms are also increasingly 'knowledge' organizations. Thus, the large international companies emphasize their global reputations and their multifaceted global capacities as providers of a wide spectrum of risk analysis and consultation services – and they are keen to stress that they are not just guarding companies. Securitas's corporate slogan – 'A Knowledge Leader in Security' – is particularly telling in this regard.

Security governance and global power

As the discussion above demonstrates, commercial security does not operate in straightforward opposition to the state, nor does it constitute autarkic enclaves within society. Such interpretations overlook

---

[63] On the function of trust in such situations, see Giddens, *Consequences of Modernity*; in terms of private security, see the insightful discussion in Loader, 'Consumer Culture', pp. 381–2.

[64] Quoted in O'Doherty, 'G4S Hopes to Push the Boat Out More'.

both the extent to which security privatization is related to neo-liberalism, and to social, political and institutional transformations in the contemporary security field. The process of privatization is often sanctioned and encouraged by governments; at the very least, it is generally tolerated and only infrequently opposed by them. Moreover, while the private security sector has grown, so too have public security organizations, and the increasingly punitive nature of criminal justice puts paid to any simple notion of the retreat of the traditional sovereign power of the state.

Contemporary criminological analyses thus commonly point to how the security sector is 'fragmenting and blurring', as public and private actors interact and combine in the provision of security.[65] However, while there is broad agreement that a pluralization of security is taking place, there is considerable disagreement about its impact and implications. For some, the result of this rearticulation of public and private actors is an almost seamless integration and a division of coercive labour. In his striking study of Los Angeles, for example, Mike Davis sees

an evolving social division of labour between public- and private-sector police services, in which the former act as the necessary support of the latter ... The private sector, exploiting an army of non-union, low-wage employees, has increasingly captured the labour-intensive roles (guard duty, residential patrol, apprehension of retail crime, maintenance of security passages and checkpoints, monitoring of electronic surveillance, and so on), while public law enforcement has retrenched behind supervision of security macro-systems.[66]

The result in his view is an increasing domination of private wealth and power via new structures of coercion.

There is clearly much to this analysis, and much – as Davis vividly argues – to be concerned about. However, presenting private security as simply the 'junior partner' of public policing in ever-stronger networks of social control not only overlooks the complexities involved in contemporary security provision but also obscures the fact that public and private security actors compete as well as collaborate and

---

[65] Jones and Newburn, *Private Security and Public Policing*, p. 255.
[66] Davis, *City of Quartz*, pp. 250–1. See also the discussion in Ericson and Haggerty, *Policing the Risk Society*, pp. 29–30.

exist in relations of considerable tension.[67] As we will argue in subsequent chapters, these tensions are constitutive elements of the field of security, and they play even more important roles when public–private security structures are simultaneously global and local.

In international politics, attempts to understand the new, pluralized security environment have tended to regard it as part of a 'shift from government to governance in security' and as part of a 'fragmentation of authority among state and non-state actors'.[68] Drawing on a combination of research in International Relations and theories of non-hierarchical forms of authority developed particularly in the study of the EU, this body of literature argues that hierarchical conceptions of government no longer capture the structure of security provision, which is increasingly dispersed geographically, functionally, normatively and institutionally.[69] Instead, 'the fragmented but overlapping networks which structure the collaboration among the growing range of state and non-state security actors are more adequately described by the concept of governance.'[70]

In common with many studies of global governance, this understanding of (private) security governance is closely concerned with the *management* of these new networks. As Elke Krahmann puts it,

[67] For a critical discussion of theories of private security that reduce it to being either a junior partner of the police or just one element in 'one big police force', see Jones and Newburn, *Private Security and Public Policing.*

[68] Elke Krahmann, 'From State to Non-State Actors: The Emergence of Security Governance', in Elke Krahmann (ed.), *New Threats and New Actors in International Security*, Basingstoke: Palgrave Macmillan, 2005, pp. 1–21; p. 12. This literature has focused primarily on the private military, and when the wider private security sector is discussed it tends to be presented as a category that can be deployed 'interchangeably' with the private military. Krahmann, 'From State to Non-State Actors', p. 8.

[69] Early formulations of global governance that remain influential in this view of security governance include James Rosenau and Ernst-Otto Czempiel (eds.), *Governance without Government*, Cambridge: Cambridge University Press, 1992; and Leon Gordenker and Thomas G. Weiss, 'Pluralizing Global Governance: Analytical Approaches and Dimensions', in Leon Gordenker and Thomas G. Weiss (eds.), *NGOs, the UN, and Global Governance*, Boulder, Col.: Lynne Rienner, 1996, pp. 17–47.

[70] Krahmann, 'From State to Non-State Actors', p. 11. See also Alan Bryden, 'Approaching the Privatization of Security from a Security Governance Perspective', in Bryden and Caparini, *Private Actors and Security Governance*, pp. 3–22; and Elke Krahmann, 'Conceptualizing Security Governance', *Cooperation and Conflict*, 38 (1) (2003): 5–26.

in a decentralized security situation 'resources are dispersed among a range of public and private actors who have to coordinate their efforts in order to solve their common problems'. While the interests of these actors may differ, the goal of security governance is to 'ensure that each actor can pursue them as uninhibited as possible'.[71] Governance thus becomes a question of how these multiple actors can work together and especially of how public authorities can establish optimal relations in the new situation.

These are important questions, and the issue of how to manage relations between public and private security actors is certainly vital if these new public–private networks are to enhance, rather than diminish security. However, this view of governance comes at a cost, in that by casting governance in such relatively narrow terms it takes the actors largely for granted and sees governance primarily as a process of ordering. The question of what has given rise to this new security architecture in terms of shifts in underlying social structures and practices of governance, and how they impact relations between its different elements, are left unanswered. In short, in addition to treating the question of governance as one of *how to govern* new structures, there is a need to understand how this problematic is produced by and reflects transformations in structures of governance at the level of micro-practices of everyday life and the macro-practices of global politics.

The most sophisticated approaches to these questions have been developed in criminology under the rubric of 'nodal security governance', which identifies the state as only one of many actors or 'nodes' in the governance and delivery of security.[72] Drawing on a range of social theories, these analyses examine the dispersed forms of power underpinning social orders – including what Foucault famously dubbed the 'conduct of conduct' – arguing that to appreciate the shifting nature of security governance we must look beyond the mere pluralization of security actors and examine the formation of

---

[71] Krahmann, 'From State to Non-State Actors', p. 13.
[72] The key literature on nodal governance includes Johnston and Shearing, *Governing Security*; Clifford Shearing and Jennifer Wood, 'Nodal Governance, Democracy and the New "Denizens"', *Journal of Law and Society*, 30(3) (2003): 400–19; Clifford Shearing and Jennifer Wood, 'Governing Security for Common Goods', *International Journal of the Sociology of Law*, 31(3) (2003): 205–25; Jennifer Wood and Clifford Shearing, *Imagining Security*, London: Willan, 2006; Jennifer Wood and

subjectivities and the shifting varieties of practices and institutions with which they are enmeshed.

In an extremely lucid summary, Les Johnston outlines the salient features of nodal security governance as those where the various nodes are perceived as 'sites of knowledge, capacity and resources that function as governance auspices or providers'. Importantly, 'the model refuses to give conceptual priority to any particular locus of power, seeing governance as a relationship contained within a shifting network of alliances rather than as a product of the realization of governing interests.'[73] Or, as two other advocates of the approach put it, 'no set of nodes is given conceptual priority. Rather the exact nature of governance and the contribution of the various nodes to it are regarded as empirically open questions.'[74] Although these new networks constitute an ordered domain, nodal arrangements do not express a single underlying logic. Instead of assuming the presence of a dominant state able to impose and regulate other security actors according to its own governance agenda, nodal governance allows for the possibility that other security actors or nodes may be more influential at particular times or in particular settings. As Johnston puts it, 'the model refuses to posit any correspondence between governing mentalities, the objectives, institutions, and technologies associated with them, and determinate governmental "outcomes".'[75] In short, decentring the state's position in security governance does not entail its direct replacement by another sovereign presence – the logic of capital, for example. Instead, the production of security within nodal networks is a relational and contingent process.

Advocates of this position are also at pains to note that while they seek to decentre the position of the state as the sole locus and driver of security practices, they do not deny that the state retains a central place in security. In Johnston's words, the model 'does not deny the state's role as a crucial site of governance', and states retain crucial legal, symbolic and material capacities that make them specific.[76] In

---

Benoît Dupont (eds.), *Democracy, Society and the Governance of Security*, Cambridge University Press, 2006.

[73] Johnston, 'Transnational Security Governance', p. 34.

[74] Shearing and Wood, 'Nodal Governance', p. 404.

[75] Johnston, 'Transnational Security Governance', p. 34.

[76] *Ibid.*, p. 34. Whether advocates of nodal security governance have taken these issues seriously enough, especially in terms of the state's place in social

particular, the capacity for legal punishment and rights of access and coercion mark the state as a special kind of node – though it must always be borne in mind that both punishment and coercion and the grounds of their legitimacy differ widely.[77] That said, the nodal governance model often actively endorses the dispersal of security governance in contrast to the exclusive and exclusionary claims of the sovereign state. This argument has been pursued with particular vigour in relation to Africa and the global South more generally, where states do not always provide security for their populations and where state security services can often be a threat to the very people they are supposed to protect. In this light, the existence of nodal security networks that include non-state actors is not just an empirical fact on the ground; it also becomes a potentially desirable alternative. Since the Third World provides some of the most striking illustrations of states that are unable or unwilling to provide security, or where state forces become predators rather than protectors, the development of progressive and accountable structures of nodal security governance is seen as part of an agenda for both enhanced security and political empowerment. Security self-reliance thus becomes a positive value, and ways in which nodal governance can be harnessed to increase democratic values and participation become part of policy advocacy.[78]

The idea of nodal structures of security governance marks a significant advance in thinking about the increasing role of private actors in security provision, and the analyses we develop throughout

cohesion, is an issue of considerable debate, and is treated extensively in Loader and Walker, *Civilizing Security*. We return to some of these issues in Chapter 6.

[77] In a pluralized setting, for example, 'vigilantes' may exercise retribution that is viewed by many social actors as legitimate, while the access of public forces to all social spaces is in many countries at best an aspiration, and sometimes not even that. For an excellent discussion of vigilantes, see Lars Buur, 'Democracy and Its Discontents: Vigilantism, Sovereignty and Human Rights in South Africa', *Review of African Political Economy*, 35 (118) (2008): 571–84; and on the limited reach of public policing in Africa, Bruce Baker, 'Beyond the Tarmac Road: Local Forms of Policing in Sierra Leone and Rwanda', *Review of African Political Economy*, 35 (118) (2008): 555–70.

[78] Wood and Shearing, *Imagining Security*, pp. 96, 148. The best illustration is the Security 21 project based around the Australian National University, in which these authors are key participants. A critique of what they term the 'Left Hayekian' underpinning of this view is developed in Loader and Walker, *Civilizing Security*.

this study are deeply indebted to its insights. Reflecting its origin in criminology, however, the approach has been primarily concerned with the domestic arena and with mapping and analysing various nodal networks contained within the territorial state. The focus of much research and controversy over alternative forms of security governance has thus centred on the relationship between the national and the local, between the state and non-state actors. Possibly the most cited case in the developing world, for instance, is the community-based Zwelethemba project in South Africa, which proponents see as an example of the virtues of plural forms of security provision. While analysts recognize that nodal security structures can also be transnational and frequently point to the existence of a global security market, relatively few attempts have yet been made to analyse the operations of transnational security networks in any depth or detail.[79]

The challenges presented by looking at global networks and dynamics are not just of scale but also of structure. To understand the integration of private security actors into global structures requires an appreciation of the impact of different forms of state, the specific relationships between states, societies and security, and an assessment of the implications of these factors for the relationship between processes of security privatization and those of globalization as a whole. The importance of these issues is clearly exhibited when analysing security privatization in Africa. While Africa is frequently perceived as marginalized by globalization, the continent is perhaps more than many other geographical territories a profoundly transnational space where the local and the global are intrinsically interwoven. Africa's long-standing 'extraversion' – its historical implication in, and to a large degree production through, global processes – means that new forms of transnational governance are taking shape as international actors of various kinds have become increasingly involved in the governance of African societies.[80] Most well known and commented upon in this regard are the international financial institutions and major bilateral donors, who, through their development policies,

---

[79] Though see Johnston, 'Transnational Security Governance', and, especially, Johnston, 'Glocal Heroes'; Wood and Shearing, *Imagining Security*.

[80] Jean-François Bayart, 'Africa in the World: A History of Extraversion', *African Affairs*, 395 (99) (2000): 217–67.

structural adjustment programmes and poverty reduction strategies have achieved an ever-stronger ability to influence policy formation and decision-making on the continent.[81] Similarly, international NGOs are increasingly 'state-like' in their functions and influences, possessing resources and providing services that frequently outstrip anything on offer from African states.[82] Transnationalization is evident not merely in terms of actors but also in terms of politically relevant (normative) discourses and audiences. Increasingly, for example, international human rights and environmental discourses play incisive roles in domestic political struggles, empowering some local actors (often at the expense of others) through their access to particular global discourses, audiences and resources.[83]

Put differently, politics in Africa increasingly takes place in 'transboundary formations', spaces that defy the neatly defined geographical boundaries of nation-states and that cannot be classified as local, national or international.[84] As James Ferguson recently commented, government in many African settings 'cannot be located within a national grid but is instead spread across a patchwork of transnationally networked, noncontigous bits'.[85] It is our contention that private security on the African continent is best analysed as part of such transnational transformations in governance and that it is best approached as part of a reconfiguration of state power and public–private relations. Here we depart from the frequently explicit normative predisposition towards private actors in much of the nodal

[81] Jeremy Gould (ed.), *The New Conditionality: The Politics of Poverty Reduction Strategies*, London: Zed Books, 2006; Graham Harrison, *The World Bank and Africa: The Construction of Governance States*, London and New York: Routledge, 2004.

[82] See Michel-Rolph Trouillot, 'The Anthropology of the State in the Age of Globalization: Close Encounters of the Deceptive Kind', *Current Anthropology*, 42 (1) (2001): 125–38.

[83] Harri Englund, *Prisoners of Freedom: Human Rights and the African Poor*, Berkeley, Calif.: University of California Press, 2006; James Ferguson and Akhil Gupta, 'Spatializing States: Towards an Ethnography of Neoliberal Governmentality', *American Ethnologist*, 29 (4) (2002): 981–1002. In the security realm, see Avant's analysis of the use of private force by international conservation NGOs in Deborah Avant, 'Conserving Nature in the State of Nature: The Politics of INGO Policy Implementation', *Review of International Studies*, 30 (2004): 361–82.

[84] Callaghy *et al.*, *Intervention and Transnationalism in Africa*.

[85] James Ferguson, *Global Shadows: Africa in the Neoliberal World Order*, Durham, NC: Duke University Press, 2006, p. 40.

governance literature and instead focus squarely on questions of power.[86] Drawing legitimacy, authority and power from a mixture of local and global institutions, capabilities and discourses, private security actors in Africa provide a striking illustration of the shifting structures of global governance and highlight the importance of prying apart the state–territory–authority triptych that has dominated analyses of politics and international relations for so long, particularly in the study of security.[87] Understanding security provision and governance within a pluralized global security environment hence requires a theoretical framework that is capable of capturing the multiple forms of power available to the participating actors. Where these nodal networks are transnational, this also inevitably entails an analysis of the relationship between global and national actors and a way of theorizing the links between these and global processes. We turn to this task of understanding global security assemblages and the forms of power within them in the next chapter.

[86] It is important to note that support for 'private' participation in security within nodal governance theory is most often framed in terms of community participation, rather than the commercial involvement that is our focus here.

[87] See Michael Barnett, 'Authority, Intervention, and the Outer Limits of International Relations Theory', in Callaghy *et al.*, *Intervention and Transnationalism in Africa*, pp. 47–67.

3 | Power and governance: global assemblages and the security field

The expansion of commercial private security in the contemporary era is not a return to the buccaneering capitalism of Cecil Rhodes, and even less the renaissance of the military mercantilism of the seventeenth century's chartered companies. Nor does it, in the majority of cases, mirror the most spectacular activities of late twentieth-century PMCs or 'neo-mercenaries', however much this image tends to capture the imagination. To the extent that these historical periods serve useful purposes, it is as metaphors and reminders of the historically and politically constructed nature of the public–private distinction and its connection to shifting structures of political power, not as templates for thinking about the emerging place of commercial security in the world order.

This chapter seeks to develop the theoretical foundations for understanding contemporary global private security. To do so, we make two moves: first, we turn for inspiration to theories of globalization that emphasize the relationship between the restructuring of national state structures and global transformations. Drawing on recent analyses of globalization, we argue that security privatization is part of a wider process of partial state 'disassembly' and a concomitant emergence of 'global assemblages' that link national and global structures.[1] In security,

---

[1] For a variety of examples, see Aihwa Ong and Stephen J. Collier (eds.), *Global Assemblages: Technology, Politics, and Ethics as Anthropological Problems*, Oxford: Blackwell, 2005; Kevin D. Haggerty and Richard V. Ericson, 'The Surveillant Assemblage', *British Journal of Sociology* 51 (4) (2000): 605–22; Randy Lippert and Daniel O'Connor, 'Security Assemblages: Airport Security, Flexible Work, and Liberal Governance', *Alternatives*, 28 (3) (2003): 331–58; Sassen, *Territory, Authority, Rights*. For a thoughtful exploration of how actor–network theory could enrich studies of global governance see Gavin Kendall, 'Global Networks, International Networks, Actor Networks', in Wendy Larner and William Walters (eds.), *Global Governmentality*, London and New York: Routledge, 2004, pp. 59–75. The theoretical literature on assemblages is enormous, complex, and extremely diverse; we make no attempt to address it here.

a result of these shifts is the emergence of what we call *global security assemblages* – transnational structures and networks in which a range of different actors and normativities interact, cooperate and compete to produce new institutions, practices and forms of deterritorialized security governance. These assemblages are reflections and components of important transformations in social and political power. To better reveal their dynamics, we turn in the second part of the chapter to the sociology of Pierre Bourdieu. In particular, we suggest that Bourdieu's understanding of *fields of practice* provides analytic categories that help clarify the resources available to public and private, as well as global and local security actors, allowing us to examine the shifting forms of power and contestation at work within global security assemblages.

Global (security) assemblages

In her recent analysis of globalization and the shifting relationship between territory, authority and rights, Saskia Sassen argues that globalization involves more than the mere existence or increase of global flows of products, capital or people. As critics of globalization theories have pointed out, these processes have long existed.[2] Nor can globalization be equated with the simple erosion of the position and power of the state, a stance often adopted in both studies of globalization and assessments of security privatization.[3] As Sassen puts it:

We generally use terms such as deregulation, financial and trade liberalization, and privatization to describe the changed authority of the state when it comes to the economy. The problem with such terms is that they only capture the withdrawal of the state from regulating its economy. They do not register all the ways in which the state participates in setting up the new frameworks through which globalization is furthered, nor do they capture the associated transformations inside the state.[4]

---

[2] For a survey, see Paul Hirst and Grahame Thompson, *Globalization in Question*, Cambridge: Polity Press, 1996; Randall D. Germain (ed.), *Globalization and Its Critics: Perspectives from Political Economy*, Basingstoke: Palgrave Macmillan, 2000; Linda Weiss (ed.), *States in the Global Economy: Bringing Domestic Institutions Back In*, Cambridge: Cambridge University Press, 2003.

[3] For a critique of this reading of globalization, see, for example, Linda Weiss, *The Myth of the Powerless State*, Ithaca, NY: Cornell University Press, 1998.

[4] Sassen, *Territory, Authority, Rights*, p. 234.

Instead of seeing globalization as a process in which states are eroded by global forces, Sassen argues that it is precisely the national state that has made today's global era possible. Many of the activities, institutions and structures now identified with globalization came into existence at the direct instigation of national governments and continue to operate through transformed national institutions that enable and facilitate their operation. More specifically, Sassen suggests that the development of contemporary global structures involves three key elements: a process of 'disassembly' in which previously public functions are increasingly transferred to private actors; the development of 'capacities' by private actors that allow them to act at a global level; and a process of 'reassembly' whereby these new actors and capabilities become part of global assemblages that are embedded in national settings but operate at a global scale. In this way, the disassembly of the national becomes constitutive of the global, in that 'the territorial sovereign state, with its territorial fixity and exclusivity, represents a set of capabilities that eventually enable the formation or evolution of particular global systems'.[5]

Two important parameters of this process need to be stressed. First, the disassembly is partial – it does not mean the national state is disappearing, or that the state is fading away. Rather, particular components of the state are undergoing a process of 'denationalization' and rearticulation, and the processes of disassembly in one part of the state may have implications for others, while shifting power relations between different agencies or organizations within the state.[6] Globalization then is not a process whereby 'outside' forces are eroding a territorially distinct 'inside'; it is entwined with a restructuring of institutions and power relations inside the state through, for example, the neo-liberal practices of privatization and regulation that we discussed in Chapter 2. Second, this realignment inside the state has generally redistributed power in favour of those elements of the state that are directly embedded in global structures, such as ministries of trade and finance, elements of the judiciary that deal with international regulation and the executive branch in general.

---

[5] Sassen, *Territory, Authority, Rights*, p. 21.
[6] *Ibid.*, p. 8; and from different perspectives, Grande and Pauly, *Complex Sovereignty*; Steven Gill, 'Globalization, Market Civilization and Disciplinary Neo-Liberalism', in Steven Gill (ed.), *Power and Resistance in the New World Order*, Basingstoke, Macmillan, 2003, pp. 116–42.

As neo-liberalism has acquired greater centrality in state policy, decisions are increasingly made with an eye to global markets and global imperatives. As Barry Hindess notes, 'the promotion of economic efficiency becomes the paramount goal in what amounts to a liberal problematic of security', and policies are judged by whether or not they contribute to or inhibit economic efficiency and global competitiveness.[7] The 'normativity of the competitive state' is thus crucial to globalization and can be seen as a 'denationalization of state agendas' whereby key 'components of the state begin to function as the institutional home for the operation of dynamics that are constitutive and crucial for "global capital"'.[8] These components of the state are in turn central in instituting the normativity of globalization at the heart of the state and often operate in complex interaction with private, transnational actors and institutions. They also facilitate globalization by allowing global actors to link directly to globalized state institutions in support of their projects and to overcome the opposition of other elements of the state. Thus, for example, the activities of politically independent central banks, their formal and informal interactions with their international counterparts, and with other key players in the international financial system, have risen in salience while that of legislatures have in relative terms declined.[9]

Like many theorists of globalization, Sassen's attention is centred primarily on the economic domain. However, a focus on these processes also illuminates important parts of global security privatization. Indeed, when set against the account of security privatization developed in the previous chapter, these categories provide a powerful heuristic for analysing global security assemblages. As we saw in Chapter 2, the process of partial state disassembly has been crucial to the rise of private security. For a wide variety of reasons – the rise of neo-liberalism and strategies of new public management, shifting attitudes towards crime and punishment and the pervasiveness of various

---

[7] Barry Hindess, 'Neoliberalism and the National Economy', in Mitchell Dean and Barry Hindess (eds.), *Governing Australia: Studies in Contemporary Rationalities of Government*, Cambridge: Cambridge University Press, 1998, pp. 126–7.

[8] Sassen, *Territory, Authority, Rights*, p. 223.

[9] *Ibid.*, for a liberal perspective that puts these developments down to legislators 'falling behind' wider processes of integration, see Anne-Marie Slaughter, *A New World Order*, Princeton, NJ: Princeton University Press, 2004.

mentalities of risk, to mention but a few – national states have often accepted and even facilitated the parcelling out of previously state-run security functions to private actors and have tolerated or encouraged the expansion of private security as a whole. In this way, the partial self-disassembly of the state, particularly in advanced liberal democracies, combined with the social, economic and political dynamics that characterize liquid modernity have been central to the growth and globalization of the private security market.

One of the consequences has been the emergence of private security firms that, like many global actors in other domains, possess a new set of capacities that enable them to act at a global level. Most obviously, partial state disassembly has been part of creating private security firms with extensive material capacities, either directly through outsourcing of previously public functions or indirectly through processes of responsibilization. Second, it has provided private security actors with ideational capacities: socially recognized forms of legitimation and recognized expertise which, when linked to processes of commodification, risk and responsibilization allow them to move effectively in the security field.

At the same time, this process has supported institutional transformations within states that legitimate the increased roles of private actors. Particularly revealing here is the role of state regulation. The capacities of global private security firms do not generally emerge from their ability to operate in the shadows of legitimate governance but from their location within state structures that legitimate and encourage their activities. Over the past decade, agencies regulating PSCs have emerged in many countries. In South Africa, for example, an enhanced and expanded Private Security Industry Regulatory Authority (PSIRA) replaced a more limited Security Officers Board in 2001. In the UK, the creation of the Security Industry Authority (SIA) in 2001 brought regulation where it was previously almost completely absent. In both their formation and operation, these two regulatory bodies include extensive participation by the private security industry itself and have often become models for regulation in other countries.[10]

[10] This is clear from interviews at the Security Industry Authority in London, as well as from our research in Uganda, Kenya, South Africa, Nigeria and Sierra Leone, which revealed several public and private initiatives seeking to develop regulatory frameworks based on the South African and the UK experiences. See also www.the-sia.org.uk and the international 'Montreux

Tellingly, there are also attempts towards regional and global regulation. With reference to Africa, representatives of the British Association of Private Security Companies (BAPSC) have argued that the drafting of a regulatory framework for the private security industry should be part of the British agenda on the continent and also that the African Union could provide a regional framework for regulation.[11] At the pan-European level, the private security association and lobby group CoESS has been heavily involved in pursuing region-wide recognition and regulation. CoESS recently published a "white paper" on the role of private security in Europe, aiming to construct a European legislative framework that is 'balanced, harmonised, efficient and conducive to the expansion of the private security industry'.[12] Europe, the paper states, can only achieve its security objectives by taking a global and integrated approach. Representing close to 50,000 security companies and 1.7 million employees, CoESS argues that it 'can and should play a key role in defining this global approach as an advisor, a central player and, ultimately, as the driving force behind policy implementation'.[13] Significantly, as we noted in the Introduction, the foreword to the "white paper" was written by the then President of the EU, President Nicolas Sarkozy of France, who provided an endorsement of the contributions of private actors to the security of European citizens.

In addition to testifying to the increasing prominence of private security and the interest of the state in attempting to manage its dynamics and impact, regulation performs a subtle legitimating function, reinforcing the accepted status of the sector. Moreover, regulation almost inevitably involves the active participation of the private security industry through consultation, standard-setting, self-regulation and best-practice guidelines. In the process, the private sector attains a role within the institutions that govern the public sphere, while the logic of market efficiency inevitably gains influence

Document' on the operations of PMCs and PSCs during armed conflict; for an overview see James Cockayne, 'Regulating Private Military and Security Companies', *Journal of Conflict and Security Law*, 13 (3) (2009): 401–28.

[11] Andy Bearpark and Sabrina Schultz, 'The Private Security Challenge in Africa: Problems and Options for Regulation', in Sabelo Gumedze (ed.), *Private Security in Africa: Manifestations, Challenges and Regulation*, Pretoria: Institute of Security Studies, 2007, pp. 73–88.

[12] CoESS, *Private Security*.   [13] *Ibid.*, p. 13.

in public policy and in the calculations this involves. In this way, as Sassen notes, regulation functions to reshape the idea of the public interest and illustrates yet another of the ways in which the public and the private have been rearticulated. In Sassen's words, 'Private logics circulate through public institutional domains.'[14]

In the field of security, the result of these processes of disassembly and reassembly has been the formation of complex, multi-sited institutional orders – global security assemblages – where a range of different security agents interact, cooperate and compete to produce new practices and structures of security governance. As a descriptive term, 'assemblage' is intended to capture the new geographies of power that are simultaneously global and national, public and private: complex hybrid structures that inhabit national settings but are stretched across national boundaries in terms of actors, knowledges, technologies, norms and values. Situating the emergence of security privatization and global security assemblages within an analysis of state disassembly and shifting institutional power relations within the state draws attention to the inadequacy of explanatory accounts that look at security only in relation to the traditional institutions of the state, such as the police, military, paramilitary forces or ministries of home affairs or justice. Instead, it is imperative to examine the relationship between these institutions and other components of the state involved in global processes. In the case of commercial security, this often involves not just regulatory agencies but also those actors concerned with relations to the global economy, particularly trade and finance ministries.

Securing the market: restriction and response in South Africa

A revealing illustration of how these processes of partial state disassembly and rearticulation relate to global security privatization can be found in the struggles that took place around South Africa's proposed Private Security Industry Regulation Bill in October 2001. As we discuss more fully in Chapter 5, South Africa has one of the world's most highly privatized and globalized security sectors and as a percentage of GDP has the largest private security sector in the

[14] Sassen, *Territory, Authority, Rights*, p. 19.

world. The immediate post-transition era saw a massive expansion of private security: by the end of apartheid in 1994, there were three times as many private security personnel as public police officers, and between 1997 and 2000 the number of private security officers grew from 115,000 to 166,000.[15] South Africa's security market thus became one of the fastest growing in the world, experiencing annual growth rates of 30 per cent in the mid-1990s.[16]

This rapid expansion attracted the interest of transnational PSCs seeking profitable acquisitions and opportunities. According to one report, foreign investors poured about 187 million rand into the private security industry in 2000–1.[17] Amongst a host of mergers and takeovers, in November 2000 Securicor acquired Gray Security Services, one of the largest security firms in South Africa, while in 2001, Group4Falck acquired two companies – Callguard Security and ASC Federal – becoming the third largest guarding company in the country, employing at the time over 8,000 people.[18] In May 2001, ADT purchased Sentry Security Services, while Chubb entered the South African market with the purchase of BBR Security in 1999.[19] Thus, within a few years, four of the largest international companies developed a significant presence in the South African market, with Securicor and Group4Falck becoming amongst the largest guarding companies, and Chubb and ADT together dominating the lucrative alarm and armed response market.

The growth of the private security sector and entrance of foreign firms did not go unnoticed and soon became a source of considerable political controversy. As the relative balance between public policing

---

[15] Mark Shaw and Clifford Shearing, 'Reshaping Security: An Examination of the Governance of Security in South Africa', *African Security Review*, 7 (3) (1998): 3–12; p. 4; data provided by a South African PSC.

[16] Credit Suisse/First Boston, *Review of the South African Private Security Industry*, Boston, 7 February 2001, p. 7.

[17] *FDI Magazine*, 'South African Security Sector Wins Bill Reprieve', 2 November 2001.

[18] Martin Schönteich, 'South Africa's Private Security Industry', *ERA's Corporate Intelligence Review*, 18 July 2002, p. 4.

[19] Reflecting a degree of division in the industry between technology and response-based companies and those focused on static guarding, Chubb sold its guarding unit to the South African firm Fidelity Security in May 2006. Employing almost 30,000 people, Fidelity is one of the largest PSCs in South Africa and also has operations in Mozambique, Botswana, Namibia, Swaziland and Lesotho.

and private security tipped in favour of the private, both in terms of personnel and firepower, the under-resourced police forces at times jealously guarded their status and role vis-à-vis a highly capitalized private sector that sported not only new patrol vehicles but frequently also the latest in surveillance and communications technologies. Police and politicians alike questioned private security's 'real' commitment to the reduction of crime, pointing to the obvious connection between commercial success and the continuation and fear of crime. The idea of companies 'profiting from crime' was antithetical to the worldview of many African National Congress (ANC) politicians; the police regarded it as an affront to their professional obligation to 'protect life and property' regardless of ability to pay; and the fact that a largely white-owned sector employed a low-paid, predominantly black labour force to guard white wealth did not fit comfortably with the new political environment. Such adverse perceptions were compounded by the fact that many of South Africa's PSCs were owned and managed by former officers of the apartheid state's oppressive apparatuses (with a predominance of former intelligence, defence and police personnel), giving rise to fears and allegations that the sector harboured right-wing sympathies and that private militias were being formed by security companies.[20] Private security was accordingly seen as an obstacle, and even a potential threat, to South Africa's fledgling democracy.

Equally significantly for our case here, suspicions were also voiced that foreign involvement in the sector might be used to destabilize the new political order. In 1995, for example, the Deputy Minister of Intelligence Services, Joe Nhlanhla, expressed concern that 'third force elements see the private security industry as a haven from where to continue their third force activities of destabilisation.'[21] Similar opinions were voiced by the Coordinator for Intelligence, Linda Mti, who maintained that 'the connection that some of the actors in the private security companies have with foreign intelligence services and

---

[20] See Jenny Irish, *Policing for Profit: The Future of South Africa's Private Security Industry*, Pretoria: Institute for Security Studies, 1999; Martin Schönteich, 'Fighting Crime with Private Muscle: The Private Sector and Crime Prevention', *African Security Review*, 8 (5) (1999): 65–75; Mike Hough, 'Private and Public Security in the RSA: Competition or Cooperation?', *Strategic Review for Southern Africa*, 24 (2) (2002): 78–96.

[21] Hough, 'Private and Public Security in the RSA', p. 4.

the similarity of objectives informed by their past co-operation in the Cold War era ... makes them free agents to be exploited for espionage activities.'[22] As the Chairman of the Parliamentary Committee on Safety and Security summed it up, 'This is a very sensitive industry.'[23]

These suspicions found concrete expression in October 2001, when the parliamentary Committee for Safety and Security proposed to ban foreign ownership in the private security sector on grounds that it constituted a threat to national security.[24] The proposal brought a swift reaction that illustrates many of the themes of this chapter. The global private security firms quickly mounted a campaign – coordinated through a South African lobbying and public-relations firm – to counter the proposed Bill. As a spokesman for Securicor Gray put it, 'We made use of as many networks as we could in our determination to get our message across to the government in a firm but non-confrontational manner.'[25] This, according to one individual central to the formulation of the strategy, involved mobilizing international as well as domestic supporters.[26] In the case of the latter, this included members of the political opposition, while the key international actors were the diplomatic representatives of the foreign companies' states of origin – the UK and Denmark in particular. A main argument of the

[22] Hough, 'Private and Public Security in the RSA', p. 5.
[23] Interview with Mululeki George, MP and Chairperson on the Parliamentary Committee on Safety and Security, Cape Town, April 2003; see also Henry E. Cauvin, 'Homegrown Guards', *New York Times*, 9 October 2001, p. B3. Although inevitably country-specific in their details, these concerns are by no means unique to South Africa. In Nigeria, for example, foreign firms are effectively banned from ownership in the private security sector and operate through complex local ownership arrangements. 'Foreign' firms remain subject to accusations of external influence and subversion, and examination (in some cases bordering on harassment) by the state security services, reflecting not only possible political concerns but also instigation at the hands of market competitors and connections to political elites. In Senegal, foreign ownership in the sector is also banned by law; see Cyrus O'Brien, 'The Dynamics of Private Security in Senegal', *Review of African Political Economy*, 35 (118) (2008): 655–9.
[24] Rita Abrahamsen and Michael C. Williams, 'Privatisation, Globalisation and the Politics of Protection in South Africa', in Jef Huysmans, Andrew Dobson and Raia Prokhovnik (eds.), *The Politics of Protection: Sites of Insecurity and Political Agency*, London and New York: Routledge, 2006, pp. 34–47; see also Cauvin, 'Homegrown Guards'.
[25] *FDI Magazine*, 'South African Security Sector Wins Bill Reprieve'.
[26] Interview, Pretoria, April 2003.

opponents of the proposed legislation was that it represented a restriction on trade in services, with the British High Commission stating that 'we are concerned' and opining that 'the proposed law could violate a 1998 trade agreement between the countries.'[27] In wider terms, it was also argued that the legislation would be taken as a clear sign that South Africa was breaching liberal economic principles and that foreign investment in all sectors (not merely security) was neither welcome nor secure in the country. As a director of BusinessMap, a Johannesburg-based investor intelligence consultancy made the connection, the 'suddenness of the announcement increases uncertainty for foreign investors in all sectors'.[28]

Tellingly, the strategy of the PSCs was not directed only – or even primarily – towards the parliamentary committee, or the Secretariat of Safety and Security. Instead, it focused on the offices of the President, the Finance Minister and the Minister of Trade. The latter quickly assured the companies through a spokesman that the Minister 'thinks there are other ways to meet national security concerns … and he will take up the matter this week with the minister of safety and security'.[29] The President and Finance Minister were both out of the country on official business when the legislative proposal was announced, and the Minister of Finance, Trevor Manuel, allegedly first heard about the issue while in Japan to encourage foreign investment. Within a matter of days, however, the proposal dropped from sight, reportedly quashed primarily by Manuel.[30] As the Chairperson of the Safety and Security Committee subsequently reflected, 'we were persuaded by the big companies to drop the ban.'[31]

The struggle over the South African Bill illustrates key features of global security assemblages. First, and most simply, the partial

[27] Cauvin, 'Homegrown Guards'.
[28] *FDI Magazine*, 'South African Security Sector Wins Bill Reprieve'.
[29] Cauvin, 'Homegrown Guards'.
[30] Interviews, Cape Town and Pretoria, April 2003. Key individuals behind the campaign also argued, probably with some justification, that the legislation was in part motivated by elements of the domestic security industry seeing an opportunity to see off competition and potentially pick up foreign owned companies at distressed prices. See Abrahamsen and Williams, 'Privatisation, Globalisation and the Politics of Protection in South Africa'.
[31] Interview, Mululeki George, MP, Chairperson Safety and Security Committee, Cape Town, April 2003.

disassembly of the state is evident both in terms of the global expansion of PSCs and their substantial entry into the South African market. Second, and more complexly, the denationalization of state agendas and the commodification of security are evident in the decision to recall the proposed Bill in light of fears that it would be detrimental to the global competitiveness of the South African economy. The ability of global PSCs to present their activities as a service and to link their operations to the authority of market principles (and sanctions) played a crucial role, as principles of free trade related to a specifically depoliticized vision of security successfully trumped concerns for national security and calls for the protection of domestic industry. By embedding security privatization in broader global norms connected to processes of commodification and responsibilization, the home states of the foreign companies were able to intercede on their behalf by using commercial arguments and forms of market-norm coercion, skirting the much more sensitive and difficult ground of 'national security' policy.

Third, the role played by the finance and trade ministries, and the executive in general, illustrates both the transnationalization of the state and the redistribution of power within the state in favour of those actors directly integrated into global structures – at the expense of the legislative branch. Within the economic strategy known as Growth, Employment and Redistribution (GEAR) adopted by South Africa in 1996, openness to international capital and compliance with international rules and norms concerning its access and mobility became a key priority. One consequence of this shift was that, as in many other countries adopting a similar agenda, the finance and trade ministries gained increasing power over policy due to their central role in the formulation of the country's international, broadly neo-liberal economic strategy.[32] The fact that South Africa's ability to participate in global economic structures was under threat by the actions of the parliamentary committee gave the Finance Ministry considerable power to intervene in what was on the surface a security issue and provided the global PSCs and their advocates with a

---

[32] In other African countries, it has been argued that the introduction of SAP, and later poverty reduction strategy papers, have similarly strengthened ministries of finance at the expense of legislatures; see Gould, *The New Conditionality*.

key strategic point of entry and set of ideological resources through which to influence government policy. In this case, the private logics of global business circulated through public institutional domains, and these public domains, operating in complex interaction with private and transnational actors, in turn became powerful agents for globalization.

Fourth, these events show how globalization cannot be seen as representing the straightforward erosion of the state or, in this specific case, the wholesale defeat of the South African state at the hands of global private actors. The outcome is indicative of broader shifts in power relations between state institutions themselves. Equally important, while this particular attempt to legislate directly against foreign ownership in the industry failed, the sector as a whole has subsequently been subject to increasing state oversight and regulation. As we show in Chapter 5, this has been part of a rearticulation of the relationship between public and private security and an increased acceptance of private security, including global firms, by the South African state as a whole. In this process, regulation, particularly through processes and bodies that involve the direct participation of those being regulated, marks a process of normalization and legitimation, as well as one that to varying degrees integrates private actors into public decision-making processes. The disassembly of the state is not, therefore, a simple process of privatization, although there is no doubt that it has contributed substantially to the power of private actors; it involves instead a rearticulation of the relationship between the public and private where the state retains a central role.

Finally, these events also reveal the degree of competition and tensions within global security assemblages. Global security assemblages do not represent a mechanistic process of disassembly and reassembly, and the rearticulation of public and private, as well as global and local, represents more than the arrival of a new set of security actors. Accordingly, analysing global security assemblages requires a variegated understanding of power. It also demands an appreciation of the particular place of security in modern politics, where its status as a public good is one of the central institutional features and legitimating principles of the sovereign state. In other words, an analysis of contemporary security calls for a theoretical framework that can identify the forms of power at work within assemblages, specify the shifting capacities of private security firms, their relationships to each other and to the state. To help address these issues, we turn to Pierre Bourdieu's analysis of social power.[33]

Capacities and capital

For Bourdieu, the variegated nature of power can be unravelled by examining the relationship of actors to specific types of what he terms 'capital'. Capital takes three main forms: economic, cultural and symbolic. As John Thompson nicely summarizes it,

> there are many different forms of capital: not only 'economic capital' in the strict sense (i.e. material wealth in the form of money, stocks and shares, etc.), but also 'cultural capital' (i.e. knowledge, skill and other cultural acquisitions, as exemplified by educational or technical qualifications), 'symbolic capital' (i.e. accumulated prestige or honour) and so on.[34]

In practice, these three forms of capital are often entwined, providing actors with different capacities.

In itself, this categorization of power is by no means novel and can be traced back at least to Max Weber. One of the most important insights of Bourdieu, however, is that there is no direct relationship between the possession of a particular form of capital and effective action or power within a given domain of practice. This is because capital is not a seamlessly transferable or fungible capacity but is only realized – that is, has practical effects – within a specific sphere of activity. Bourdieu calls these spheres of activity 'fields'. Different fields are characterized, constituted and dominated by specific forms, distributions and relations of capital – of what is valued and what provides power within the field. A field is, therefore, in Bourdieu's words, a 'structured space of

---

[33] For other applications of Bourdieu to the security field, see Benoît Dupont, 'Security in the Age of Networks', *Policing and Society*, 14 (1) (2004): 76–91 and Benoît Dupont, 'Power Struggles in the Field of Security: Implications for Democratic Transformation', in Wood and Dupont, *Democracy, Society and the Governance of Security*, pp. 86–110. In international security, Michael C. Williams, *Culture and Security: Symbolic Power and the Politics of International Security*, London and New York: Routledge, 2007, elements of which we draw on here.

[34] John Thompson, 'Introduction', in Pierre Bourdieu, *Language and Symbolic Power*, edited by John Thompson, Cambridge, Mass.: Harvard University Press, 1991, pp. 1–31; p. 14.

positions in which the positions and their interrelations are determined by the distribution of different kinds of resources or "capital"'.[35] Since a particular field is structured by the operation and distribution of particular forms of capital, the ability to move in that field is tied to an agent's possession of the relevant forms of capital.

Thus, to use an illustration that many readers may be familiar with, the academic field is structured through the distribution of particular forms of cultural and symbolic capital and only secondarily through economic capital. Traditionally, economic capital has been fairly limited in its direct impact on the functioning of the academic field: one cannot become a professor simply by having enough money. Instead, issues such as the extent and origin of academic degrees, the relative prestige of academic positions and the number and status of publications (themselves viewed in terms of cultural and symbolic capital, not economic return) are central to the operation of the field. To play the academic game is necessarily to operate in a field constituted by these dynamics and to confront the distributions of capital that structure that field. This is not to say that economic capital is unimportant in providing the conditions for success in the educational field, whether in terms of providing the economic and cultural backgrounds attuned to success or in terms of access to prestigious educational institutions and the resources and opportunities they afford.[36] Similarly, the cultural and symbolic capital of educational institutions is by no means unconnected to their economic capital but, crucially, a focus

---

[35] Pierre Bourdieu, *In Other Words: Essays toward a Reflexive Sociology* (Palo Alto, Calif.: Stanford University Press, 1987), p. 64.

[36] In this analysis we explicitly bracket another dimension of Bourdieu's analysis of fields, that of the habitus. The habitus embodies specific forms of capital. It also constitutes an inclination to express and recognize the forms of capital that operate within specific fields and to orient oneself towards them in particular ways, providing both a way of adjusting one's behaviour in conformity with one's position in a specific field and, to a degree, contributing to the reproduction of one's place in that field. Thus, for example, Bourdieu argues that different social classes will differ in their access to higher education not only due to the economic constraints they may encounter in gaining access but also due to the structures of the habitus which incline them both by disposition and experience to see themselves as not cut out for that world. Similarly, those who acquire a habitus which does so incline them will tend to act on it. So, Bourdieu argues, social structures reproduce themselves; and so also we can understand how they reproduce relations of inequality and domination. Although it is important to keep in mind their dynamic and relational dimensions, these aspects can

on cultural and symbolic capital highlights how practices take shape in the relationship *between* fields and forms of capital and are not wholly determined by a single form. The cultural and economic capital of prestigious universities, for example, are continual objects and instruments of struggle and competition between them as they seek to convert economic capital into cultural capital (by, for instance, competing for the best students or 'star' faculty) and to convert this cultural capital into economic capital via high fees, endowments and donations.

Finally, a focus on the relationship between forms of capital and a specific field also allows an examination of how capital can be translated across fields. For example, the accumulation of certain forms of cultural capital, such as specific kinds of educational degrees, can – in specific circumstances – be converted into access to other forms of capital. More concretely, consider the ability of an Ivy League MBA to command a high price on the job market, or the conversion of a university's large financial endowment into acquiring or maintaining cultural and symbolic capital. A key concern for investigation accordingly becomes the forms and relations of capital that operate within a specific field, the ways in which they are related and the processes of transformation and conversion which take place.

Neither the distribution of capital nor its valorization within or between fields is fixed. Indeed, fields are characterized both by struggles over the distribution of currently recognized forms of capital and by struggles to change the social relationship by transforming the structures of valorization within the field. While some forms of capital may retain their value both within and across fields at particular points in time, they by no means do so easily, fixedly or universally. The structures of a field are in constant tension and potential flux. Yet the possession of a specific habitus and particular forms of capital serves to reproduce (though not determinately) the fields within which agents tend to move, their possibilities for moving in other fields and the options for action which they are likely to adopt. Thus habitus,

be represented symbolically as: '([habitus] + [capital]) + field = practice'. Bourdieu, *The Logic of Practice*, Cambridge: Polity, 1992, p. 101. Bourdieu frequently and pointedly argues that scholars would have a far better understanding of practice if they used an analysis of their own practices as a model for theorizing rather than constructing models based upon particular theoretical visions of practice.

capital and field act in a reciprocal relationship tending to reproduce regularities of behaviour at the same time as they are continual arenas of struggle and power.

The advantages of a Bourdieuian analysis for an understanding of contemporary global security assemblages are numerous. Most importantly, perhaps, the concept of forms of capital allows us to specify the new normative and material capacities of private security as forms of symbolic and material capital while still appreciating that capacities do not necessarily translate directly into power and effective action, much less the domination of security practices. In other words, since forms of capital are only realized in a security field structured by the valorization of diverse forms of capital and populated by a variety of actors who themselves possess capital specific to the field, there is no direct relationship between capital and effective action. In fact, the increasing accumulation of a given form of capital in the absence of other forms may paradoxically *dis*empower actors while empowering competitors in a field. For example, the increasing military capabilities and expertise of private military actors such as the South African firm EO in the 1990s – enhanced weaponry, transport capacities and even air support – certainly marked an increase in its material capacities and power. However, it also contributed to increased alarm about the company and its activities and to a reassertion of the legitimacy of state actors and their dominance in the security domain. The increase in material capital thus led, paradoxically, to a decrease in the effective capacity of the company to operate – a paradox that reflects the structure of the field and the relative lack of symbolic and cultural capital possessed by this type of private military firm. Power in a specific field is thus practical, not arithmetic, and it depends on the forms and distribution of capital relevant to that field. Effective participation in a field thus depends on the actors' ability to comprehend their place within the field and the relative distribution of forms of capital within it – what Bourdieu calls having 'a feel for the game'.[37]

The private in the security field

It follows from the above that to appreciate the forms of capital (material, symbolic and cultural) acquired by private security actors as part

[37] See Bourdieu, *In Other Words*, p. 64.

of recent processes of state disassembly and reassembly demands a more specific analysis of the security field. To begin such an exploration, it is necessary to stress the field's specific relational structure, to see how it is structured by the *relation* between public and private, not by their straightforward opposition or their seamless cooperation, and how this relation between public and private permeates the actual practices of security provision. In other words, while it is analytically helpful to see the public and private as structuring oppositions constituting the field, it is equally important to note how in practice public and private are already always interpenetrating in the constitution of both public and private security actors and how this impacts security as a field of practice. By interpenetration we do not just mean that private actors function in settings that also include public agents (military, paramilitary, police), but that the positions of these actors have to be seen in the context of their relative possession of the multiple forms of capital constituting and operating in the field. As such, an analysis of the security field requires both the location of shifting forms of material, symbolic and cultural capital and an excavation of the deep historical roots of the security field and its connections to the conceptual and institutional structures of modern understandings of politics and sovereignty. Recognizing these connections is by no means a purely academic exercise; on the contrary, it is essential to an appreciation of the distribution of capital in the security field and hence to who gets secured and how.

To begin with the shift in forms of capital, perhaps the most obvious transformation in capacities involves the accumulation of economic capital and material resources by PSCs. Historically, these capacities have remained very limited in comparison to the resources of the state, and, seen in the round, they continue to be so. Yet, as demonstrated in Chapters 1 and 2, the considerable expansion both numerically and functionally of private security actors has brought about a corresponding augmentation of their technical, material and organizational resources. In material terms, the enhanced capacities of private security firms arise in part from the partial disassembly of the functions of the national state. The outsourcing of public sector security functions, combined with policies (and politics) of responsibilization have contributed to the development of private firms with resources that dwarf their predecessors. Publicly traded on major stock exchanges, with substantial assets and earnings derived from a wide field of commercial operations, with thousands or even hundreds of thousands of personnel, and with highly developed and differentiated organizational structures and technological capabilities, the private security firms that have emerged from these transformations have the material capacity to play substantial roles in the provision of security, and sometimes to become sophisticated transnational corporate entities.

A second part of the power of private security lies not in its own material or economic capital, but in its connections to that of its clients via property rights. The integration of private security into the day-to-day operations of firms and individuals means that it derives considerable power from its connection to clients and from their view of the provision of private security as a legitimate and necessary aspect of their operations and daily life. As we show in Chapter 4, this is a key element in the relationship between global capital and global private security, where the ability of PSCs to operate in national settings is strengthened by the demand from foreign resource extraction firms that regard PSC services as necessary for overseas investment and operation. This is particularly important in politically unstable parts of the world, where public security capacities may be limited (or perceived to be so) and where risk-averse corporations hesitate to venture without a form of private security. Here, the power of private security arises not only from its direct economic or material capital, but from its ability to deploy these capacities in the service of clients who possess significant material (and often symbolic and cultural) capital.

However, shifts in material capacities alone are not enough to explain the power of contemporary global private security. Equally important is the acquisition of symbolic and cultural capital by private security actors. Cultural capital takes many forms, but, broadly speaking, it can be understood as recognized status or authority, whether deriving from personal charisma or social background (class, for example), or conferred by institutional membership or organizational leadership. Symbolic capital is grounded in symbolic systems, pre-eminently language. But it also arises from abstract symbolic forms such as knowledge systems and the capital generated by their possession. Cultural and symbolic forms of capital are linked to specific forms of power. Most broadly, Bourdieu holds that cultural and symbolic power is a power that is *recognized;* in his formulation: 'I contend that a power or capital becomes symbolic, and exerts a specific effect of domination, which I call symbolic power or symbolic violence, when it is known and recognized, that is, when it is the object of an act of knowledge and recognition.'[38] As Bourdieu is at pains to stress, however, the two forms of capital and power are often related in practice.

One of the most important reasons for locating private security against the backdrop of broader shifts in global governance is that it allows us to see the degree to which private security actors have been able to acquire these forms of capital and the impact that this has had on the operation of the security field and on the formation and operation of global security assemblages. Once we dispense with the mercenary misconception, we can see that far from operating in the shadowy margins of contemporary societies, security privatization is linked to some of their most powerful dynamics and transformations. In this sense, security privatization is far from illicit; on the contrary, it draws legitimacy – that is, accrues cultural and symbolic capital and power – from its connection to transformations in the security field as a whole. This capital provides PSCs with the ability to move within the existing security field and provides resources which they can wield in attempts to defend and expand their activities, markets and global operations.

The most basic (as well as the oldest) linkage between economic and cultural capital in security privatization derives from the protection of liberal property rights, and from the 'principal–agent' relationship between private security and the private property of its clients. As Rick Sarre points out, 'Unlike the public police, whose power is found generally in the various law enforcement statutes, the power of private security personnel derives principally from their being legal 'agents' of those who control or own private property.'[39] In a majority of cases, the authority of private security arises from the right to enforce a

---

[38] Bourdieu, *In Other Words*, p. 111; see also Ian Loader, 'Policing and the Social: Questions of Symbolic Power', *British Journal of Sociology*, 48 (1) (1997a): 1–18.

[39] Rick Sarre, 'The Legal Basis for the Authority of Private Police and an Examination of Their Relationship with the Public Police', in David Biles and Julia Vernon (eds.), *Private Sector and Community Involvement in the Criminal Justice System*, Canberra: Australian Institute of Criminology, (1994): 167–82; p. 169.

combination of the 'law of contract' dictating an implied or actual contract between the owners of property and those who come onto it (such as, for example, conditions for the conduct of visitors to a site); the 'law of property' declaring the right to control the use of property and access to it (particularly the right of exclusion); and the 'industrial law' concerning the relations between employers and employees (a typical example being the rule that employees are subject to search when entering or leaving the site). PSCs thus derive capital from their status as agents of legitimate principals, whose position is itself based in the legitimating principles and legal status of property rights. The basis of this position is not only that private security is necessary for economic activity, but that it is a legitimate extension of the principles underlying those activities. As we discuss in Chapter 5, the extension of this principle beyond industrial site security to residential spaces (from individual homes to gated communities), to mass private–public space (such as malls or urban developments), and even to the private patrolling of formally public spaces such as central business districts, is one of the most significant and controversial aspects of security privatization.

The combination of authority arising from principal–agent relationships (where PSCs act on behalf of the rights possessed by those who own or control property) and the treatment of security as a 'service' to be provided in the market represents important forms of cultural capital possessed by private security firms and reflect a shift in the structure of the security field. In a social context marked by increasing responsibilization, security privatization is able to appear as an effective and appropriate response to increasing demands for security. This capital is further enhanced by links to the privatization ethos and the general valorization of private sector activities and its purported efficiency that has played such a prominent role in the wider political domain. Abetted by state advocacy of public–private partnerships in many areas of public policy, including aspects of security, private security has increasingly carved out a recognized role as a domain of market actors providing a service that can be bought and sold on a free market.

As neo-liberal political and economic structures have become widespread, this cultural capital is not restricted to a specific jurisdiction: it is extendable across borders and, as providers of a legitimately traded service/commodity, private security actors are able to connect their activities to the broader structures of market liberalism and free trade. Commodification, combined with the increasing salience of risk mentalities that render security an increasingly apolitical, technical issue of design, planning and prevention, rather than an issue of reactive policing and public policy, have further enhanced the capacity of private actors to claim expertise – to acquire cultural and symbolic capital and to exercise power across national boundaries. As the fate of the South African legislation discussed earlier illustrates, the status of security as a service has facilitated its globalization by placing it within the logic of free trade, shifting the distribution of capital within the security field in favour of private, global actors.

At the same time, the increasingly technological nature of security provision is not neutral in its impact on the security field. The fact that CCTV, alarm systems and the like are developed, installed, maintained and often responded to by private firms means that private actors can claim expert knowledge and legitimate (and even indispensable) participation in security provision, making their integration into networks with public actors a burgeoning area in which the sector can claim a high degree of expertise increasingly recognized by both its clients and by public authorities.[40]

Approached as a field of practice, the growth of private security can be understood as both a result and a reflection of its increasing acquisition of forms of capital and as part of a reconfiguration of the security field. Transformations in perceptions of security are not therefore just a matter of shifting norms; they are forms of power that provide private actors with new possibilities and change their relations with public actors. The state, however, frequently adopts a regulatory function in the sector, and even where the capacity for regulation is weak or even non-existent it generally retains a crucial position in the field. Indeed, the symbolic and cultural capital of private security does not lie in denying the connection between security and the state, but in rearticulating the relationship between actors and activities. Private security providers portray themselves as legitimate and competent actors in a field that continues to include the state,

---

[40] In many jurisdictions, for instance, public police will not respond to private alarm signals unless these have first been responded to by the PSC responsible, in no small part because the number of false alarms these systems generate would otherwise overwhelm police resources. Technology and individual choices are thus not neutral; they have systemic consequences.

responding to the legitimate demands of private individuals, corporations and other actors, as well as responding to the desire of the state for greater private-sector partnerships. Whether this is cast as helping an overstretched state, as stepping in where an incompetent, inefficient or ineffective public authority is incapable of meeting its obligations, or just as a prudent measure taken by responsible private actors responding to a condition of increased 'ambient insecurity'[41] (and often all these arguments are in play at the same time, albeit to different audiences), the key point is that important forms of capital accrue to private actors by stressing their relation to the public. This in turn draws attention to the manner in which security as a field of practice is structured and constituted by the relation between the public and the private and how the very notion of 'the public' constitutes a vital form of capital.

Symbolic struggles of 'the public'

History weighs heavily on the security field, which continues to be structured by norms and institutions (and forms of power) that have evolved from specific historic relations between security and the public sphere and by the positions occupied by public security actors embedded within them. Like the categories of public and private themselves, public and private security actors coexist within historically shifting boundaries. As has been pointed out numerous times, there is nothing natural about the public–private distinction, nor is this a neutral or purely technical–managerial division.[42] Instead, it is historically constructed, reflecting particular social interests and power relations at particular points in time. In the security field, the relationship between public and private is intimately connected to the symbolic relationship between security and the state. At one level, the very origins of the modern (and later liberal democratic) state were defined by its opposition to the notion of 'private' security. Security was not to be decided on or provided by private individuals, nor was violence to be wielded differently by different classes (as exemplified until very late

---

[41] Yoshida and Leishman, 'Japan', pp. 222–38.
[42] For useful discussions, see A. Claire Cutler, 'Artifice, Ideology and Paradox: The Public/Private Distinction in International Law', *Review of International Political Economy*, 4 (2) (1997): 261–85; Owens, 'Distinctions, Distinctions'.

in the aristocratic privilege of duelling). In the modern state, security was to be a public function, applying equally to all subjects, a process which became further intensified when those subjects became recast as citizens. The consolidation of modern sovereign power, the creation of a public political sphere separated in principle from private interests – and especially from the exercise of private violence – thus corresponded with a conception of security as a public good and was an essential element in liberal (and later democratic) visions of individual liberty and proper governance.

Similarly, the evolution of liberal capitalism reveals a long and intimate history between the realms of political economy and security, even if the two are often treated in isolation. The constitution of a private economic sphere was in important ways made possible by the removal of the control of violence and coercion – what we today call security – from private hands into the public or political domain. This transition was a key feature of the move from feudalism to absolutism, in the consolidation of the modern state, and in the shift of social power from a landed aristocracy that wielded violence as part of its socio-economic position and dominance, towards the rising commercial classes whose position and property was underpinned by liberal conceptions of rights and an increasingly formalized and centralized monopoly of state violence that could enforce and secure them. The subsequent development of nineteenth-century liberal capitalism was linked to the construction of individuals whose economic liberty was part and parcel of their freedom from violent coercion by other private individuals, and the corresponding location of these individuals within new forms of market discipline and coercion. In short, the existence of a public sphere of security in principle applying uniformly to all subjects was, as both Max Weber and Karl Polanyi stressed, a key element in the evolution of liberal capitalism and its specific articulation of the relationship between the economy and society.[43]

---

[43] See the collection in H. H. Gerth and C. Wright Mills (eds.), *From Max Weber: Essays in Sociology*, Oxford: Oxford University Press, 1958; Karl Polanyi, *The Great Transformation*, Boston, Mass.: Beacon Press, 1991 (first published 1944); also Perry Anderson, *Lineages of the Absolutist State*, London: Verso, 1974 and Ellen Meikins Wood, 'The Separation of the Economic and Political in Capitalism', *New Left Review*, 127(1) (1981): 66–95.

In sum, the idea of security as a *public* good is historically a key component and reflection of the development of modern politics, and the progressive restriction of private actors in security long seemed almost pre-given.[44] Importantly, this is not to say that modern state formation was a rosy story, or that the notion of security as a public good should be taken at face value. Historically, the concentration of security in the hands of state authorities and agencies was often far from consensual, with the initial phases of state-making often resembling, in Charles Tilly's well-known and evocative phrase, a form of 'organized crime'.[45] The agents and agencies of state security always possess the potential to pose dangers to the very citizens they claim to protect, and they continue to do so today, with the actions undertaken by public actors in the name of security all too frequently bearing at best a tenuous connection to the substantive promotion of the public good or the security of citizens. The publicness of security should also not conceal the extent to which public force was, and often still is, wielded in support of private or sectional interests under the guise of the public good – suffice to mention the history of the policing of labour disputes and other forms of social unrest, as well as the centuries-long philosophical and legal disputes over the nature of the public interest.[46] Finally, but in a somewhat different vein, the evolution of concepts of abstract citizenship also created a situation in which security as the invocation of danger

[44] As David Slansky has nicely put it: 'for most people, the police are the government incarnate: the street-level embodiment of the state's monopolization of legitimate force. That is why it seemed so natural, in the middle decades of the twentieth century, for Pinkerton's guards, private eyes, and the whole old-fashioned apparatus of private peacekeeping and criminal apprehension to be dwindling away. By the end of the 1960s public law enforcement already employed more people than private security, and it appeared that the disparity would soon be two to one. The socialization of order maintenance and crime control seemed almost foreordained, part and parcel of the gradual triumph of the rule of law'. 'Private Police and Democracy', *American Criminal Law Review*, 43 (89) (2006): 89–105; p. 89.

[45] Charles Tilly, 'War Making and State Making as Organized Crime', in Peter B. Evans, Dietrich Reuschemeyer and Theda Skocpol (eds.), *Bringing the State Back In*, Cambridge: Cambridge University Press, 1985, pp. 169–91.

[46] As traced in the very revealing study by J. A. W. Gunn, *Politics and the Public Interest in the Seventeenth Century*, London: Routledge & Kegan Paul, 1969.

became a powerful political technology in the service of creating common identities or advancing particular interests through a politics of fear.[47]

For the purpose of our analysis, however, the key point to note is that the idea that security *ought* to be a public good continues to inform and underpin many, if not all, of these perspectives. If, for example, the policing of a protest is seen as illegitimately handled, or the security services are accused of endangering those whom they are supposed to protect, criticisms generally arise from a conviction that security should be a good equally provided and applied to all. Disagreements about the correct relationship between security and liberty, or conflicting judgements about the nature of the public interest or the greater good abound, but few reject the claim that security should be a public good in principle applying equally to all. The notion of security as a public good is thus an almost inescapable aspect of modern politics. Indeed, one could claim that within the dominant traditions of modern political thought it is almost impossible *not* to think of security in this way.

It is not our intention here to engage in the numerous political and theoretical debates that arise from this understanding of security. Instead, our point is a rather simple one: that the centrality of security as a public good – and its opposition or contrast to security as a 'private' good – in modern conceptions of politics is one of the defining oppositions constituting the field of security. It is also a source of power within that field. Most obviously, it is a key aspect of the institutional and material power of modern police forces, which generate political support and material resources on the basis of their recognized role as agents and guardians of the public good of security. It also underpins the unique universal jurisdictional reach of the police – their right to go anywhere – that so clearly distinguishes them from private security.[48] Equally, it links the agencies of state security directly with the operation of the judiciary and, through this, to the powerful idea of the rule of law, of a legal (and security) order applying equally to all. Finally, of course, it is part of the ability *in extremis*

---

[47] For example, David Campbell, *Writing Security: United States Foreign Policy and the Politics of Identity*, Minneapolis, Minn.: University of Minnesota Press, 1998; Huysmans, *Politics of Insecurity*.

[48] See Jones and Newburn, *Private Security and Public Policing*, p. 258.

to mobilize other coercive agencies of the state, including the military and intelligence services, to secure the public good and to exercise legally legitimated (and potentially lethal) force if necessary. As Bourdieu points out, the combined acquisition of dominant physical force, economic, informational (or cultural) and symbolic capital was central to modern state formation.[49]

More broadly, as Ian Loader and Neil Walker have argued at length, the idea of security as a public good represents an important part of the 'structure of feeling' of citizens of modern polities.[50] One need perhaps not go as far as Loader and Walker in their declaration that the public good of security is *the* constitutive feature of societies capable of providing a full range of other public goods to recognize that this claim – and the corresponding charge that this principle is under threat from processes of security privatization – is not just a personal value or an abstract philosophic principle, it is also a symbolic and cultural resource, a form of capital that represents considerable power within the security field. Public authorities retain significant symbolic and cultural capital in the security field on this basis and acquire material capital as a consequence.[51]

At the same time, the modern liberal state justifies and legitimizes its role precisely on the basis of the security of the individual and, in many cases, of property.[52] This simultaneous commitment to public security and/as the security of the individual and private property

---

[49] An argument sketched in 'Rethinking the State'.

[50] Loader and Walker, *Civilizing Security*; and the insightful argument in Loader, 'Consumer Culture', pp. 82–3.

[51] Seen in this light, security has an inescapably *moral* dimension that is interesting not only normatively but also as an element in symbolic struggles.

[52] This sets up an obvious and long-standing tension in liberal (and especially contractarian) visions of government, often played out in the old contrast between Hobbes and Locke: if the ultimate justification of the state is the security of its citizens, then what right does the state have to prevent them from doing whatever they deem necessary for their own security? Even if one took Mill's famous harm principle – whereby individuals should not do anything that *actively* imperilled their fellows – as a limiting condition to this right, there would still seem little reason why individuals should not provide for a measure of their own security in addition, and potentially in contrast, to that provided by the state. Much here depends on what one thinks the *consequences* of this are for public security. If privatization is seen as leading to a loss of legitimacy by the state and to an erosion of social trust and cohesion, then its effects are seen as a damaging and potentially downward spiral into enclavism and anomie. For an exploration of the public

constitutes an intrinsic ambivalence between security as a public and a private good. This tension plays out within a security field still structured by the domination of public security with its connections to conceptions of legitimate sovereignty and legality, the institutional capacities that follow from these connections and broad social perceptions that security ought to be a public good. In no small part, of course, this is connected to fears over the social breakdown and violence that are seen as likely to arise from competition between private security providers in a situation where the state is severely weakened – a situation where private security would in fact be difficult to distinguish from organized crime.[53]

In sum, the state retains a key place in the security field, materially, symbolically and culturally, possessing forms of capital that structure its relationship to the private and that structure the field as a whole. In the security field, in other words, we do not have a 'state' pole that stands self-sufficiently in contrast to a 'private' pole. While it may be useful to use these two concepts as abstract parameters, in actuality the public–private relationship and its tensions are intrinsic to the place of the state in the security field. In terms of power, this means that the position and symbolic capital of the state is not one-dimensional and linear: it is already implicated in a tension-filled relation to the private. Symbolic power, as grounded in recognized knowledge, in categories of what Bourdieu calls 'visions and divisions', is thus connected to struggles over the nature of the public/private divide and relationship, not over attempts to do away with it.[54]

In the context of global security assemblages, the dynamics of the security field play out not only within the parameters of public and private but also to an increasing extent between the global/national and global/local levels. If privatization poses questions for the 'publicness' of security within the state, situations where those agents are also 'foreign' (either as individuals or as foreign-based PSCs) add further layers of complexity to the field. Just as security has been seen as a public good in modern politics, that public

---

as the securing of the private in modernity, see also Owens, 'Distinctions, Distinctions'.

[53] An excellent analysis of the dynamics of such a situation in immediately post-Soviet Russia can be found in Volkov, *Violent Entrepreneurs*.

[54] Bourdieu, 'Rethinking the State', pp. 62–3.

domain has been overwhelmingly defined in terms of the national, territorial state – a connection that has often been seen as an inextricable and perhaps even defining feature of sovereignty itself.[55] Here, the emergence of *global* private security represents an issue for state sovereignty that cuts across that constituted by the public–private distinction, but that also reinforces the structure of the field in important, if complex, ways.

At the most straightforward level, the presence of global PSCs may, paradoxically, allow national states to mobilize their symbolic capital by linking public provision of security to the defence of sovereignty. Globalized security privatization can thus potentially be cast as an issue of national security, enhancing the power of state actors who draw upon their institutional positions and their symbolic power as the representatives of *national public* security to define themselves, and the provision of security in general, in opposition to the impact of *global private* security and to limit its influence.[56] As we saw in the case of the proposed South African legislation, these linkages can play important roles in struggles in the security field.

Yet while the exclusionary public–national security logic is powerful, states and their security agencies, strategies and imperatives are today deeply embedded in global structures that can significantly impact their relationship to security privatization and their ability to mobilize the symbolic and cultural capital provided by an exclusionary sovereignty. The spread of global norms, practices and institutions ranging from human rights regimes to 'good governance' programmes and policy measures designed to counter international terrorism means that all states operate in a context where, to differing degrees, they are subject to internationally dominant understandings of how security is best provided and of the appropriate relationship

---

[55] Clearly, we cannot engage here with the extensive controversies over the nature of sovereignty, much less the relationship between nationalism and the modern state. Two treatments with interesting connections to our argument are Jens Bartelson, *A Genealogy of Sovereignty*, Cambridge: Cambridge University Press, 1995; and Huysmans, *Politics of Insecurity*.

[56] It also, as demonstrated in the South African episode, provides nationally based PSCs with symbolic resources in their competitive struggles against foreign-based firms, although the latter in turn often possess forms of symbolic and cultural capital linked to claims of expertise or globally recognized standards, not to mention their economic capital. We illustrate these dynamics in more empirical depth in Chapters 4 and 5.

between the individual and the security institutions of the state.[57] The growing influence of neo-liberal ideas and policies and the transformations in security governance discussed in Chapter 2 have provided a global dimension to the public–private relationship. Global private security firms are now able to contest sovereign claims concerning the necessary monopoly of state security by linking private provision to a wide variety of legitimating discourses and institutions. Whether this involves the rights of individuals and property-holders to provide for their own security, logics of commodification whereby security is portrayed as a service legitimately flowing like any other across borders in a liberal world economy or a myriad of other possibilities arising from the transformations we have examined thus far, the result is that a pure logic of 'state' security, in which decisions about the provision of internal security are completely divorced from transnational influences, is increasingly rare. As part of this process, the individual's right to security, and the question of how best to provide for it, is implicated in global norms about legitimate sovereignty and security governance.

As noted previously, one of the benefits of seeing capital in terms of its realization within a field is that it warns against assuming that the possession of any one form of capital will result in effective power within all fields. The possession of specific forms of capital can be both enabling and constraining within a given field, and there is no direct relationship between the possession of forms of capital and action or outcomes. Specifically, there is no one-to-one equation of the possession of increasing amounts of economic, material or symbolic capital by PSCs with their domination of the security field as a whole. Despite expanding privatization, security continues to be viewed to a significant degree as a public good, and an important part of the power of state actors arises from this fundamental belief, which is grounded in broader understandings of political legitimacy. This provides state actors with their own source of symbolic capital. Yet, because symbolic power is power that is *recognized*, a key question always concerns whether actors are recognized in their claims and status, and by which audiences (domestic, as well as international). Recognition is therefore also a field of struggle, and the forms of

---

[57] See Ole Jacob Sending and Iver B. Neumann, 'Governance to Governmentality', *International Studies Quarterly*, 50 (3) (2006): 651–72.

capital possessed by private and public actors thus exist in a dynamic tension. Each is also subject to reversals that are crucial in the operation of the security field as a whole. The state's symbolic claim to the public good of security, for example, is a source of tremendous power. However, this can be eroded or reversed if the state fails in this task or is perceived as doing so. In this way, its source of symbolic power can paradoxically become a resource for others to challenge its monopoly – to assert that in light of the state's failure to perform its necessary role it is necessary to legitimate the entrance of other – for example, private and/or global – actors into the security field, even if this is only to support the state's limited abilities or to exercise a partial right to self-protection in the absence of adequate (or what is perceived as inadequate) public protection. The technified nature of security as a service, along with its particular moral and political entailments, makes this possible; and the state has often actively encouraged these developments.

At the same time, the claim of private actors to political neutrality is always subject to potential reversal, and privatized security can be presented as illegitimately eroding the public good of security and the capacity and symbolic significance of the state. In this way, the growing symbolic and economic capital of private security does not necessarily equal a corresponding increase in its domination of the security field. On the contrary, the expansion of private security risks undermining its own symbolic capital and legitimacy if it comes to be seen as eroding the public good of security and its constitutive social role. Similarly, at the global–national level, the activities of transnational PSCs are always subject to the charge of transgressing the status of security as a *national* public good connected to national authorities, and/or as being beyond legitimate political control. In each case, the growth of private security is likely to yield a response, as can be seen in the attempts at regulation that tend to accompany its expansion. Regulation as public control over private security, and regulation as public legitimation of private security are thus not opposites. They are aspects of a field of struggle, where the precise configuration of these roles is contested and is played out in the context of their differing forms of capital and the strategies they enable. The outcomes reflect not only the capital of private security but also the standing and capacity of state actors recognized as legitimately representing the public good, or claiming to do so.

Towards an analysis of the field

It might be objected that these formulations are too abstract, that they miss the operation of specific fields in particular settings and that they make the mistake of assuming that states are uniform entities when in fact they – and their relationship to security – vary widely. These are important points. To the first, we can only say that even a full analysis of every field of practice including specific micro-analyses of national, and even local, practices, still requires an abstract analytic framework if it is to rise above the descriptive level. To the second, as we seek to demonstrate in the next two chapters, security practices are undoubtedly conditioned by the specific state form in question, as well as its particular place in the global order. Nonetheless, however variable state forms and practices may be, few (if any) fail to operate with (and within) some conception of sovereignty that specifies a particular relationship between (public) security and the state – and few state actors fail to avail themselves of the symbolic and material resources that follow from this linkage. As a result, the relational structure of public and private forms an essential structure for analysis, however differently its dynamics may play out in practice.

Globalization is not a uniform process, and, by the same token, the processes of security privatization do not represent a general process of global homogenization but a specific set of articulations in which the national mediation of the global becomes more rather than less important. Our approach thus draws attention to the need for 'grounded theory', for investigation at the point where the global is inserted and translated into the local. As Sassen puts it in a different context, 'as the national becomes a more complex site for the global, the specific and deep histories of a country become more, rather than less, significant and hence produce distinctive negotiations with the new endogenous and external global forces.'[58] Following the processes of state disassembly and reassembly, contemporary security is replete with global and local, public and private agents whose relationships are deeply competitive as well as cooperative, conflictual as well as coordinated.

The concept of global security assemblages allows us to capture these contemporary rearticulations of territory and authority and the

---

[58] Sassen, *Territory, Authority, Rights*, p. 227.

presence of actors and forms of capital not tied to a specific national territory. The new geographies of power found within global security assemblages cannot be reduced solely to questions of more or less state power or weakened domestic government. Instead, they involve the production of new modalities of power through which the very categories of public and private and global and local are reconstituted and reconfigured. In the next two chapters, we offer an analysis of different global security assemblages in Nigeria, Sierra Leone, South Africa and Kenya, showing the very different and localized forms of capital at work. In this way, analysing global security assemblages helps bring into view what lies *between* the global and the national: zones of politico-economic interactions that produce new institutional forms and novel relationships of power stretched across territories.

4 | Of oil and diamonds: global security assemblages in resource extraction

In a well-known essay, Zygmunt Bauman compares contemporary capital to the absentee landlords of the early modern age, notorious for their neglect of the needs of the populations that fed them.[1] But, unlike the absentee landlords of yesteryear, Bauman argues, the corporations of the twenty-first century are untied from even the locality of the estate, enjoying a new mobility by virtue of their liquid resources. Thus, if one locality proves too inhospitable, capital can always move on to more welcoming sites when the challenges of doing business require 'a costly application of force or tiresome negotiations. No need to engage, if avoidance will do.'[2]

Bauman's metaphor captures an important part of modern capitalism, one that many analysts of globalization – whether proponents or critics – would doubtlessly endorse. But while capital is clearly more 'footloose and fancy-free' today than in the past, it does not inhabit a completely deterritorialized world. Corporations still choose to operate in difficult and dangerous settings, providing the rewards are high enough. This is particularly the case in resource extraction, where the mobility of capital is highly qualified; capital is not free, for example, to move from the oil-rich and conflictual Niger Delta to the stormy but non-violent shores of west Wales. Instead, geology is destiny, and the oil companies must stay where the oil and the profit is to be found, and the same is true of companies involved in other types of resource extraction. Bauman's observation that contemporary capital never has to 'encounter otherness' and thus be faced with 'the temptation to reduce difference by force or take up the challenge of communication' accordingly requires modification: the continuation of much contemporary global commercial activity involves creating

---

[1] Bauman, *Globalization*, p. 10.
[2] *Ibid.*, p. 11.

security environments that permit its operations, and PSCs are key intermediaries in these arrangements.[3]

Put in Bauman's terminology (but in contrast to his claims), private security is often indispensable in contemporary capital's attempt to deal with otherness, whether in terms of 'the application of force' or in terms of 'tiresome negotiations' that seek to understand, shape, and control the security environment of its clients. Often this takes the shape of spatial and physical enclaves – highly secured sites where externally traded commodities such as oil and diamonds are extracted for the benefit of local elites and their transnational business partners, largely bypassing the surrounding communities. Resource enclaves are, in Ricardo Soares de Oliveira's useful description, 'outward oriented'; they do not provide mass local employment and have few linkages with other sectors of the domestic economy. Moreover, even in otherwise 'weak' states that exercise only limited control over large swathes of their territory, enclaves are sites with a high level of 'stateness' since these are the areas that ensure the economic survival and reproduction of the political elite.[4] Ensconced behind layers of barbed wire, secured by regular patrols and monitored from watchtowers and by surveillance cameras, resource extraction is often cut off from its immediate surroundings and its benefits are largely enjoyed elsewhere, in the national capital and in the boardrooms of transnational corporations.[5]

In the resource extraction sector, more than in any other area of private security involvement, the mercenary misconception holds a powerful sway. The reasons are many and understandable: notorious historical examples of resource extraction sites secured by mercenary forces abound, and today relatively few people actually visit these

---

[3] For different discussions of such involvements in the past and present, see William Reno, 'Order and Commerce in Turbulent Areas: 19th Century Lessons, 21st Century Practice', *Third World Quarterly*, 25 (4) (2004): 607–25; and Drohan, *Making a Killing*, pp. 7–133.

[4] Ricardo Soares de Oliveira, *Oil and Politics in the Gulf of Guinea*, London: Hurst, 2007, p. 106.

[5] In Africa, private security can in this way be seen as contributing towards the re-emergence of the French colonial separation between *Afrique utile* and *Afrique inutile*, between a useful/useable and a non-useful/expendable Africa; see William Reno, *Warlord Politics and African States*, Boulder, Col.: Lynne Rienner, 1999. The use of private security in resource enclaves naturally varies historically and today takes specific forms.

areas: access is difficult, fieldwork may be dangerous, and information is often withheld or controlled by companies and governments
alike. The result is that assumptions, perceptions, misperceptions and
dated second-hand accounts often come to pass as evidence. As James
Ferguson notes with admirable honesty in his chapter on 'governing
extraction' in Africa, in this area the risk of 'not knowing what one
is talking about' is thus 'even greater than usual'.[6] Drawing primarily on the work of William Reno and Peter Singer (who both analyse
the involvement of companies such as EO in the 1990s with great
insight), Ferguson, and many others like him, argues that contemporary resource extraction is dependent on the protection of PMCs.
'The use of private military forces', he avers, 'has become routine in
many parts of Africa.'[7] Similarly, Soares de Oliveira, in his illuminating study of the petro-states of the Gulf of Guinea, infers that private
security in the oil sector is primarily provided by PMCs, yet again
using EO's activities in Angola in the 1990s as an illustration of the
dangers this holds.[8] The impression created by such accounts is that
private security in Africa, especially in resource extraction, is primarily provided by heavily armed private soldiers, often operating outside
the bounds of legality.

Yet much has changed since the 1990s. EO, for one, no longer exists;
and although PMCs have become deeply entrenched and increasingly
influential on the African continent, their role is frequently of a different kind.[9] Rather than fighting the wars of beleaguered governments, or shifting the military balance in civil wars, the largest PMCs
now train the continent's military forces and conduct security sector reform programmes, often on behalf of Western donors. Non-
combat PMCs have extensive roles in this sector. MPRI, for example,
is involved in training the Nigerian Army, an activity that clearly has
a bearing on the army's ability to protect the oil industry but one
that does not involve MPRI itself in the direct protection of the oil
enclaves. While some companies engaged in resource protection in
Africa can undoubtedly and justifiably be described as military, most

---

[6] Ferguson, *Global Shadows*, p. 195.
[7] *Ibid.*, p. 205.
[8] Oliveira, *Oil and Politics*, pp. 114–19.
[9] For an account of some of the contemporary roles of PMCs in Africa, see
Aning *et al.*, 'The Role of Private Military Companies in US–Africa Policy',
and McFate, 'Outsourcing the Making of Militaries'.

notably perhaps in conflict zones such as the Democratic Republic of the Congo and the Sudan, a large part of security provision in the resource extraction sector is provided by PSCs whose main business is in non-military, non-conflict activities.[10] These companies do not operate outside the bounds of legality (which, of course, is not to say that they may not break the law or avoid regulations) but are generally legal entities and perceived as legitimate businesses providing a 'service like any other'. They are often listed on international stock exchanges, and their other clients may include embassies, NGOs and donor agencies. In other words, their power stems not exclusively or primarily from the barrel of the gun, and, in fact, they are in many cases completely unarmed. Instead they are empowered by virtue of being embedded in broader legitimated structures of security governance, and this in turn has implications for their effects, both locally and for global capital expansion.

In this chapter we analyse the role of private security in the oil industry in Nigeria and in diamond and rutile mining in Sierra Leone. These are clear examples of resource enclaves, in the sense that they are highly protected sites largely cut off from the surrounding communities. However, privileging their 'enclave' nature risks overlooking the more complex and extensive links between state, security and market; for while these locations may be spatially identifiable as enclaves, they are also institutionally and normatively embedded within broader structures of global governance. In the enclaves we examine here, private security actors operate alongside and often with the active encouragement of the state and public security forces. They are located within complex and highly politicized public–private, global–local security structures, and any understanding of their political and social significance needs to take account of this embeddedness and the positions of private actors within public power and discourse. In short, despite their spatial segregation, these enclaves are part of intricate global security

---

[10] Very little reliable information is available from these areas; but see Jana Hönke, 'Transnationalised Pockets of Territoriality: Western Mining Companies and Security Governance in Katanga (DRC)' (forthcoming). There are also a number of settings where companies' operations straddle the private military/private security boundary. Perhaps the most notable of these were the activities of the British firm Armorgroup, which was acquired by G4S in March 2008, a development which may well mark an increase in the latter's involvement in more quasi-militarized activities.

assemblages, where public and private, global and local actors combine
and interact and where global private security actors have considerable
influence on security strategies and governance.

Private security and the Nigerian petro-state

'After oil, security is the second biggest money spinner in Nigeria.' The
fact that the accuracy of this statement is impossible to verify matters
less than the crispness with which it captures the centrality of private
security to the continuation of oil extraction in Nigeria. As this long-
time Niger Delta campaigner and human-rights activist observed from
his Port Harcourt base, private security in all its various guises has
expanded rapidly throughout the country and has in recent years come
to pervade the oil industry. Reliable statistics in this area are a rare commodity in Nigeria, but the best estimates indicate that there are currently
between 1,500 and 2,000 PSCs in the country, employing in excess of
100,000 people.[11] Although foreign-owned security companies are prevented by law from operating in the country, there is nevertheless an
expanding presence of international security personnel and companies,
operating either through various intricate ownership arrangements, 'sis-
ter' companies, or by embedding their personnel as employees of their
clients. G4S, for example, has over 7,000 employees across Nigeria,
while risk and consultancy firms such as Control Risks have a number
of contracts and personnel embedded with various multinational corporations. Private security companies, whether local or global, are by
no means confined to the oil sector. Their clients include embassies, corporations and private residents, but, as with everything else in Nigeria,
it is in oil that the most lucrative opportunities are to be found.

As many countries in the industrialized North, including the USA,
seek to diversify their petroleum imports away from dependence
on the Persian Gulf, West Africa has been identified as an important future source of high-quality, low-sulphur oil and is becoming
increasingly central to world energy security.[12] Nigeria is at the heart

---

[11] Keku and Akinbade, *Industrial Security in Nigeria*; Abrahamsen and
Williams, *The Globalisation of Private Security: Country Report – Nigeria*.
[12] See Paul M. Lubeck, Michael J. Watts and Ronnie Lipschutz, *Convergent
Interests: US Energy Security and the 'Securing' of Nigerian Democracy*,

of this strategy: it is the world's fifteenth largest oil producer, contains the largest natural gas reserves in Africa, and its geographical proximity to Western markets adds a further strategic advantage. At the same time, the long-standing conflict in Nigeria's oil-producing areas continues. Persistent violence in the Niger Delta has reduced oil production by around a quarter, and frequent kidnappings and attacks on oil installations have forced some oil companies to close or curtail operations.[13] In this climate, it is not only the presence of Nigeria's public security forces that is growing. The oil companies are also enlisting the services of an expanding range of private security actors, ranging from formal and informal local organizations and vigilantes to a variety of national and international commercial security personnel.[14]

Oil and the production of insecurity

The key to unravelling the Niger Delta's persistent insecurity lies in the nature of the state and its rentier economy.[15] After oil was discovered at Oloibiri in May 1956, petroleum revenues as a percentage of

Washington, DC: Centre for International Policy, 2007; Tom McCaskie, 'The United States, Ghana and Oil: Global and Local Perspectives', *African Affairs*, 107 (428) (2008): 313–32.

[13] International Crisis Group, *Nigeria: Seizing the Moment in the Niger Delta*, Abuja, Dakar and Brussels: International Crisis Group, 30 April 2009; Andrew Walker, '"Blood Oil" Dripping from Nigeria', *BBC News Africa*, 27 July 2008. Available online at http://news.bbc.co.uk/2/hi/africa/7519302.stm.

[14] In addition, both the UK and the USA have increased their security involvement in the region, and the controversial AFRICOM is also to be understood in part in this light; see William Wallis and Matthew Green, 'UK and Nigeria Aim to Stop Oil Theft', *Financial Times*, 15 July 2008; and Sean McFate, 'Briefing: US Africa Command: Next Step or Next Stumble?', *African Affairs*, 107 (426) (2008a): 111–20. On the use of local and vigilante groups, see Kenneth Omeje, *High Stakes and Stakeholders: Oil, Conflict and Security in Nigeria*, Aldershot: Ashgate, 2006.

[15] Rentier in this context is a largely descriptive term, and can be traced back to David Ricardo's classic reference to rents as the opposite of profits, the result not of the ingenuity of work, but of nature. See also Douglas A. Yates, *The Rentier State in Africa: Oil Rent Dependency and Neo-Colonialism in the Republic of Gabon*, Trenton, NJ: Africa World Press, 1996.

total national revenue grew from less than 25 per cent in the 1960s
to over 70 per cent from the 1970s onwards.[16] As the importance of
oil increased so too did the intensity of the politics of resource control: 'petro-states', as political economists of oil are fond of reminding us, 'are not like other states'.[17] The results of petroleum riches are
often 'perverse', as the easy availability of oil revenue builds a centralized state, independent of its population for taxation and production
and prone to authoritarianism and secrecy.[18] In line with this reading,
Nigeria is commonly characterized as a state dominated by constant
elite struggles for access to power and resources, a zero-sum struggle
of winner takes all, where those in power defend their position by
almost any means available and those outside seek entry at nearly any
cost.[19] Centralization began in earnest with the military government
of General Yakubu Gowon, who with Decree 13 of 1970 'strengthened the federal government's role as the sole allocative and distribu-
tive authority and gave it a domineering fiscal position'.[20] A policy of
indigenization in the 1970s made the state the main equity holder in
joint venture arrangements with all oil companies operating in the
country. These joint ventures are managed by the Nigeria National
Petroleum Company (NNPC), Nigeria's largest company with over
17,000 employees and a turnover of more than $1.6 billion a year.
The largest such venture is with Shell, where the NNPC owns 55 per
cent, while its equity share in the joint ventures with ExxonMobil and

[16] The Oloibiri find was made by Shell–BP Petroleum Development Corporation
   of Nigeria Ltd, and Shell has since enjoyed a privileged status within
   Nigerian oil production.
[17] Terry Lynn Karl, 'The Perils of the Petro-State: Reflections on the Paradox of
   Plenty', *Journal of International Affairs*, 53 (1) (1999): 31–48. On Nigeria's
   turbulent political history, see Eghosa E. Ogashe, *Crippled Giant: Nigeria
   since Independence*, Bloomington, Ind.: Indiana University Press, 1998.
[18] Terry Lynn Karl, *The Paradox of Plenty: Oil Booms and Petro-States*,
   Berkeley, Calif.: University of California Press, 1997, p. xv. For a recent
   study of the petro-states of the Gulf of Guinea, see Soares de Oliveira, *Oil
   and Politics*.
[19] The literature is extensive; for a selection see Richard A. Joseph, 'Class,
   State, and Prebendal Politics in Nigeria', *Journal of Commonwealth
   and Comparative Politics*, 21 (3) (1983): 21–38; and Richard A. Joseph,
   *Democracy and Prebendal Politics in Nigeria: The Rise and Fall of the
   Second Republic*, Cambridge: Cambridge University Press, 1987; Peter
   Lewis, *Growing Apart: Oil, Politics and Economic Change in Indonesia and
   Nigeria*, Ann Arbor, Mich.: University of Michigan Press, 2007.
[20] Osaghae, *Crippled Giant*, p. 73.

Chevron is 60 per cent. All in all, the Nigerian state takes over 70 per cent of the total revenues from the joint venture operations, including taxes, rents and royalties, and collects about 90 per cent of the export value of oil.[21]

As in many petro-states, the Nigerian state is almost entirely independent of the production and taxation of its national population. Taxes, as Atul Kohli states matter-of-factly, were 'essentially eliminated with the coming of oil revenues', with important implications for the material basis for liberal democratic struggles.[22] Politics in Nigeria has thus come to revolve around the distribution of rents, as the state has more or less abandoned any pretence at productive activities and governs instead through federal largesse and coercion.[23] The various institutions of governance are primarily means for allocating patronage, and, because economic resources and opportunities are centralized in the state, access to it becomes a precondition for economic success of any kind. In this way, political offices become 'prebends' or personal goods to be appropriated by the office-holders for their own material benefit, and that of their associates, friends and family, with any notion of the public good downgraded to a secondary concern.[24] One result of this form of politics has been an increasing administrative fragmentation, as each new administrative unit provides another opportunity for distribution and appropriation of resources. Thus, the number of states in the Nigerian federation has increased from only three at independence to thirty-six today, while the number of local governments has grown from fifty in 1966 to

---

[21] Omeje, *High Stakes and Stakeholders*, p. 49; Menachem Katz, Ulrich Bartsch, Harinder Malothra, and Milan Cuc, *Lifting the Oil Curse: Improving Petroleum Revenue Management in Sub-Saharan Africa*, Washington, DC: International Monetary Fund, 2004, p. 5. For useful overviews of the legal framework relating to the oil industry in Nigeria, see Jedrzej George Frynas, *Oil in Nigeria: Conflict and Litigation between Oil Companies and Village Communities*, Berlin: Lit Verlag, 2000.

[22] Atul Kohli, *State-Directed Development: Political Power and Industrialization in the Global Periphery*, Princeton, NJ: Princeton University Press, 2004, p. 350; and Jane I. Guyer, 'Representation without Taxation: An Essay on Democracy in Rural Nigeria, 1952–1990', *African Studies Review*, 35 (1) (1992): 41–80.

[23] Charles Gore and David Pratten, 'The Politics of Plunder: The Rhetoric of Order and Disorder in Southern Nigeria', *African Affairs*, 102 (407) (2003): 211–40; Joseph, 'Class, State, and Prebendal Politics'.

[24] Joseph, *Democracy and Prebendal Politics*.

almost 1,000.[25] As Michael Watts puts it, 'Nigeria as a modern nation state has become a machine for the production of ever more local political institutions, and this process is endless. The logic is ineluctable and, of course, terrifying.'[26]

The much-celebrated return to multi-part democracy in 1999 has done little, if anything, to change the basic logic of this situation, which is often perceived locally to have worsened since the 1990s.[27] Despite some recent improvement, Transparency International continues to rank Nigeria as one of the most corrupt countries in the world, with corruption scandals a part of daily life.[28] As part of a high-profile anti-corruption campaign in 2003, for example, the anti-corruption chief Nuhu Ribadu claimed that 70 per cent of the country's oil wealth was stolen or wasted; by 2005, this had decreased to 'only' 40 per cent.[29] These processes of appropriation show few signs of change, regardless of formal political transformations. Thus, one of the first acts of President Umaru Yar'Adua, elected in 2007, was to send the anti-corruption tsar on a 're-education' programme, again defying any easy equation between liberal democracy and the end of corruption.[30]

The 'politics of plunder' is accompanied by a highly unequal society. According to the World Bank, some 80 per cent of oil revenues are accrued by 1 per cent of the population, while 70 per cent of private wealth is held abroad.[31] At the same time, about 70 per cent of Nigeria's population live below the poverty line, with deprivation acute in parts of the oil-producing states. Average life expectancy is as low as

---

[25] Michael Watts, 'Development and Governmentality', *Singapore Journal of Tropical Geography*, 24 (1) (2003): 6–34.

[26] *Ibid.*, p. 25.

[27] Gore and Pratten, 'The Politics of Plunder'.

[28] See the annual *Global Corruption Report* (www.transparency.org/publications/gcr). For a wider survey, Giorgio Blundo and Jean-Pierre Olivier de Sardan (eds.), *Everyday Corruption and the State: Citizens and Public Officials in Africa*, London: Zed Books, 2006.

[29] Lubeck *et al.*, *Convergent Interests*, p. 7.

[30] It should be noted that both the 2003 and especially the 2007 elections have been characterized by blatant fraud and rigging; see Human Rights Watch, *Nigeria's 2003 Elections: The Unacknowledged Violence*. Available online at http://hrw.org/reports/2004/nigeria0604; and Ben Rawlence and Chris Albin-Lackey, 'Briefing: Nigeria's 2007 Elections: Democracy in Retreat', *African Affairs*, 106 (424) (2007): 497–506.

[31] Lubeck *et al.*, *Convergent Interests*, p. 7.

fifty years in some states, and many communities are without electricity, safe water and basic infrastructure. Although consecutive federal governments have gradually increased the amount of oil revenue allocated to the oil-producing states, from a low point of only 1.5 per cent during the military dictatorship of Sani Abacha to 13 per cent today, little appears to find its way to local communities. The Niger Delta Development Commission (NDDC), established in 1999 by President Olusegun Obasanjo, also appears to have made scant impact and is dismissed by critics as elitist and top-down.[32] Thus, Cyril Obi describes the Delta as a place with 'virtually no development, with the people torn between a life of subsistence and the stark reality of unemployment'.[33]

This situation is exacerbated by the widespread environmental damage caused by petroleum extraction in a fragile eco-system of swamps, mangroves and lowland rain forest. Spills and leaks from the pipelines that criss-cross the region have polluted and destroyed farmland, fisheries and aquatic life, and, although matters have improved somewhat in recent years, the record is still devastating.[34] The causes of oil spillage, however, remain a bone of contention, with the oil companies inclined to blame sabotage by local communities, who in turn point to a lethal combination of company negligence and ageing pipelines. Whatever the causes, the environmental damage is made worse by extensive gas flaring that releases toxic chemicals into the atmosphere. Nigeria is the largest flarer of gas in the world, accounting for 12 per cent of the world total.[35] The oil companies' commitment to cease the practice has been continually delayed since the late

---

[32] See Omeje, *High Stakes*, and Dimieari Von Kemedi, 'The Changing Predatory Styles of International Oil Companies in Nigeria', *Review of African Political Economy*, 30 (95) (2003): 134–9.

[33] Cyril Obi, 'Global, State and Local Intersections: Power, Authority, and Conflict in the Niger Delta Oil Communities', in Callaghy *et al.*, *Intervention and Transnationalism in Africa*, pp. 173–95; p. 176. The Delta region consists of eight states, containing some sixty different ethnic groups and a population of approximately 28 to 30 million – a small minority when compared to the three dominant groups of Yoruba, Hausa and Igbo that make up the majority of the country's nearly 140 million inhabitants.

[34] See Ike Okonta and Oronto Douglas, *Where Vultures Feast: Shell, Human Rights, and Oil*, London: Verso, 2001. In 2001, Shell alone reported 221 spills, totalling some 9,900 barrels of oil. Shell Petroleum Development Corporation, *2001: People and the Environment – Annual Report*, Lagos: Shell Petroleum Development Corporation, 2002, p. 7.

[35] Lubeck *et al.*, *Convergent Interests*, p. 9.

1970s. A December 2008 deadline was recently postponed until 2010 or 2011, and communities neighbouring these installations continue to bathe in an eerily constant daylight and suffer the attendant environmental consequences.

The persistent unrest in the Delta is best understood in this context of economic marginality and exploitation and a highly unresponsive state where the easy availability of rent revenue reduces the political and economic significance of the citizenry. In conditions of extreme disenfranchisement and exclusion, the struggles in the Delta are, in effect, ways of making claims to a share of the oil wealth. As such, there is, as Charles Gore and David Pratten observe, an inherent duality to the struggles: they are simultaneously demands for inclusion in patronage networks and protests against the coercive dominance of the state.[36] The result has been what Michael Watts refers to as a 'veritable jigsaw of militant particularisms', where ever more groups turn to protest and violence as the only language that seems to gain any recognition.[37] The international oil companies are an intrinsic part of this situation, and they have over the years become deeply entangled in Nigerian politics.[38] The alliance between the state and the companies means that many people in the oil-producing areas make little distinction between the two, and the oil majors are often seen by the population as legitimate targets in the struggle for a more equitable distribution of wealth.

Yet there is no simple way to describe the crisis in the Niger Delta, and, over the years, political opposition, ethnic struggles for self-determination and social justice have come to blend and overlap with

[36] Gore and Pratten, 'The Politics of Plunder'.
[37] Watts, 'Development and Governmentality', p. 24.
[38] For some observers, the oil companies are the real holders of power in Nigeria, with the state a mere dependent 'puppet'. For a discussion and critique of these views, see Omeje, *High Stakes*, pp. 1–12. Our analysis does not directly address this problematic, but the focus on global assemblages has much in common with Pamela Burke's observation that transnational oil companies in Ecuador have a 'semi-public role' and should be seen as 'quasi-public actors that function on multiple levels within the international system, including subnational, national, and transnational'. Pamela L. Burke, 'Embedded Private Authority: Multinational Enterprises and the Amazonian Indigenous Peoples Movement in Ecuador', in Cutler *et al.*, *Private Authority and International Affairs*, pp. 223–4.

criminal activity and political corruption. Alongside more organized movements, such as the Ogoni struggle in 1995 and the 1998 Kaiama Declaration, everyday resistance against the oil companies has persisted.[39] As the state has increasingly abandoned its responsibilities towards the population, the companies have become the focus of people's social demands. State neglect, as Ricardo Soares de Oliveira writes, has led to a 'shifting of popular expectations away from the state towards the private sector'.[40] Neglected, poor communities often find protests against the oil companies more rewarding in terms of development programmes and social benefits than protests against an unresponsive state, and, for numerous local groups and communities, attacks on oil companies and their property have become prime sources of income. Small-scale crude oil theft and intentional pipeline damage, for example, may be rewarded by compensation for the resulting oil spills and environmental damage, while intentional damage can bring contracts to repair and guard the pipelines against future sabotage. Through such practices, the oil companies have, over the years, contributed to intercommunal conflict, as compensations, payments for land rent, contracts for informal security and protection services, development programmes and social funds have been unequally distributed between communities and have become spoils to be fought over. As Shell put it, in a veiled acknowledgement of this dynamic, 'we recognise that our development activities in the past may have been less than perfect.'[41] In particular, the youths hired on more or less formalized security contracts have become a source of community violence, rivalry and instability, sometimes leading to the

---

[39] Internationally, the conflict is epitomized most tragically in the hanging of Ken Saro-Wiwa and eight other Ogoni leaders in 1995, but despite this brutal response from the state, protest and violence continued to escalate. The Kaiama Declaration, issued by a conference of over 500 Ijaw youth to the Government and the oil companies, demanded self-government and control over resources within a federation of ethnic minorities. Effectively issuing an ultimatum to the oil companies to comply or to leave by the end of the year, the declaration (predictably) sparked another military onslaught by the Government that further intensified the militarization of the region.

[40] Soares de Oliveira, *Oil and Politics*, p. 103.

[41] Shell Petroleum Development Corporation, *2003: People and the Environment – Annual Report*, Lagos: Shell Petroleum Development Corporation, 2003, p. 1.

formation of ethic militias and vigilante groups.[42] For the oil companies, as Kenneth Omeje observes, such security contacts are a two-edged sword in that they do not provide effective security but equally cannot be abandoned without increasing the threat to oil personnel and facilities.[43]

In recent years, the conflict in the Delta has taken a more violent turn, with the emergence of heavily armed militias. The fact that some of these groups were initially linked to powerful politicians and used as political thugs during the 2003 elections shows how the lines between those fighting for social justice and self-determination and those simply 'on the make' in a politically permissive environment have become yet more porous and difficult to disentangle. In December 2005, the emergence of MEND (the Movement for the Emancipation of the Niger Delta) signalled a new level of violent capacities on behalf of the militias. Calling for the percentage of oil revenues allocated to the Delta states to be increased from 13 to 25 per cent, as well as for a $1.5 billion compensation payment from Shell for environmental damage, MEND has mustered sufficient military capacity to at times seriously challenge the state security forces. As the International Crisis Group reports, since mid-2008, the conflict has spread in unanticipated ways to sea, land and air. MEND has demonstrated capacity to attack oil installations 120 kilometres off the coast, the Joint Military Task Force (consisting of the combined forces of the Army, Navy and paramilitary Mobile Police, MoPol) has several times bombed militants' camps and other suspected locations, whereas MEND in February 2009 for the first time attacked a civilian helicopter.[44] While MEND vigorously rejects the view that its struggle is being criminalized, the human costs of

---

[42] See Omeje, *High Stakes*, pp. 73–101. On the emergence of vigilantes in Nigeria more generally, see David Pratten, 'The Politics of Vigilance in South-Eastern Nigeria', in Christian Lund (ed.), *Twilight Institutions: Public Authority and Local Politics in Africa*, New York: Wiley, 2006, pp. 33–60; Rufus T. Akinyele, 'Ethnic Militancy and National Stability in Nigeria: A Case Study of the Oodua People's Congress', *African Affairs*, 100 (401) (2001): 623–40.

[43] Omeje, *High Stakes*, p. 131.

[44] International Crisis Group, *Nigeria: Seizing the Moment*. Piracy has also increased, making Nigerian waters second only to Somalia in terms of danger. See also Ukoha Ukiwo, 'From "Pirates" to Militants: A Historical Perspective on Anti-State and Anti-Oil Company Mobilization among

the escalation in fighting are tremendous. According to Amnesty International, oil-related deaths in the Delta were 680 in 2003 and over 1,000 in 2004.[45] The latest figures from the government suggest that 1,000 people were killed in the first nine months of 2008 alone, with the costs in terms of lost oil revenues estimated at nearly $24 billion.[46]

A further aspect of the ongoing crisis is the frequent kidnapping of expatriate personnel for ransom. Between May and August of 2006, there were at least three such kidnappings per month, and the first nine months of 2008 recorded 300 hostage situations.[47] Armed militias such as MEND are responsible for many of these incidents but there are also suggestions that rings of hostage-takers have emerged, sometimes established by government officials.[48] The same complicity of state officials and high-ranking politicians can be found in the growing business of 'illegal bunkering', or large-scale crude oil theft. This has become a huge enterprise, with oil-smuggling rings netting at least $5 billion annually, often more than 500,000 barrels a day.[49] Tankers filled with tens of thousands of litres of oil have simply 'disappeared' while in the care of the Nigerian Navy and Police, and, in a rare case in 2005, two rear admirals were court-martialled and dismissed for allowing the tanker *African Pride* to escape the navy port in Lagos.[50] President Umaru Yar'Adua has sought to name this 'blood oil', drawing a parallel to the 'blood diamonds' that fuelled the civil wars in neighbouring Sierra Leone.[51] The President's call for international assistance to curb illegal bunkering was met with a

the Ijaw of Warri, Western Niger Delta', *African Affairs*, 106 (425) (2007): 587–610.

[45] Quoted in Lubeck *et al.*, *Convergent Interests*, p. 8.

[46] International Crisis Group, *Nigeria: Seizing the Moment*, p. 2.

[47] BBC Africa, 'Nigeria Oil Unrest Kills 1,000', 10 April 2009. Available online at http://news.bbc.co.uk/2/hi/africa/7994152.stm; Lubeck *et al.*, *Convergent Interests*.

[48] According to Ukiwo, the kidnappers often target the so-called 'security votes', funds budgeted by federal, state and local governments for the maintenance of law and order and managed by the chief executive of each tier of government, with no obligation to disclose the extent of these funds or how they are spent.

[49] Wallis and Green, 'UK and Nigeria Aim to Stop Oil Theft', p. 7.

[50] See Dayo Aiyetan, 'And the Navy Lied'. *Tell Magazine* (Lagos), 27 September 2004, pp. 12–15.

[51] Walker, '"Blood Oil" Dripping from Nigeria'.

promise of military training support from the UK – and with scepticism by many activists, who pointed to the involvement and collusion of politicians, security personnel and company officials in the international oil-smuggling cartels. In short, while the bunkering syndicates may enlist the services of unemployed Niger Delta youth and militias and operate under the cover of the ongoing conflict between the local population and the oil companies, many suspect that the real money accrues to people in much more powerful positions.[52] Curbing this massive illegal trade may thus require more than strengthening a military and security apparatus itself embedded in the very fabric of violence and illegality.

The security situation in the Delta is such that many of the activities associated with oil extraction take place in fortified enclaves; operations behind layers of barbed wire, staff inside gated compounds, transports with armed escorts. While the risk to personnel and property is very real, there is also little doubt that the extensive security presence is in itself perceived as an aggressive and exclusionary act by many local people and hence perpetuates an environment of hostility and violence. Security, in this sense, begets insecurity. On coming to power in 2007, the Yar'Adua Government initially signalled a renewed intention to solve the conflicts through dialogue and inclusion, but subsequent efforts have been at best 'ambiguous and at times incoherent'.[53] For example, while setting up the Technical Committee on the Niger Delta, the Government has subsequently failed to respond to its recommendations, instead convening yet another committee to study the issue. In short, it seems that the government has fallen back on the well-worn tactics of a militarized solution. As one human rights activist commented to the BBC, 'Everything in Yar'Adua's budget for the Delta has gone on security, not sustainable development.'[54]

---

[52] According to the International Crisis Group, for example, the Joint Military Task Force is widely suspected of involvement in oil bunkering. *Nigeria: Seizing the Moment*, p. 5.

[53] International Crisis Group, *Nigeria: Seizing the Moment*, p. 1.

[54] Andrew Walker, 'Elusive Peace in Nigeria's Oil Delta', *BBC News*, 18 July 2008. Available online at http://news.bbc.co.uk/2/hi/africa/7500472.stm. For an overview of the Government's recent policies, see International Crisis Group, *Nigeria: Seizing the Moment*.

Global security assemblages in the Niger Delta

In a militarized, conflictual and intensely political situation such as this, there might seem to be few roles for the kind of PSCs we are concerned with in this book. In reality, however, commercial firms have come to play increasingly important roles across the spectrum of security provision in the Delta, both in terms of 'a costly application of force' and in terms of 'tiresome negotiations' with local populations, to return to Bauman's terminology. In fact, the enclave appearance of petroleum production belies the extent to which it takes place within a wider structure where private and public security actors are integrated into new hybrid arrangements or global security assemblages. These assemblages are not unified or linear, and the security field is characterized and constituted by tensions and divisions as well as synergies and collaboration. Within them, actors draw on a range of different forms of capital, producing a new architecture of security that requires empirical investigation in order to analyse its effects and implications for global capital, state authority and local populations.

As noted in Chapter 3, however tenuous it may sometimes be in practice, the state's monopoly of force is an important form of both material and symbolic power in the security field. One expression of this power in Nigeria is that, although there is little direct regulation of the sector, PSCs are prevented from carrying firearms by the Private Guard Companies Act (1986).[55] This unarmed status has given rise to close collaboration between PSCs and the police and a general fusion of public and private force across a number of security operations. The generally high level of violence and insecurity means that most leading PSCs, whether local or global, find it necessary to offer armed protection for certain key contracts, as well as the possibility of armed response in cases of emergency. The solution comes in the form of cooperation with the Nigerian police whereby members of MoPol – often armed with fully automatic weapons – are more or less permanently seconded to PSCs and integrated into their everyday operations. MoPol officers are paid supplementary wages by the companies and are supervised by PSC officers, but continue in principle to

---

[55] Private Guard Companies Act (1986), Cap 367 Laws of the Federal Republic of Nigeria.

take orders from their own commanders, thus creating a significant fusion of public and private authority and responsibility.[56]

In the oil sector, this integration is even more extensive and multi-faceted. To start, private security personnel cooperate extensively with the so-called supernumerary or 'spy' police – officers recruited and trained by the Nigerian police force at the direct request of the oil companies and deployed as an unarmed police force (used primarily for manned guarding) under the direct pay and control of the oil companies, and with police powers only on company property. The numbers of spy police are extensive: Shell alone has 1,200 at its operations, including an intelligence unit, while ExxonMobil deploys between 700 and 1,000, and Chevron approximately 250. As the security situation in the Niger Delta has worsened, the oil companies have also integrated armed components of the public police directly into their operations. These range from armed officers of the Nigerian police force, who also act as dog handlers, to the more heavily armed MoPol. Again, the numbers are considerable, with Shell utilizing approximately 600 police and MoPol officers in its operations. Police and MoPol alike are paid a stipend by the companies and are also sometimes provided with food and accommodation. Unlike the spy police, however, the oil companies do not have direct control over these forces. While operational authority is in the hands of a senior company security official and police officers are instructed to comply with the oil company's 'guidelines for the use of force' or code of conduct drawn up by its security officials, the police have their own commanders and supervisors and receive their orders within this line of command. These arrangements amount to a significant, if partial, privatization of public force and a blurring of authority between company security officials and public officers.

In addition, private security personnel interact on a daily basis with the military forces, or government security forces (GSF), which are increasingly used to protect oil operations defined as national key assets. The GSF are allocated directly to the oil companies, who pay an administrative fee to the commander and a direct stipend, as well

---

[56] Our research revealed that in all these various arrangements involving the secondment of public officers to private companies, the lion's share of the stipend went to the commander, within a hierarchy of distribution down the chains of command.

as food and accommodation, to the soldiers. The oil companies also frequently supply and maintain the equipment, vehicles and boats of the GSF. In highly conflictual situations, the GSF provide more direct protection of sites, such as flowstations and terminals, and the Navy is also used to supply operations in the swamp and offshore. In response to the deteriorating security situation of the past few years, the number of GSF assigned to the various oil companies has grown, and Shell alone has a total of 700 army and navy personnel deployed at its various locations.

A more detailed image of the global security assemblages in the Niger Delta can be found in G4S's contract with Chevron Nigeria Ltd (CNL), the most extensive PSC involvement in Nigeria's oil industry and one of G4S's biggest and most valuable contracts on the African continent. Chevron is the third largest oil major in Nigeria, after Shell and ExxonMobil. It is also the largest shareholder in the consortium contracted to build the West African Gas Pipeline, an ambitious project to construct a 681-kilometre onshore–offshore gas pipeline from Escravos in the western Niger Delta to Benin, Togo and Ghana.

Chevron has been described as one of the most 'embattled' oil companies in Nigeria, due to its location on the 'front line' of the petro-violence.[57] In the Warri area, long-standing conflicts between the three ethnic groups, the Ijaw, the Itsekiri and the Uhrobo, have been intensified by oil extraction, and persistent violence has caused most other oil companies to relocate from Warri to Port Harcourt. Chevron, however, is compelled by its valuable concessions to stay. The company's operations are mostly onshore, in relatively close proximity to local communities, and its infrastructure is geographically dispersed across vast areas.[58] As a result, it is a prime target for demands for compensations, development programmes and other benefits. One of the most dramatic displays of these fraught community relations occurred in July 2002, when a Chevron refinery near Warri was occupied by more than 600 Itsekiri and Ijaw women, demanding company investments and jobs for the local population. The peaceful occupation closed down oil production and export for almost two weeks,

---

[57] Omeje, *High Stakes*, pp. 121–54.
[58] Many companies have sought to secure production by moving to deep-water offshore platforms. Even this has proven vulnerable, however, as militants have acquired more powerful boats.

imposing significant losses on the company and presenting it with an uncomfortable public relations situation.

Following this 'invasion' and other similar incidents, Chevron undertook a major review of its security strategy and in 2002 signed an extensive security contract with the South African company Gray Security, operating in Nigeria as Outsourcing Services Ltd (OSL).[59] At the time, Gray was one of South Africa's most prominent and entrepreneurially aggressive security companies. Employing predominantly ex-military personnel, often with experience from combat in the front line states, the company had expanded quickly to establish operations in some twenty countries across the continent. Shortly after gaining the Chevron contract, Gray was bought by the British company Securicor, which in turn merged with Group4 to form Group4Securicor in 2004.[60]

When commencing the contract, OSL replaced seven local PSCs that Chevron's security review had determined were below acceptable standards. It also reduced Chevron's reliance on the spy police. Initially, the contract was for guarding at CNL's headquarters in Lagos, the two logistical bases in Port Harcourt and Warri, as well as the operational base in Escravos, but G4S's engagement with Chevron has since expanded significantly beyond more traditional guarding activities. In total, G4S now provides a security force of 1,200 persons for CNL, and their operations are integrated in a complex and intricate assemblage with the various elements of the public security forces.[61]

A clear illustration is provided by the role played by OSL in providing marine security for CNL, especially around Escravos. A small sand island, set in an estuary, accessible only by boat or via Chevron's private airstrip, and surrounded by security fencing and watchtowers, Escravos fits the classic image of a resource enclave. Yet its physical isolation is misleading, as the facility is set within a dense public–private, global–local security assemblage that is crucial

---

[59] The arrangement gets around the legal prevention of foreign ownership of security companies, and is one reason why OSL has been highly controversial among local security companies in Nigeria.

[60] See the discussion in Chapter 1.

[61] For the company's own accounts of this contract, see Securicor 'Focus on Nigeria', *Securicor Magazine*, May 2004, pp. 38–42; and Gavin Greenwood, 'The Thin Black Line', *G4S International*, June 2008, pp. 17–20.

to its operation. As a consequence of the spread of CNL's production throughout the mangrove swamps, and the isolation of Escravos itself, maritime security is essential to the company, and OSL plays a central role in its provision. In close interaction with Nigerian naval personnel, the company is responsible for daily routine patrols both offshore and in the surrounding swamp's rivers and creeks, and OSL boats also provide escort and protection for supply vessels, drilling rigs and work barges. Fast-response craft equipped with high-calibre machine guns are deployable at short notice in emergency cases, and in 2007 OSL acquired two high-speed patrol boats further enabling the movement of rapid reaction force personnel. While OSL mariners (usually ex-navy personnel) operate and command the boats, each patrol vessel includes a contingent of armed naval personnel. Detailed 'convoy/patrol orders' specifying the number of GSF forces required for these tasks are issued on a daily basis, with varying patrol routes and departure times. A satellite tracking system allows the OSL control room to follow the boats' movement through the narrow waterways around Escravos, providing constant surveillance and communications, and allowing for rapid deployment of security personnel. In day-to-day operations, the OSL mariner is in control of the vessel, but at the point when a 'life-threatening situation' develops, authority passes to the senior GSF officer. Although the division of labour and authority between OSL and the GSF is in principle clearly outlined, the definition of 'a life-threatening situation' is by no means straightforward. The GSF retain ultimate authority, but they are to a significant extent embedded within structures, routines and procedures developed by OSL and CNL.[62] As the situation is described in a G4S publication, 'OSL also liaises between the Nigerian security forces and CNL, a delicate task requiring a high degree of cultural sensitivity and diplomatic skills.'[63]

These interactions are facilitated by the integration of high-ranking ex-navy personnel directly into the CNL–OSL security management structure as security coordinators. The role of these officials is both

---

[62] This structure also reflects the embedding of the security network within the normative constraints provided the Voluntary Principles on Security and Human Rights, to which Chevron subscribes. The principles favour unarmed private security and restraints on the use of force by public authorities. See www.voluntaryprinciples.org. We return to this issue in Chapter Six.

[63] Greenwood, 'The Thin Black Line', p. 18.

formal and informal or, to use more analytic terms, both symbolic and cultural. Symbolically, their experience of naval procedures furthers private-sector claims to expert knowledge about security. Technical, international and local–national forms of symbolic capital are thus melded into the private security operations. Equally significant, however, is the cultural capital provided to the company by these coordinators. They provide personal links into the Nigerian military and political establishment and possess forms of symbolic and cultural capital recognized by military personnel. As such, they are important points of mediation (and articulations of power) between national military forces and private, largely expatriate personnel.

A similar fusion of public and private security is found in the land-based protection of Chevron's facility at Escravos. As mentioned, the facility has been subject to a number of attempted 'site invasions' by local communities with grievances against the company, the government, or both, and at times such protests have forced Chevron to close production and evacuate personnel. Following its appointment, OSL designed and implemented strategies to counter such events: the facility is enclosed behind three layers of fencing, with additional razor wire ready to be dispatched from a mobile unit at speeds of up to 40 kilometres per hour. Watchtowers are strategically placed along the perimeter fence. A new access control system and entry regulations for local workers from the community were also introduced, including a central entry gate and a fingerprinting system. While these measures were designed to keep the surrounding populations out, a 'closed camp' policy was adopted to prevent Chevron workers from leaving the facility for social visits to the surrounding villages. As a result of these various strategies, incidents such as fence-cutting, theft and attempted 'invasions' decreased significantly. Should an 'invasion' occur, OSL has devised a tactical plan which incorporates private security personnel, the spy police and MoPol. These various security actors are trained by OSL officers as an integrated 'quick response force' consisting of OSL personnel, supernumerary police, MoPol, and – in the last instance – GSF forces. In case of an 'invasion', public police and GSF forces will act within the structures devised by a global PSC, not by their local commanders, and they will act side by side with private security officers. Again, ultimate authority and responsibility lies with the police and GSF commanders, but the structures and tactical plans are developed and supervised by senior OSL officers.

Governing the Niger Delta

Private security in the Niger Delta plays an important role in securing not only the operations of the oil companies but also, by extension, the authority of the Federal Government, which depends upon the income from oil extraction. Importantly, however, these international actors are not mercenaries operating on the fringes of legality and outside the purview of the state, or even PMCs with an armed capacity. Instead, the ability of a global PSC to influence security arrangements and tactics stems in large part from its international legitimacy, expertise and material capabilities and (in the case of OSL, for instance) their ability to operate effectively within the cultural field of Nigerian security politics. The unarmed status of PSCs, as well as their connections to the protection of property rights and the principal–agent relationship, embed them within legitimating norms and institutions and reflect the capacities that global PSCs have acquired as part of the transformations in contemporary governance. As a result, OSL is able to deploy its recognized expertise and to bring to bear organizational techniques and technological resources that state forces and local private security firms are unable or unwilling to exercise and that are valued by both the oil companies and Nigerian political authorities and have a significant impact on the security situation, the exercise of force and the balance of social power in the area.

In this setting, private security is not simply a 'junior partner' to the state: it is a key component in the operations of state forces.[64] Integrated into complex assemblages of governance, and often operating in close integration with public forces, private security provides technology, expertise and expatriate personnel that substantially influence the security situation. Its political effects should also not be underestimated. As noted earlier, the Nigerian state is largely independent of its population, but, like many petro-states, it is dependent on external relations and strong state–oil firm partnerships. These partnerships, as Soares de Oliveira observes, are characterized by mutual dependency. Oil extraction cannot take place without the state, and this means that oil companies generally increase the power of the state through diplomatic leverage exerted on its behalf, assistance in

---

[64] For a discussion of private security as a 'junior partner', see Jones and Newburn, *Private Security and Public Policing*, pp. 98–101.

obtaining loans and, most importantly, by allowing it to profit from resources that it would otherwise lack the expertise to access.[65] In today's Nigeria, PSCs are key parts of this relationship, since without them the maintenance of the state–firm partnership would be considerably more difficult, especially as growing local resistance threatens both oil production and state income.

Yet these global security assemblages are not without tensions, and they are constantly evolving as the political and security situation changes. The legitimate application of force is a case in point. In the past, the oil companies have (at the very least) tolerated – and at times even promoted – the highly coercive security strategies of the Nigerian police and military.[66] Both these forces have been criticized for their brutality and lack of respect for human rights. According to Amnesty International, the 'Nigeria Police Force and the State Security Services (SSS) continue to commit human rights violations with impunity, including extra-judicial executions ... the police execute people for refusal to pay bribes during road checks, saying they are criminal suspects'.[67] In a shocking statement in 2007, the Inspector General of Police Mike Okiro informed the Nigerian public that between June and August 2007, some 785 suspected armed robbers were killed by the police.[68] The military's record is no better, with Amnesty International pointing to rape as a particular strategy of coercion and intimidation in the Niger Delta.[69]

[65] Soares de Oliveira, *Oil and Politics*, p. 53. A prime example of this mutual dependency is Shell's announcement of its intention to lend Nigeria $3 billion to sustain oil production and investment threatened by falling government funding. Ed Crooks, 'Shell to Lend Nigeria $3 Billion', *Financial Times*, 20 February 2009.

[66] Human Rights Watch, *The Price of Oil: Corporate Responsibility and Human Rights Violations in Nigeria's Oil Producing Communities*, New York: Human Rights Watch, 1999; Okonta and Douglas, *Where Vultures Feast*; Karl Meier, 'Shell "Feeds" Nigeria Conflict, May End Onshore Work', *Bloomberg News Service*, 10 June 2004; Jedrzej George Frynas, 'Corporate and State Responses to Anti-Oil Protests in the Niger Delta', *African Affairs*, 100 (398) (2001): 27–54.

[67] Amnesty International, *Nigeria: "Pragmatic Policing" through Extra-Judicial Executions and Torture*, 16 May 2008, p. 2.

[68] Amnesty International, *Nigeria: "Pragmatic Policing"*, p. 3.

[69] Amnesty International, *Nigeria: Amnesty International Report 2008*, New York: Amnesty International, 2008.

There are now signs that the oil companies are seeking at least in part to distance themselves from the coercion of public security services, recognizing both the failure of these policies and the considerable international opposition and negative publicity they have generated. Instead, they are exploring more 'comprehensive' security strategies incorporating community engagement and development.[70] To be sure, the depth of this commitment remains questionable and largely untested, and a common response is simply that it is 'too little, too late'. At the same time, the use of PSCs and consultants are potentially important components of these strategies.

Global PSCs provide the oil companies with an increased capacity to manage their own security arrangements. The presence of PSCs allows oil companies to insulate themselves to some degree from the violence of the state, but it also allows them potentially to influence the exercise of violence through the introduction of more technology-based security responses and also (perhaps) to discipline public forces through their integration into different security strategies and normativities. Through OSL, for example, Chevron exercises influence not only over its own security personnel but also – albeit to a lesser degree – the forces of the Nigerian state that operate alongside and act within strategies influenced (and in some cases devised) by the global PSC. At the simplest level, these 'disciplining strategies' can be seen in the code-of-conduct cards carried by all police employed on Shell property, reminding officers of restrictions on the use of force as well as warning against involvement in 'illegal road blocks or other unethical activities that will jeopardise your operation and tarnish the Company's image' (see Figure 4.1). While any best-practice guideline is of limited practical effect, such initiatives are nevertheless clear attempts to change behaviour, and an illustration of how in such security assemblages global normativities influence security practices, seeking to embed them within corporate structures of responsibility and accountability.[71]

More complexly, by partially embedding state security forces within structures provided by global PSCs such as G4S, international

---

[70] See Omeje, *High Stakes*; and Shell Petroleum Development Corporation, *2001: People and the Environment.*

[71] For a critical appraisal of corporate social responsibility, see Ronnie Lipschutz, *Globalization, Governmentality and Global Politics*, London and New York: Routledge, 2005, pp. 130–70.

GUIDELINES TO NIGERIA POLICEMEN ON
SPECIAL DUTY IN SPDC ASSET AREAS

1. All SPDC rules must be strictly adhered to and respected.

2. Ensure that all persons entering SPDC Locations are authorized.

3. It is your statutory responsibility to detect and prevent crimes, most specially Armed Robbery/Stealing within SPDC Loactions.

4. You should ensure the Security/Safety of Personnel and Property in SPDC Locations.

5. You should act as a deterrent to intending saboteurs, thieves or other anti-social elements harbouring untoward intents against SPDC assets.

6. **You must report promptly to SPDC Base any case of security breach in your area of operations. This involves Intelligence Gathering and timely dissemination of same to Base with a view to forestalling planned threats against SPDC Asset Areas.**

7. You should be guided by Force Order 237 in your use of firearms.

8. Ensure you always wear Safety Protective gear provided for you, especially during escort.

9. You must never be involved in illegal road blocks or other unethical activities that will jeopardise your operations and tarnish the Company's image.

10. The use of company recreational facilities such as the swimming pool is strictly forbidden.

11. Always be polite in any interactions involving SPDC staff, spouses and dependants, especially in the Residential Areas.

12. Always seek clarification from a SPY Senior Police Officer when in doubt on any issue in the course of performing your duties.

13. Any act of indiscipline of any sort on your part will be subject to severe disciplinary action including prompt return to Base.

WISHING YOU A SUCCESSFUL DUTY TENURE IN SPDC ASSET AREAS.
-RCL-SEC-

Figure 4.1 Guidelines to Nigeria policemen on special duty in Shell Petroleum Development Corporation asset areas.

oil companies can also influence security structures and strategies in much more direct ways than in situations where the monopoly of public security provision is stronger. The recognized expertise of a global PSC, its substantial material capacities and its status as the agent of a powerful principal provide forms of power in the security field that may allow direct influences on the behaviour of state forces. As two directors of CNL put it in an interview, one of the perceived benefits of employing a global private security firm was that 'OSL helps discipline the GSF', a claim that, as we have shown, is not completely fanciful. However, this process is by no means straightforward. Ultimate legal authority and control over the exercise of coercion, especially at the level of lethal force, remains in the hands of public officials, and private actors operate in a setting where the symbolic dominance of the public security forces remains central. To be effective, the practices of private security actors must always account for this element of the security field. The need for what one G4S publication calls a 'high degree of cultural sensitivity and diplomatic skills'[72] in Nigeria can be rendered analytically as the need for what Bourdieu called a 'feel for the game' – a delicate and constantly reflexive movement within a security assemblage that is part of a wider field of practice and power. While private security actors can influence the capacities and even the applications of public force, they by no means control it, and this means that they inevitably become entwined in political struggles that in part involve disputes over the legitimacy of the Nigerian state itself.

The impacts of PSCs in the Niger Delta are thus in many ways contradictory. On the one hand, private security can enhance the coercive powers of the state by providing material and technical capacities (strategic planning, management expertise, fast-response craft and real-time command and control, for example) beyond those otherwise possessed by state forces, and in the process extend their coercive capacities. From a slightly different angle, the ability of global PSCs to introduce more effective technical exclusionary solutions and risk-management strategies (as opposed to directly coercive strategies) may provide greater insulation for the oil companies and the government from the activities and protests of local actors and thus to a degree depoliticize the setting and disempower those whose previous modes of protest are rendered less effective.[73] In both ways, by offering security capabilities that would otherwise be absent, global PSCs help facilitate the continuation of unjust societies where security

---

[72] Greenwood, 'The Thin Black Line'.
[73] This may in turn lead these actors to adopt increasingly violent methods and to increased support for such violent opposition among the general population.

solutions become the dominant logic and response to underlying political questions of distribution and participation.

On the other hand, the petroleum companies and global private security firms might through their incorporation into global discourses and practices and their subscription to various ethical principles help facilitate a less directly coercive environment. Moves in this direction need not be seen wholly or mainly as shifts in ethical or political consciousness. They also reflect the limited ability of previous coercive strategies to provide the security the extractive companies require, the pressure placed upon them by domestic and international groups who call into question their corporate responsibility, and the impact of wider normative frameworks such as the international Voluntary Principles on Security and Human Rights or the United Nations' Global Compact.[74] In this regard, global PSCs may be important instruments allowing non-state actors of various kinds (the oil companies themselves, foreign governments, international governmental organizations and NGOs) to have a concrete impact on the day-to-day provision of security in the Niger Delta and beyond. Indeed, the security companies may themselves even become susceptible to such pressures and, as a result, become potential agents of transformation. Such voluntary approaches inevitably have limitations and importantly do not challenge the broader political and social order. They do, however, point to the potential for pressure to be brought to bear on global PSCs and to the existence of a political arena that, like the global security assemblage, stretches beyond the immediate locality of the Niger Delta. We return to this topic in the final chapter of the book.

Private security in post-conflict Sierra Leone

Based on the fashionable maxim 'no security, no development', post-conflict Sierra Leone has been the target of an extensive international Security Sector Reform (SSR) programme aimed at restoring the state's monopoly of force and rebuilding what had come to be seen as an ideal-typical failed state. Inevitably, this programme has taken place in the shadow of EO's notorious exploits during the civil war and has sought to reconstruct the distinctions between a military focused on external defence and a police force centred on domestic enforcement

---

[74] See Meier, 'Shell "Feeds" Nigeria Conflict, May End Onshore Work'.

of law and order. Yet this does not mean that private security has disappeared from post-conflict Sierra Leone. On the contrary, it has flourished, albeit primarily in the guise of commercial security companies rather than PMCs or neo-mercenaries.

Prior to the war, there were only two PSCs in the country: Mount Everest Security Agency, founded in 1984, and Dynamic Security, established one year later. Today there are at least thirty and, according to some observers, perhaps as many as fifty. Although no accurate employment figures exist, the Office of National Security estimates total employment in the sector at approximately 3,000 persons, while other calculations by industry sources suggest that it may be as high as 4,000 to 5,000.[75] By comparison, the Sierra Leone Police employs 9,300 persons, including some 2,000 support staff. There is also a significant international presence in the private security sector: G4S has a number of important contracts, partly as a result of the presence of Wackenhut and the South African company Gray Security in the country prior to their takeovers by Group4 and Securicor and eventual incorporation into G4S. Moreover, a number of ex-United Nations (UN) peacekeepers have remained in Sierra Leone and are engaged in the private security sector, as are several former soldiers from EO and its offshoots Lifeguard and Southern Cross. Today, mining companies that have returned to Sierra Leone employ these former soldiers in a variety of in-house security arrangements as directors, employees or consultants, as do the plethora of international aid agencies and NGOs that flocked to the country in the aftermath of the civil war. Thus, while it is an exaggeration to say with one of our interviewees that 'the Sierra Leonean private security sector is rooted in EO', it is undoubtedly the case that the company's legacy is highly pertinent to the present situation.

Diamonds and the production of insecurity

Any analysis of contemporary global security assemblages in Sierra Leone requires a brief review of the causes and course of the civil

---

[75] The legislation covering private security in the country is set out in the National Security and Central Intelligence Act, 2002. Supplement to the *Sierra Leone Gazette*, 132 (42), 4 July 2002a. Part IV, Section 19 deals with the 'control and licensing of private security companies'.

war and the involvement of private military actors.[76] The decade-long war has to be understood in the context of an intensely patrimonial polity, built from the 1970s onwards by President Siaka Stevens through his personal distribution of access to the country's main asset: diamonds. Before this period, diamonds had generated about $200 million in state revenue, but by 1987 the diamonds that passed through formal, taxable channels were valued at only $100,000. The rest were appropriated by Stevens and his allies.[77] This privatization of public assets sent the economy into rapid decline, as formal state institutions were deprived of resources and their effectiveness deteriorated accordingly. By the late 1980s, there were shortages of many basic commodities, and public health and education services had all but collapsed. When Joseph Momoh inherited the presidency as Stevens' chosen successor in 1985, this situation also became a security challenge, since Momoh gained only formal control of the state apparatus while Stevens and his allies remained at the helm of the informal networks of accumulation. By 1988, official diamond exports yielded a meagre $22,000 in public revenues, while illegal exports were estimated at $250 million.[78]

The economic crisis was not helped by the structural adjustment package agreed with the Bretton Woods institutions in 1991. While the agreement released new loans to a desperately cash-strapped administration, it also further undermined state capacity while simultaneously leaving informal networks in control of the diamond sector. The IMF and the World Bank insisted on reforming the public sector,

---

[76] No attempt will be made at a full discussion of either the civil war, or the role of EO. For discussions of the conflict, see Ibrahim Abdulla, 'Bush Path to Destruction: The Origin and Character of the Revolutionary United Front (RUF-SL)', *Africa Development*, 22 (3/4) (1997): 45–76; Richard Fanthorpe, 'Neither Citizen Nor Subject? "Lumpen" Agency and the Legacy of Native Administration in Sierra Leone', *African Affairs*, 100 (400) (2001): 363–86; Lansana Gberie, *A Dirty War in West Africa: The RUF and the Destruction of Sierra Leone*, Indianapolis, Ind.: Indiana University Press, 2005; Paul Richards, *Fighting for the Rainforest: War, Youth and Resources in Sierra Leone*, Oxford: James Currey, 1996. For discussions of EO's involvement, see Avant, *The Market for Force*, pp. 82–97; Howe, *Ambiguous Order*, pp. 187–242; Singer, *Corporate Warriors*, pp. 101–18; Ian Douglas, 'Fighting for Diamonds: Private Military Companies in Sierra Leone', in Cilliers and Mason, *Peace, Profit, or Plunder?*, pp. 175–200.
[77] Reno, *Warlord Politics*, p. 116.   [78] *Ibid.*, p. 120.

which was deemed responsible for inefficiency and unproductive spending, and, by 1994, 40 per cent of state employees had been dismissed.[79] In an effort to increase tax revenues – and thus the country's ability to service its debts – foreign firms were contracted to operate and police the country's ports, to collect customs duties and royalties from offshore fisheries and to stop smuggling activities.[80]

The neo-liberal disassembly of the state through structural adjustment and the general collapse of the economy coincided with the incursion by the Revolutionary United Front (RUF) in March 1991. Backed by the Liberian warlord (and later President) Charles Taylor, the RUF attacked the diamond fields that were the economic base of Sierra Leone's patronage network.[81] Initially, the RUF forces presented themselves as championing the cause of young men and their families, and many saw their fight as a protest against their systematic exclusion from the benefits of the state.[82] But as the civil war continued, the RUF unleashed unspeakable violence on the population, making it increasingly difficult to locate any clear political objective in their actions. Instead, the dislocation and turmoil caused by the incursion encouraged rebels, miners, military personnel and politicians alike to seek their private fortunes in diamond mining and violence. The final report of the Sierra Leone Truth and Reconciliation Commission (TRC) subsequently noted the 'factional fluidity' among the different armed groups and militias, commenting that both 'overtly and covertly, gradually and suddenly, fighters switched sides or established new units' in what are described as 'chameleonic tendencies'.[83] What is clear, however, is that prolonged social and political exclusion was a main factor behind most youth involvement in the war. As Richard Fanthorpe puts it, 'the common social denominator here was a youth cohort modernized by education and exposure to mass consumption,

---

[79] William Reno, 'Ironies of Post-Cold War Structural Adjustment in Sierra Leone', *Review of African Political Economy*, 23 (67) (1996): 7–18; p. 11.

[80] Reno, 'Ironies', p. 12. One of the British nationals involved in the company contracted to secure the port in Freetown subsequently started a PSC in Sierra Leone. It is still one of the largest in the country.

[81] The involvement of Liberia illustrates the importance of trans-border links in many contemporary wars and the regional dimensions of West African security; see Duffield, *Global Governance and the New Wars*.

[82] Richards, *Fighting for the Rainforest*.

[83] Truth and Reconciliation Commission of Sierra Leone, *Final Report*, 2004 paras 95–7.

yet thwarted in its projects of self-realization by poverty and political exclusion.'[84] The report of the TRC is unequivocal in its condemnation of Sierra Leone's political elite for 'plundering the nation's assets' and concludes that the 'Commission holds the political elite of successive regimes in the post-independence period responsible for creating the conditions for conflict'. In this situation, the report notes, many Sierra Leoneans, and particularly the youth, 'lost all sense of hope in the future' and were 'easy prey for unscrupulous forces who exploited their disenchantment to wreak vengeance against the ruling elite'.[85]

The involvement of PMCs in the civil war began after Momoh was overthrown in a military coup by disgruntled soldiers led by Captain Valentine Strasser in April 1992. Strasser's first strategy to contain the advances of the RUF was to introduce conscription, an initiative that expanded the size of the army but not its effectiveness. His next move was to turn to external military help. First, he hired the UK firm Gurkha Security Guards to help train the Sierra Leone special forces and officer cadets, but several of the company's employees were killed in an encounter with the RUF and the contract subsequently collapsed when the company refused to take on a more combat active role.[86] In March 1995, Gurkha was replaced by EO, which had no such qualms. The company primarily enlisted former soldiers from the various battalions and divisions that had spearheaded South Africa's destabilization strategy in the front line states during the apartheid era, including the 32 Battalion, the Reconnaissance Commandos, the Parachute Brigade and the paramilitary Koevoet (Crowbar). Founded by Eeben Barlow, formerly the second-in-command of the 32 Battalion's reconnaissance unit, EO's top echelon generally emerged from elite South African military backgrounds, whereas approximately 70 per cent of the soldiers were black Africans, including many Angolans who had fought with South African Defence Forces during the apartheid era. The company also benefited from its ability to mobilize extensive

---

Farnthorpe, 'Neither Citizen Nor Subject?', p. 29.
[85] Truth and Reconciliation Commission of Sierra Leone, *Final Report*, paras 13–18. For a discussion of the influence of local chiefly structures and traditions on the conflict, see Paul Richards, 'To Fight or to Farm? Agrarian Dimensions of the Mano River Conflicts (Liberia and Sierra Leone)', *African Affairs*, 104 (417) (2005): 571–90; Fanthorpe 'Neither Citizen Nor Subject?'
[86] See Alex Vines, 'Ghurkas and the Private Security Business in Africa', in Cilliers and Mason, *Peace, Profit, or Plunder?*, pp. 123–40.

post-Cold War connections and resources, and its equipment included Russian Mi7 and Mi24 attack helicopters.

EO began an intensive training programme for the Republic of Sierra Leone Military Forces (RSLMF), involving a three-week cycle for approximately 120 soldiers at a time. According to Venter, three such groups were trained in the first three months.[87] EO also trained and mobilized local groups of fighters, which subsequently became known as the Civil Defence Forces. The largest and strongest of these forces were the Mende *kamajoisia*, or kamajors, traditionally hunters empowered by local customs to use firearms and occult 'medicines' in the pursuit of big game and the defence of their rural villages.[88] As government forces failed to protect Mende communities against the ravages of the RUF, the kamajors had during the course of the war become the main community defence throughout the south-eastern parts of the country. For EO, the kamajors represented valuable local knowledge and skills, and they were trained in counter-insurgency, supplied with weapons and deployed alongside EO against the rebel forces.

In military terms, the EO intervention was highly successful. Within a month of their arrival, EO and the RSLMF cleared the capital Freetown of RUF rebels. Hundreds of RUF fighters are reported to have been killed in the operation, while even more reportedly deserted.[89] In July and August of the same year, EO-led forces reconquered the all-important diamond-mining areas, again inflicting significant losses on the RUF, and later, in January 1996, they helped recapture the southern coastal rutile and bauxite mines belonging to Sierra Rutile and Sieromco.[90] The same month, Strasser was overthrown by his defence chief, Julius Maada Bio, in a coup that EO is often said to have favoured but not actively supported. By now effectively defeated, the RUF agreed to negotiate with the Bio government, and in February 1996 multi-party elections resulted in victory for Ahmed

---

[87] A. J. Venter, 'Executive Outcomes: Mixing Business with Bullets', *Jane's Intelligence Review*, November 1995, pp. 65–8.
[88] See Joe Alie, 'The Kamajor Militia in Sierra Leone: Liberators or Nihilists?' in David Francis (ed.), *Civil Militia*, London: Ashgate, 2005, pp. 51–70; Danny Hoffman, 'The Meaning of a Militia: Understanding the Civil Defence Forces in Sierra Leone', *African Affairs*, 126 (425) (2007): 639–62.
[89] See Douglas, 'Fighting for Diamonds'.
[90] We will return to Sierra Rutile below.

Tejan Kabbah of the Sierra Leone People's Party. The newly elected president continued to rely on the services of EO until January 1997, when the contract was terminated. Explanations for this decision vary. On the one hand, the Abidjan Peace Accord signed in November 1996 stipulated the withdrawal of all foreign military presence. On the other, both the IMF and the World Bank are believed to have become concerned about the costs of the EO contract, though many donors privately expressed their (albeit reluctant) appreciation for the stability brought by the PMC.[91]

The fragility of the negotiated peace was cruelly demonstrated when President Kabbah was forced into exile in neighbouring Guinea a mere ninety-five days after terminating the contract with EO. The May 1997 coup that led to his flight was instigated by an alliance of mid-level army officers, led by Johnny Paul Koroma, and RUF soldiers, and heralded another period of looting and killing in Freetown. When an intervention by ECOMOG (Economic Community of West African States Monitoring Group) forces consisting primarily of Nigerian soldiers failed to recapture the capital but held the main airport at Lungi, the exiled president turned to another PMC, the British-based Sandline International. Sandline's contract was to train and equip 40,000 kamajors, to coordinate the recapture of Freetown, to provide arms, ammunition, transportation and food for the assault coalition, to coordinate with the ECOMOG troops in control of the airport and to provide air support and intelligence gathering.[92] In collaboration with ECOMOG, forces trained by Sandline succeeded in retaking Freetown and other major towns including Bo and Kenema. The Sandline intervention, however, came to a halt when the firm's shipment of arms was declared in contravention of the UN arms embargo and was impounded by Nigerian forces at Lungi. In response to legal proceedings by the British customs agency, Sandline claimed that its operations had been in full knowledge of the British Foreign and Commonwealth Office. The ensuing 'Sandline Affair' was to cause the newly elected Labour Government much embarrassment

---

[91] See Howe, *Ambiguous Order*, p. 234; and Reno, *Warlord Politics*, p. 135.
[92] Abdel-Fatau Musah, 'A Country under Siege: State Decay and Corporate Military Intervention in Sierra Leone', in Musah and Fayemi (eds.), *Mercenaries*, pp. 76–116.

and provided the first significant dent in its recently proclaimed 'ethical approach to foreign policy'.[93]

Important details of both these PMC contracts are clouded in controversy. In the case of EO, the key concern has been the link between the PMC and mining interests, most notably the company Branch Energy, headquartered in London. The exact details are difficult to establish, but one of Branch Energy's directors, Michael Grunberg, is said to have introduced Strasser to EO, while Tony Buckingham, the CEO of Heritage Oil and Gas, a subsidiary of Branch Energy, negotiated the contract. According to Avant, the agreed price for EO's services was $2 million per month, most of which was never paid.[94] Instead, the company was to be awarded with tax revenues from the recaptured Sierra Rutile mine as well as with lucrative diamond concessions.[95]

The Sandline contract had similar links to international mining interests and to Branch Energy. The main financier behind the operation was the former Thai banker Rakesh Saxena, at the time under house arrest and awaiting extradition in Canada in connection with his role in the Bank of Credit and Commerce International banking fraud. Saxena had several mining interests in Africa and had promised to underwrite the Sandline operation in return for diamond concessions from the restored Kabbah government. When Saxena was arrested in Canada, Sandline itself fronted the money for the equipment, which was subsequently impounded by ECOMOG. Importantly, Sandline was owned by the same consortium as EO, namely the Branch-Heritage group in London.[96] Again, as with the EO contract, the Sierra Leonean Government was mortgaging its future income and economic assets in exchange for immediate survival.

[93] See the Parliamentary Legg Report, and the treatment in Christopher Kinsey, *Corporate Soldiers in International Security*, London and New York: Routledge, 2006.

[94] Avant, *The Market for Force*, p. 86.

[95] See Drohan, *Making a Killing*. Pech claims that 'EO's operations facilitated the granting of some of the richest diamond concessions in the world, valued at over US $3 billion'; Khareen Pech, 'Executive Outcomes: A Corporate Conquest', in Cilliers and Mason, *Peace, Profit or Plunder?*, pp. 81–109; p. 90.

[96] See Drohan, *Making a Killing*. Sandline's Director Tim Spicer, a retired British colonel in the Scots Guards, now runs the company Aegis, which acquired substantial contracts with the US Government in Iraq.

Sierra Leone's civil war was not declared over until January 2002, by which time over 75,000 people had been killed and 10,000 maimed. More than half the population had fled the country or was internally displaced. The ensuing peace was enforced by a UN peacekeeping mission which at its peak reached 17,500 personnel before being gradually reduced until responsibility for domestic security was officially handed over to the Sierra Leonean police in 2004 and the mission brought to an end in 2005. This followed an extensive and wide-ranging SSR programme, started in 1998 and sponsored by international donors, particularly by the UK Department for International Development. SSR was deemed an essential part of the post-conflict reconstruction effort, since by the end of the civil war little in the way of a credible and trustworthy security apparatus and framework existed. The country's armed forces were in disarray and deeply tainted by their involvement in human rights atrocities and economic looting. The numerous rebel armies, factions and civil defence militias were similarly discredited. The police emerged from the civil war with significant weaknesses – throughout the country, police stations, posts and barracks had been destroyed, and the police were widely seen as symbols of an oppressive state and lacked the trust and support of the public.[97]

The broad aim of the SSR programme has been to ensure effective management, transparency and accountability of the security sector so that it does not threaten democracy, human rights or other development goals. Police reform has been a key part of this agenda, and significant resources and international advising (most notably from the Commonwealth Community Safety and Security Project) have been devoted to retraining and re-equipping the Sierra Leonean police with a view to improving both its effectiveness and its public reputation. Although the reform and restructuring of the Sierra Leonean police is widely perceived as having achieved significant results, it is fair to say that the level of public distrust of the police continues to be high. Police wages are low, and corruption and abuse of power, though much improved, remain a concern.[98]

---

[97] See Mark Malan, Sarah Meek, Thokozani Thusi, Jeremy Ginifer and Patrick Coker, *Sierra Leone: Building the Road to Recovery*, Pretoria: Institute for Security Studies, 2003.

[98] For an assessment of the reform efforts, see Brian Thomson, *Sierra Leone: Reform or Relapse? Conflict and Governance Reform*, London: Chatham House, July 2007.

Another aspect of the SSR programme was the Disarmament, Demobilization and Reintegration (DDR) programme, which disarmed and demobilized over 67,000 ex-combatants from various junta and rebel forces.[99] The SSR programme also sought to reduce the size of the Republic of Sierra Leone's Armed Forces (RSLAF) and to refocus its mission, moving it firmly away from an active role in internal security towards an external orientation aimed at securing borders. The broad goal, in the words of one senior UK military official, is to make the military 'affordable, accountable, and admired'. This has involved a consistent reduction in the size of the RSLAF, from 14,000 to 10,517 by the end of 2007, with some suggesting that a force of 6,000–7,000 is ultimately an appropriate and affordable target.

An obvious challenge to this process involves the reintegration of ex-soldiers and combatants into the broader economy and society. As part of the DDR programme, ex-combatants were offered training, often in carpentry, taxi driving, agriculture or computer skills, but many found these options unattractive or unprofitable, a problem exacerbated by the country's difficult economic situation. However, many former combatants and soldiers have found work in newly founded PSCs. Indeed, in an economy with little growth and few employment opportunities, private security has been one of the few sectors of employment demand. Although it is impossible to determine what percentage of security guards are former soldiers or combatants, many companies reported that a significant number of their guards were ex-combatants, particularly young men from the RUF. From the companies' point of view, ex-RUF employees represented no particular problems or challenges, but some international police advisers expressed concern that they might use PSCs as vehicles to regroup, although it must be added that since PSCs in Sierra Leone are unarmed, it is difficult to see an obvious causal chain here.

By contrast, there are reports that unemployed former combatants were deployed as thugs and informal security by all political parties

---

[99] Paul Richards, Steven Archibald, Khadija Bah and James Vincent, 'Where Have All the Young People Gone? Transitioning Ex-Combatants toward Community Reconstruction after the War in Sierra Leone', unpublished report submitted to the National Commission for Disarmament, Demobilization, and Reintegration, Government of Sierra Leone, February 2003.

contesting the elections in September 2007.[100] While unarmed, these informal vigilantes used their wartime reputation to intimidate political opponents and potential voters alike. That said, the elections were relatively peaceful, and, according to the International Crisis Group, this is widely acknowledged in Sierra Leone and abroad as 'a testament to the efficiency of the police … who deployed well-trained forces, anticipated potential outbreaks and used non-lethal crowd control methods'.[101] In a remarkable turnaround, the elections saw the defeat of the Kabbah Government and victory for the All People's Congress, the former party of Siaka Stevens and Joseph Momoh. In no small part this was due to the absence of socio-economic improvement, with the UN Secretary-General observing prior to the elections that 'there is a general perception that the Government's inability to deliver basic services or respond to the needs of the population is due to corruption and mismanagement of public resources, and this has become a source of tension.'[102] Sierra Leone remains at the bottom of the Human Development Index, with an average life expectancy of forty-two years and 70 per cent of the population living below the national poverty line. The country is heavily dependent on foreign aid, and in 2005 alone Official Development Assistance amounted to $336 million, with loans and grants totalling 46 per cent of national revenue.[103]

As this brief review shows, security is one of the few areas where Kabbah's government (and its international advisers) has been credited with a degree of success. The UN, for example, while expressing general concern with the country's economic performance and governance, commented in 2006 that the 'national security sector is generally functioning well. The capacity of the Sierra Leone Police to maintain law and order and discharge its security responsibilities continues to develop.'[104] In large part this is seen as a result of the SSR programme's progress towards reconstructing a public monopoly of

[100] Maya M. Christensen and Mats Utas, 'Mercenaries of Democracy: The "Politricks" of Remobilized Combatants in the 2007 General Elections, Sierra Leone', *African Affairs*, 107 (429) (2008): 515–39.

[101] International Crisis Group, *Sierra Leone: A New Era of Reform?*, 31 July 2008, p. 2.

[102] United Nations, *Third Report of the Secretary General of the UN Integrated Office for Sierra Leone*, New York: United Nations, 28 November 2006, p. 3.

[103] International Crisis Group, *Sierra Leone: A New Era of Reform?*, p. 27.

[104] United Nations, *Third Report of the Secretary General*.

security and disarming the various private forces. Thus, contrary to widespread belief, private security in Sierra Leone is not licensed to carry firearms of any sort. Although the government in 2002 passed legislation that in principle allows PSCs to hold arms, this remains overruled by the UN arms embargo of October 1997, preventing the sale of weapons to non-state actors.[105] With one significant exception that we discuss later, private security in Sierra Leone is therefore entirely unarmed – indeed, private security is no longer a major topic of debate in the country, and little or no attention has been awarded to private security in the SSR process.[106] Yet, despite its low profile, private security plays a key role in the country, whether in the form of local, informal initiatives, vigilantes or commercial PSCs.[107]

In fact, what has emerged in the post-conflict period is far from a traditionally conceived security sector with the police at its centre; it is instead a series of global security assemblages involving a range of public, private, global and local actors. In a situation where the resources, expertise and credibility of the public security forces are limited (or perceived to be so), private security firms have been able to use their new capacities – material resources, market legitimacy, technical expertise, global linkages and claims of political neutrality – to wield significant influence in security provision and governance. In no small part due to Sierra Leone's conflictual history, the past activities of PMCs and the extensive involvement of international public security advisers, the notion of the 'public' exercises considerable symbolic power within these assemblages, perhaps more so than in many other countries. The general invisibility of the private security sector is thus in large part testimony to its location within more or less legitimated structures of security governance, a status that its private military predecessors never managed to achieve. At the same time, as in Nigeria, these assemblages are sites of competition as well as cooperation, and the symbolic struggles over the public are crucial to an understanding of the security field.

---

[105] UN Security Council Resolution 1132, 8 October 1997.

[106] See Rita Abrahamsen and Michael C. Williams, 'Security Sector Reform: Bringing the Private In', *Conflict, Security and Development*, 6 (1) (2006): 1–23.

[107] On informal policing in Sierra Leone, see Bruce Baker, *Multi-Choice Policing in Africa*, Uppsala: Nordiska Afrikainstitutet, 2008, Chapter 7.

Global security assemblages in diamond and rutile mining

A striking and instructive example of the new structure of private security in Sierra Leone can be found in diamond mining. Since the end of the war, formalized diamond exports have increased steadily, and in 2007 amounted to $142 million.[108] The country's second-largest diamond exporter is the company Koidu Holdings, which has acquired all of the country's known kimberlite deposits and operates the largest hardrock mine. When Koidu Holdings reopened its operations in Kono (the epicentre of the civil war) in November 2003, it marked the return of corporate, kimberlite diamond mining to Sierra Leone, where most diamond mining is alluvial and organized along informal, artisanal and highly exploitative lines. Koidu Holdings' success is accordingly regarded by the Government and its international backers as vital in restarting and renewing the sector along more regulated lines, increasing government royalties from exports and reducing the dynamics seen as central in starting the conflict. Moreover, in the government's view, success for Koidu Holdings would increase the country's attractiveness to other foreign investors. As then-President Kabbah put it,

A primary focus now is to attract foreign investment. We have had tremendous success with Koidu Diamond Holdings. They are easier to monitor. They keep a paper trail, and they are bringing a lot of revenue in the form of taxes and employment. The alluvial mines are a problem. They always have been.[109]

Koidu Holdings' history is of considerable interest. The company is jointly owned by the Israeli diamond magnate Beny Steinmetz and DiamondWorks, the parent company of Branch Energy Ltd. The rights to the mine were obtained by Branch Energy under the National Provisional Revolutionary Council (NPRC) of Valentine Strasser in 1995. Drafted as the Koidu Kimberlite Mining Lease Agreement ML

---

[108] Partnership Africa Canada, *Diamond Industry Annual Review, 2006: Sierra Leone 2006*, Ottawa and Freetown: Partnership Africa Canada and Network Movement for Justice and Development, p. 1. Total diamond production is estimated at $400 million a year, testifying to the continuation of illegal mining and smuggling.

[109] Partnership Africa Canada, *Sierra Leone, 2005*, p. 1.

6/95, it was awarded and ratified as NPRC Decree No. 12 and adopted as an act of parliament on 23 December 1996. Essentially, this was a key part of the payment for EO's services. Operations at the mine began in 1996, but when Kabbah was overthrown in the 1997 coup, the expatriates at the mine were evacuated, with the exception of a security team, which stayed behind to defend the mine's assets while the area was under RUF control. The company's current managing director, Jan Joubert, was part of that team. Despite this controversial legacy, Koidu Holdings is today generally billed as a transparent and responsible corporate player. As Lansana Gberie of the Diamond and Human Security Project noted in a review of the diamond sector in Sierra Leone in 2004, staff at Koidu Holdings are overwhelmingly hired locally and are better paid than most. The mine employs some 500 local people, plus about fifty expatriates.[110]

Although the security situation in Kono district bears scant resemblance to conditions during the civil war, security remains a key concern for Koidu Holdings. Like many commercial establishments in Sierra Leone, the company relies as much on private security providers as it does on the state, and while the capacity and integrity of the police service is much improved, the company is reluctant to place its security entirely in the hands of the public police. The result has been the development of a three-tier security structure, where public police, private security officers and in-house security experts work in close coordination. The mine area is guarded by G4S (trading as SecuricorGray), in a contract that was originally obtained by Gray Security. The PSC provides a force of eighty-six unarmed guards at the mine. In addition, Koidu Holdings has a dedicated armed police contingent of twenty-three officers from the Operation Support Division (OSD), the special armed division of the Sierra Leone Police, and these officers receive supplementary wages from the mining company.[111] Overall supervision of security is in the hands of seven expatriate specialist personnel employed by Koidu Holdings, all specially chosen for their previous combat experience, often from

[110] Partnership Africa Canada, *Diamond Industry Annual Review: Sierra Leone 2004*, Ottawa and Freetown: Partnership Africa Canada and Network Movement for Justice and Development, 2004. The company now claims to be the largest private employer in Sierra Leone.

[111] The OSD was formed as part of the SSR process, replacing the paramilitary Special Services Division.

the conflict in Sierra Leone itself. Importantly, the OSD is under the direct operational control of these in-house security specialists, who accompany OSD officers on mobile patrols throughout the concession (patrols consist of one officer from Koidu Holdings and two from the OSD). SecuricorGray is also responsible, in coordination with armed OSD officers, for the security of the diamonds when in transit from the mine to Freetown and onwards to Antwerp.

What is evidenced here is a global security assemblage: a hybrid structure of public and private, local and global security actors who combine to make possible economic activities aimed at a global market and deemed by both the government and international development donors as essential to state reconstruction and economic recovery. The structure represents a complex and multi-layered arrangement in which global capital, transnational private security, state authorities, local police and international police advisers are integrated in the planning and provision of security. Public police, trained by international advisers and funded through development assistance, are utilized for the exclusive protection of the private assets of a transnational corporation; they are paid supplementary wages and food allowances by foreign capital and are under the supervision and to some degree control of private expatriate security operatives. While the police retain their formal authority and the monopoly of armed force, the practical coordination of their activities with those of the PSC is one of continual and often delicate negotiation. In other words, these are not hierarchical or vertical relationships, where power and authority run in only one direction or from one particular and clearly defined centre. Instead, the authority and goals of the state and its international advisers are routinely exercised and negotiated with those of private security providers and their clients.

A second example of a global security assemblage where private security actors (this time in the form of an armed in-house security force) exercise considerable influence and authority can be found at Sierra Rutile, a rutile mine situated in the south-west of the country. Before the war, the foreign-owned company was the country's largest private employer, accounting for 57 per cent of Sierra Leone's total export earnings and providing annual tax revenues of $7 million. As a consequence, the reopening of the mining operation was widely considered to be the single most important economic issue in post-conflict Sierra Leone.

Today, the mine is owned by the Titanium Resource Group and operates through its subsidiary Sierra Rutile Ltd, registered in the British Virgin Islands and listed on the Alternative Investment Market stock exchange in London. The main shareholder is Jean Raymond Boulle, a businessman originally from Mauritius, now resident of Monaco, and a former De Beers manager in Sierra Leone. The company's board of directors also includes the former US Assistant Secretary of State for African Affairs, Walter Kansteiner. The mining concession is one of the largest natural rutile deposits in the world and in 2005 had an estimated mine life of approximately twenty years.[112] Since operations were restarted in 2006, the mine has proceeded to recapture nearly 30 per cent of the rutile market and, according to the company's Executive Director John Sisay, aims to be the world's leading producer within three years.[113]

As in the case of Koidu Holdings, the economic viability of Sierra Rutile is inextricably bound up with its security situation. In 1995, the (unarmed) mine was overrun by a relatively small group of RUF fighters, who also kidnapped several foreign employees and local workers. As a result, the mine closed its operations, and the facility was subsequently looted by the very police contingent assigned to protect it. In January 1996, rampaging RSLMF soldiers caused a further $20 million damage to the site. After this, the inoperative mine was protected by a series of PMCs, including the Gurkha Security Guards, EO, Lifeguard and Southern Cross Security Services. According to Herbert Howe, the Kabbah Government in early 1997 even considered granting Lifeguard, through Sierra Rutile, responsibility for a 25-kilometre radius around the concession. The plans would have required the country's military to request permission to enter the Lifeguard-controlled area and allowed Lifeguard to monitor the national army while on its territory.[114] The May 1997 coup meant that the plan never came to fruition, but it usefully illustrates the importance assigned to Sierra Rutile by successive governments.

---

[112] Rutile is an ore high in titanium, mined from sand in man-made lakes and used in the paint and plastics industries. The company also has a bauxite mine in the area.

[113] James Knight and Katrina Mason, 'Interview: Sierra Rutile Aims to Be No. 1 in Three Years', *Reuters Business and Finance*, 4 April 2007. Available online at http://uk.reuters.com/article/oilrpt/idukl0472258020070404.

[114] Howe, *Ambiguous Order*, pp. 187–242.

The contemporary security arrangements at Sierra Rutile represent the most extensive private security provision in Sierra Leone and are a direct legacy of the events of the civil war. The mine possesses the only armed private security force in the country; in fact, specific legislation (the Sierra Rutile Act of 1989 [2002]) allows that, 'In order to achieve an effective security regime, the Company may create and maintain a security force to provide a deterrent, defence and reaction capability to incidents.'[115] It also gives the company the authority to 'import such arms and ammunition that are appropriate to such a security force subject only to the prior approval of the Government and the security force may carry and use such arms and ammunition for the purpose of carrying out its functions'.[116]

The in-house security arrangements are directed by three expatriates, again with direct combat experience and links to past security arrangements at the mine. They are in charge of a force of 155, of whom 130 are unarmed, static guards, positioned at numerous key points (equipment sites, depots, generating stations) throughout the 30-square-kilometre concession. These unarmed personnel are reinforced by a mobile rapid-reaction force of twenty-five men, armed with AK-47 rifles. During the night, the rapid-reaction force conducts patrols throughout the concession. In addition to the weapons carried by the rapid-reaction force, Sierra Rutile Security at one point also possessed a number of heavier weapons, including RPGs and an anti-aircraft gun. However, as one of Sierra Rutile's directors stressed, 'No shot has ever been fired' by the mine's security force.

Nevertheless, Sierra Rutile Security has been the source of considerable controversy. The Government and its international advisers for many months pressed for, and finally succeeded in, removing the company's heavier weaponry. In the eyes of some government officials and international advisers, this was the first stage of a clear and non-negotiable process which in its second phase will see Sierra Rutile surrender all weapons and move towards a situation similar to that at Koidu Holdings: an unarmed security force backed up

---

[115] The agreement was ratified by the Sierra Leone Government as the Sierra Rutile Agreement (Ratification) Act, 2002. Supplement to the *Sierra Leone Gazette*, 133 (5), 31 January 2002. Notably, a similar right was granted to the Koidu kimberlite project by decree in 1995.

[116] Sierra Rutile Agreement (Ratification) Act, 2002, Clause 11, § Q(2) and (3).

by a dedicated OSD presence. Indeed, a contingent of twenty OSD officers has already been assigned to the company in preparation for this arrangement, but they have not been fully integrated into the security strategies of Sierra Rutile, and both company directors and security officials express a degree of puzzlement as to their utility. The company's owners and managers remain reluctant to disarm completely, and the legacy of the events of 1995 and the heavy investment ($74 million) required to rehabilitate the operation have led to a unwillingness to place security in the hands of a police force that has so conspicuously failed to provide protection in the past. As a global security assemblage, Sierra Rutile is thus notable for the relative absence of a direct public security presence, and, importantly, the efforts by international security advisers to disarm the mine can be seen as an attempt to assert the authority of the Sierra Leonean state as the only legitimate locus of armed force.

Governing resource extraction in Sierra Leone

Today, Sierra Leone provides as significant an illustration of security privatization as it did in the 1990s, but its form and implications are different. Rather than an exemplary case of external private military activity undermining an already weak state (or supporting a 'shadow state') and operating on the darker side of legality and international norms, the current security situation testifies to the existence of global security assemblages that include not only private security firms and state actors but also international development officials and security advisers. Here, private security actors' power and capacities arise from their incorporation into broader structures of governance, their material resources and symbolic status as experts in a commodified security field and their status as agents of powerful principals – in these cases, international mining firms – with connections to wider political imperatives, most notably the need to foster economic development and encourage foreign investment.

As argued in Chapter 3, the forms of capital possessed by private and public security actors exist in a dynamic tension. Each is also subject to reversals that are crucial in the operation of the security field as a whole. The state's symbolic claim to the public good of security, for example, is a source of tremendous power. However, this can be eroded or reversed if the state fails in this task or is perceived as doing so. In this way, its source of symbolic power can paradoxically become a resource for others to challenge its monopoly – to assert that in light of this failure it is necessary to legitimate the entrance of other (e.g. private or global) actors into the security field, even if this is only to support the state's limited abilities or to exercise a partial right to self-protection in the absence of adequate (or what is perceived as inadequate) public protection. The commodification of security, along with its connections to the rights conferred by private property, further help make this possible.

In Sierra Leone, the symbolic power of the public is of crucial relevance in the security field and has interestingly ambiguous effects. On the one hand, the power and authority of private security actors, as well as the bargaining power of foreign capital, is in important respects strengthened by the legacy of state weakness and the lack of a public monopoly of violence. In this situation, the position of global PSCs and actors reflects their economic and technological superiority vis-à-vis an under-resourced and still distrusted police force. Both G4S and the in-house security experts at Sierra Rutile are able to claim considerable technical expertise in the security field. It is clear that both Koidu Holdings and Sierra Rutile regard the private management of their security as absolutely essential, as past policing failures and complicity in looting and war atrocities have left continuing doubts about the police's capacity to provide adequate protection, and it is highly unlikely that either of the companies could (or would) operate without private security. For the government and its international backers, attracting foreign investment is a key priority given the country's dire economic situation. As former President Kabbah indicated, foreign companies bring revenues: about 40 per cent of Koidu Holdings' profits, in the form of corporation tax, surface rents and royalties, ultimately go to the state. Accordingly, government and development donors alike have, through legislation and regulation, signalled that they regard private security as a means of exercising and consolidating state authority and legitimacy by supplying the conditions for foreign investment and economic growth. In this sense, private logics circulate through the Sierra Leonean state, whose symbolic power in part depends on its ability to deliver economic success.[117] Thus, while PSCs have certainly stepped into the breach created by the incapacity of the Sierra Leonean state, they cannot in any meaningful way be seen to simply undermine or supplant public authority – even though, as we have seen, they often exist in tension with it.

While it might be the case that Koidu Holdings' 400 reasonably well-paid employees can be 'proudly advertised', economic development based on resource extraction carries high political risks in desperately poor countries, and, like in Nigeria, resource extraction in Sierra Leone (especially that which is foreign-owned) is not without local opposition. Relations between mining companies and local communities have often become strained, and the exclusionary strategies and technologies provided by PSCs are crucial aspects of these tensions, as they are frequently experienced as aggressive and disempowering by local communities. In the case of Koidu Holdings, strained community relations date back to 2003, when an environmental impact assessment produced at the request of the company concluded that nearly 300 households comprising some 4,500 people would be adversely affected by the mine's blasting. The company had acquired the land from the government as 'unoccupied' and hence argued that the residents were illegally squatting on its land. When new houses were eventually built, the residents argued that they were of inferior quality, and, in December 2007, when local residents protested against what they perceived as the company's inadequate compensation package, the police shot and killed two people. Although the shots were fired by the public police (and not by the unarmed private officers), the OSD is frequently referred to as the mine's security force, reflecting the perception that the OSD exists for the private protection of Koidu Holdings rather than public safety and security. The Government closed Koidu Holdings' operations for several months, and pressure from a number of civil society organizations succeeded in forcing the Government to set up a commission of enquiry to review

---

[117] As observed by the Diamond Industry Annual Review, Koidu Holdings' 'reasonably well-paid staff of about 400 – mainly Sierra Leoneans – can be advertised proudly in a country with widespread unemployment and poverty'. Partnership Africa Canada, *Sierra Leone, 2005*, p. 7. By comparison, Sierra Leone's approximately 120,000 artisanal miners have no written contracts and earn little more than subsistence wages.

the country's mining policies, a review that resulted in a white paper setting out new guidelines for corporate social responsibility.[118]

There is little doubt that in the absence of a responsive state that addresses the fundamental grievances of people, the presence of private security actors may help consolidate productive enclaves whose economic returns fail to benefit sufficiently the local populations. At this point, the paradoxical reversals in the security field come into view, with the integration of the private and the public meaning that the state risks being seen as complicit in private (and global) exploitation and exclusion. Rather than simply supporting state legitimacy by providing security conducive to economic development, these dynamics risk undermining the legitimacy of the state. Importantly, however, this is not because the private is supplanting the state and delegitimizing it by diluting its authority. It arises instead from the close *integration* of the private and the public.

The legacy of state weakness and the symbolic power of the public also weigh powerfully in attempts to regulate and keep the private security sector unarmed. It is in this light that we must understand the symbolic significance (as opposed to the actual security threat) of the armed security force at Sierra Rutile. Unlike in Nigeria, foreign development agencies and security advisers play prominent roles in Sierra Leone, providing substantial financial support and international expertise on state-building and security sector reform. It is clear that for these actors the image of the Weberian legal-rational state, where security is by definition a public good, informs and underpins the reform process. These international advisers were notably more insistent on the non-armed status of private security than the Kabbah Government, which in 2002 passed legislation that in principle allows PSCs to be armed. Similarly, those within the private security and resource extraction sectors that favour an armed capacity for PSCs frequently stressed that their lobbying found greater

---

[118] Lansana Fofana, 'Sierra Leone: Activists Cry Foul over Mining Policy', *Inter Press Service*, 26 August 2008. Available online at http://ipsnews. net/africa/nota.asp?idnews=43679 (accessed 24 June 2010). Partnership Africa Canada, *Diamonds and Human Security: Annual Review 2008*, Ottawa: Partnership Africa Canada, 2008, pp. 14–15; Richard Fanthorpe and Roy Maconachie, 'Beyond the "Crisis of Youth": Mining, Farming, and Civil Society in Post-War Sierra Leone', *African Affairs*, 109 (435) (2010): 251–72.

favour in government circles and regarded international development actors as the main obstacle to achieving their agendas. Koidu Holdings, for example, has lobbied the Government to replicate the highly militarized security characteristic of diamond mining in other parts of Africa and has twice, with the help of South African security consultants, applied to arm its own internal security force. Both applications were rejected, in decisions that were strongly influenced by international donors and especially the Government's police and security advisers. Their deeply held convictions that the public must retain the monopoly of armed violence and that the diamond mine must be integrated into the overall structure of national policing has led to the current security arrangements.

The security structure at both Koidu Holdings and Sierra Rutile reflects a fluid situation, itself influenced by a combination of local and global actors and imperatives. Both also draw attention to the extent to which international development actors have been able to influence (and perhaps even determine) state agendas as part of their deep involvement in key institutions and ministries concerned with defence, policing and justice reform. The particular reassembly of a post-conflict state is thus of crucial relevance, both in terms of strengthening certain executive elements of the state and the prominent role of donors. Global security assemblages in Sierra Leone also illustrate the continued power of the notion of security as a public good and its influence on global strategies of state-building. The merging of security and development, and the dominant concepts and policies of state-building that accompany them mean that security is not seen as a purely internal issue for the Sierra Leonean Government. Instead, the logic of the security–development nexus, where failed states are seen as global threats, combines with doctrines such as the 'responsibility to protect' to make internal security structures an area of legitimate concern and intervention by international actors. For donors, the effort at state- and capacity-building is simultaneously a struggle against the neo-patrimonial and informal structures that are perceived to permeate the Sierra Leonean 'shadow state', and hence the public represents a particular kind of symbolic, legal-rational capital against the cultural, traditional capital of informal networks. These positions are in turn often linked to claims about the changed nature of international security in an age when global networks make instability in one part of the world a potential threat to others.

Struggles in the Sierra Leonean security field are thus structured not only by the logics of global private security but also those of global *public* security, and the field of practice reflects the positions of these global actors and forms of capital, as well as their relationships to the Sierra Leonean state.

Conclusion

Private security is pervasive in both Nigeria and Sierra Leone and in both countries acquires its power not through the barrel of the gun but through its incorporation into broader, legitimated structures of global security governance. Approached in this manner, resource enclaves are not enclaves in any simple sense. Spatially and physically they are often cordoned off from the surrounding populations, but institutionally and normatively they are simultaneously embedded within the public security apparatus of the state and the normativity of the global security order. In fact, the effectiveness and the invisibility of private security actors are in part a result of their ability to function *through* the state and practices of global governance in a legitimating process.

Our analysis also shows that while the activities of private security clearly act in the service of global capital, this cannot be understood as a straightforward return to mercantilism or the buccaneering capitalism of the eighteenth century. In both Nigeria and Sierra Leone, private security plays key roles in its independent capacity and in coordination with public forces. In both countries, it helps secure resource extraction and, by implication, the reproduction of the state elite. However, the manner in which private security actors mediate between global capital, the state and local populations matters. Whether in terms of 'the costly application of force' or 'tiresome negotiations', the strategies and technologies adopted by PSCs have important implications. Observations about the deterritorialized nature of contemporary capital thus need to take account of the way in which the reconfiguration of the relationship between public and private actors may also influence the provision and governance of security. These impacts, as we have demonstrated, are not uniform but require specific investigation. The impact of private security actors is influenced by local histories, social relations and forms of power. While clearly containing elements of the national, in terms of being embedded in a specific territory, drawing on particular laws and regulations and leaving largely intact the state's monopoly of legitimate armed force, these security arrangements are simultaneously a complex assemblage of cross-border networks constituted by a variety of institutions and practices that cannot be contained within the territorial boundaries of the nation-state.

5 | Safer cities or cities of walls? The politics of urban global security assemblages

While the role of private security in resource extraction and conflict situations has attracted considerable attention, its place in the provision of everyday security in the developing world has been the subject of much less debate. Yet it is here, in the routines of daily life, that private security is most pervasive and has some of its most extensive impacts and implications. This is particularly the case in the world's fast expanding cities. For the first time in history, more than half the world's population live in urban areas, and in Africa and Asia the urban population is forecast to double between 2000 and 2030, by which time towns and cities in the developing world will make up 81 per cent of urban humanity.[1] In the past few years, urban security has become an issue of increasing prominence on the agendas of national governments, development agencies and international organizations, whether in the guise of human security or as part of more contentious claims about the potential connections between 'feral cities' and international terrorist networks.[2] In the ever-shifting politics of security, the urban looks set to become one of the next big things.

For urban residents in most of Africa, private security in one form or another is a fact of life. The inadequate resources of public police forces, coupled with their all-too-frequent penchant for coercion and

---

[1] UN Population Fund, *Unleashing the Potential of Urban Growth: State of the World Population 2007*, New York: UN Population Fund; see also Mike Davis, *Planet of Slums*, London: Verso, 2006.

[2] In the words of a UN report, 'insecurity will be a growing concern in cities of the developing world in the future'. *State of the World's Cities 2006/07*, New York: Earthscan/UN-HABITAT, 2007, p. 204. See also Small Arms Survey, *Small Arms Survey 2007: Guns and the City*, Cambridge: Cambridge University Press, 2007; Rita Abrahamsen, Don Hubert and Michael C. Williams (eds.), 'Special Issue on Urban Insecurities', *Security Dialogue*, 40 (4–5) (2009); humansecurity-cities.org, *Human Security for an Urban Century*; Richard J. Norton, 'Feral Cities: The New Strategic Environment', *Naval War College Review*, 56 (4) (2003): 2–15.

corruption – or what René Lemarchand has described as the 'moral discredit incurred by the state, both as a concept and institution' – remains an acute political fact, as it does across much of the developing world.[3] It is also a key reason why corporations, organizations, neighbourhoods and individuals are reluctant to place their security wholly in the hands of the public security apparatus, thus making the uniformed guards of PSCs an ever more familiar feature of the urban landscape. But, like the police, PSCs are the potential providers of both security and insecurity. Stories of private security guards turned villains, robbers and even murderers abound in many contemporary cities, coexisting with tales of their heroism and indispensability. Even if the evidence on both counts is oftentimes, but not always, anecdotal, there is little doubt that a disordered and unregulated private security sector can add significantly to the violence and turmoil of urban space.

The politics of private security in urban environments is inescapably bound up with questions of security as a public good. When private security does work, it can add to feelings of safety and security, with all its attendant social and economic implications. But frequently these benefits extend primarily or exclusively to the inhabitants of the city's lusher and more prosperous neighbourhoods, and private security can be the guarantor of social divisions and inequalities – a symbolic and material consolidation of fragmented and divided cities. These have been prominent themes in criminology and political sociology, which have drawn attention to the almost worldwide retreat of the rich to gated communities and fortified enclaves of work, leisure and consumption.[4] In the most apocalyptic interpretations, the street as a place of commonality and equality – an essential part of classical conceptions of the public sphere so eloquently defended by writers such as Jane Jacobs – is

---

[3] René Lemarchand, 'Uncivil States and Civil Societies: How Illusion Became Reality', *Journal of Modern African Studies*, 30 (2) (1992): 177–91.

[4] See Caldeira, *City of Walls*; Davis, *City of Quartz*; Charlotte Lemanski, 'A New Apartheid? The Spatial Implications of Fear of Crime in Cape Town, South Africa', *Environment and Urbanization*, 16 (2) (2004): 101–11; Low, *Behind the Gates*; Eric Dennis, 'Cairo as Neo-Liberal Capital? From Walled City to Gated Community', in Diane Singerman and Paul Amar (eds.), *Cairo Cosmopolitan: Politics, Culture, and Urban Spaces in the New Middle East*, Cairo: American University in Cairo Press, 2006, pp. 47–71.

deserted and abandoned to the poor and the predatory, the destitute and the homeless.[5]

While urban security is frequently treated as a domestic issue of policing, cities are prime sites for the emergence of new forms of security governance that span the global–local and public–private divides.[6] Global processes and discourses of security privatization and state reform have encouraged the partial disassembly and reassembly of the security field, and increasingly private companies are embedded in urban security assemblages, interacting with public security providers, transnational actors and discourses and informing and influencing security decisions in the world's urban centres.[7] The patterns are diverse, and the question of how the emergence of public–private, global–local security assemblages influence the politics of protection is a crucial one; but it is not one that can be deduced a priori, or assumed to be the same across time and space. Instead, the relative power of actors within security networks must be carefully assessed in order to determine how their interaction affects various groups and populations.

In this chapter we analyse the role and impact of private security within global security assemblages in two highly insecure African cities: Cape Town and Nairobi. In both cities, private security plays a key role and exists in a field of competition with public security forces as well as with other actors. Yet the dynamics and outcomes are very different, reflecting the cities' different histories and politics, as well as their location within national and transnational dynamics. The politics of protection within these globalized security fields clearly reflects the material power of PSCs and their clients; however, the symbolic capital of the public and national security also plays key

---

[5] Jane Jacobs, *The Death and Life of Great American Cities*, New York: Modern Library, 1961.

[6] Stephen Graham (ed.), *Cities, War, and Terrorism*, Oxford: Blackwell, 2004; Saskia Sassen (ed.), *Global Networks, Linked Cities*, London and New York: Routledge, 2002; Michael P. Smith, *Transnational Urbanism: Locating Globalization*, Oxford: Blackwell, 2001; Fran Tonkiss, *Space, the City and Social Theory*, Cambridge: Polity Press, 2001.

[7] More informal policing and security groups, such as neighbourhood watches and/or vigilantes, are also part of this picture, but are not included in our investigation. In the African setting, a growing literature includes Buur, 'Democracy and Its Discontents'; David Pratten and Atreyee Sen (eds.), *Global Vigilantes*, Cambridge: Hurst, 2007.

roles. The political economy of security is thus much more complex than can be captured within a simple dichotomy of 'safer cities' or 'cities of walls': it is part of a wider struggle over security and its place in public life.

Cape Town: city improvement or urban exclusion?

South Africa has one of the world's most highly privatized and globalized security sectors, and, measured as a percentage of GDP, its security sector is the largest in the world.[8] In the space of a short decade, the post-apartheid private security industry moved from being regarded by the Government as politically suspect and potentially subversive to becoming increasingly integrated into public–private partnerships which are perceived as crucial to the maintenance of law and order. This transformation has taken place in a profoundly transnational space, where PSCs have drawn on material capital that includes their extensive financial and material resources, the enhanced symbolic capital derived from the commodification of security, their positions in global markets and claims to expert knowledge, as well as the turn to neo-liberal modes of governance by the South African government. As such, South Africa displays highly globalized security assemblages. However, the country also shows how the relative power of actors within these assemblages is conditioned by particular histories and contemporary political challenges that have significant impacts on the structure of the security field.

From apartheid guardians to security 'partners'

The immediate context for South Africa's massive private security expansion is, of course, the transition to majority rule in 1994, which was accompanied by high crime rates and pervasive fear among the white minority. A less truncated historical perspective is however required in order to reveal the deep roots and complex lineages of the contemporary security field, and apartheid as a political system with security at its heart provides a better point of departure. Apartheid policing was a profoundly political enterprise, primarily concerned with controlling the black population in order to preserve white

---

[8] Credit Suisse/First Boston, *Review.*

privilege.[9] Preoccupied with repression of black opposition and political activities, the police devoted relatively little time and capacity to regular policing duties and the prevention of crime.[10] Instead, spatial segregation played a key role in crime control, and the boundaries of apartheid were rigidly policed through pass laws that ensured that black people's access to white areas was limited to those periods when they were economically useful as cheap labour. Through such means, black people, perceived as potential criminals, were kept physically separate from white people, their potential victims. At the same time, the police paid little attention to crime and crime prevention within black areas, and police presence in the townships was characterized by 'fire-force' responses to collective challenges to apartheid.[11] Apartheid, in other words, functioned as an effective form of crime prevention for the white minority, while simultaneously ensuring that the conditions for violence and crime were rife, but largely contained, in the black townships. As the political climate turned more turbulent and violent during the 1980s, the wealthy minority and the corporate world became increasing concerned with their security. The state of emergency from 1985 to 1990 did little to help in this regard, and as the structures and boundaries of the apartheid state began to crumble, so too did the minority's ability to insulate itself from crime.

With police resources directed towards political repression, private security has long played an important role in South Africa. The initial growth of the sector dates back to the late 1970s and early 1980s, when the wealthy minority was actively encouraged to protect itself through the use of private companies and initiatives and the development of the private sector was regarded as a necessary and welcome supplement to the increasingly overstretched apartheid state. As one local security provider put it: 'Instability and war within and on the borders of the front line states put severe pressure on the state's resources to provide security and maintain acceptable levels of order.

---

[9] Mike Brogden and Clifford Shearing, *Policing for a New South Africa*, London and New York: Routledge, 1993; Shaw and Shearing, 'Reshaping Security'; Mark Shaw, *Crime and Policing in Post-Apartheid South Africa*, Bloomington, Ind.: Indiana University Press, 2002.

[10] The South African Police's official historian points out that during the Apartheid years only one in ten members of the police force was engaged in crime detection and investigation. Marius De Witt Dippenaar, *The History of the South African Police, 1913–1988*, Pretoria: Promedia, 1988.

[11] Shaw and Shearing, 'Reshaping Security'.

For these reasons, the state believed that there was a need for a close relationship with private security.'[12]

The pre-1994 period was accordingly characterized by a convergence of interest between public and private security forces, with the private sector freeing the public from everyday policing and allowing it to concentrate on suppressing growing political unrest. Successive apartheid governments thus actively encouraged the commercial provision of security, as exemplified by the National Key Points Act of 1980. The Act required strategic installations and factories to employ commercial protection, creating a lucrative market and substantial growth opportunities for the sector.[13] While any characterization of private security providers as direct agents of the apartheid state would be an exaggeration, there is no denying the intersection of their interests, practices and effects. This common purpose was clearly evident at a 1987 conference entitled 'Security: A National Strategy – The Integration of Security in the Public and Private Sector', where the Minister of Defence, General Magnus Malan, argued for a shared will to 'resist destructive forces' through the 'joining of forces and efforts and the optimum use of human and financial resources'.[14] A brigadier at the conference similarly maintained that public–private partnerships required 'an integrated action in which both the public and the private sector play an indispensable role towards achieving the common goal, namely survival of the total population of our country'.[15] The point could hardly be made more succinctly; the state and the private companies had joined forces in the protection of a particular racial, political and social order.

Inevitably, this close relationship was disrupted by the transition to black majority rule, and the first few years of ANC government were marked by suspicion towards the burgeoning private security sector. Where the apartheid state had seen a partner with shared political objectives and sentiments, the ANC saw a white-owned security sector, often managed by former officers of the apartheid

---

[12] Quoted in Shaw, *Crime and Policing*, p. 111.

[13] See Irish, *Policing for Profit*.

[14] P. J. Schalkwyk, 'Security and the Defense Force: The National Key Points Experience', in R. L. Jackson (ed.), *Security: A National Strategy – The Integration of Security in the Public and Private Sector*, Cape Town: Lex Patria, 1987.

[15] Schalkwyk, 'Security and the Defense Force'.

state's oppressive apparatus, employing a poorly paid black guard force to protect white wealth. Private security thus appeared not only as a relic of the old order but also as an impediment to the creation of the 'new' South Africa. The predominance of former intelligence, defence and police personnel in the PSC sector also gave rise to fears and allegations that individuals were involved in criminal activity and organized crime, that they harboured extreme right-wing sympathies and that private militias were being formed by security companies.[16] In short, in the space of a few years, the private security sector went from being seen as a defender of the social order to being viewed as an obstacle, or even a potential threat, to South Africa's fledgling democracy.

While suspicion towards private security was clearly rooted in historical lineages, political outlooks and ideologies, it gained added force from the sector's phenomenal expansion. By the end of Apartheid, there were already three times as many private security personnel as public police officers, and from 1997 to 2000 their number grew from 115,000 to 166,000.[17] As the armed forces were downsized and career opportunities for previously privileged groups were curtailed in both the police and the armed forces as part of the transition, scores of white officers fled the public sector to join the burgeoning private security business. These developments provided the immediate context for the emergence of PMCs such as EO, but, more importantly for our argument, they also contributed towards making South Africa's security market one of the fastest growing in the world, with annual growth rates of 30 per cent in the mid-1990s.[18]

The rapid expansion of the market was accompanied by its increasing globalization, as transnational PSCs looked to South Africa for profitable acquisitions and opportunities. By 2004, the South African private security industry was valued at 14 billion rand, an increase from 9 billion rand in 1997. Foreign investment in the sector was

---

[16] See Irish, *Policing for Profit*; Schönteich 'Fighting Crime with Private Muscle'; Hough 'Private and Public Security in the RSA'. Given the apparent strength of right-wing groups, including the Afrikaner Weerstandsbeweging (AWB) in the immediate aftermath of the transition, this suspicion is understandable.

[17] Shaw and Shearing, 'Reshaping Security', p. 4; Data from South African security firm.

[18] Credit Suisse/First Boston, *Review*, p. 7.

estimated at approximately 2 billion rand.[19] Three of the largest international companies have gained a significant presence in the country: G4S occupies a key position as one of the leading guarding firms with over 15,000 employees, while Chubb and ADT together dominate the lucrative armed response market.[20] In 2009, Securitas also acquired a foothold in the country through its acquisition of a small Johannesburg PSC.

Currently, there are 6,392 registered and active PSCs in South Africa, employing 375,315 active security officers with access to 80,000 vehicles.[21] By comparison, the South African Police Service (SAPS) has 114,241 sworn police officers and only 37,000 vehicles.[22] In the nine years from 1997 to 2006, the number of security guards grew by over 157 per cent, while in the year from March 2008 to 2009, the number of active guards increased by over 10 per cent. Importantly, private security officers in South Africa are generally armed, sometimes with semi-automatic weapons.

As we discussed in Chapter 3, this rapid increase, the influx of foreign firms and private security's historical engagement with the apartheid state led some members of the Government to seek to ban foreign ownership of PSCs. Today, however, these reservations and suspicions have faded, giving way to a more conciliatory and cooperative atmosphere. To be sure, some unease towards the private security sector survives among both the ANC Government and the SAPS. Former President Thabo Mbeki, for example, expressed his concerns over inadequate regulation of the sector in his State of the Nation Address in 2007, and a three-month strike by security guards

---

[19] Martin Schönteich, '2001 Crime Trends: A Turning Point?', *SA Crime Quarterly*, 1 July 2002; D. Albert, 'New Security Company Identifies Niche Market', *Security Focus*, 22 (1) (2004): 56; Anthony Minaar, 'Crime Prevention, Partnership Policing and the Growth of Private Security: The South African Experience', paper presented at Policing in Central and Eastern Europe – Dilemmas of Contemporary Criminal Justice, Ljubljana, Slovenia, 23–5 September 2004.

[20] Before their merger, both Securicor and Group4Falck had entered the country separately in the 1990s.

[21] Private Security Industry Regulatory Authority, *Annual Report 2008/2009* and *Annual Report 2006/2007*, Pretoria: Private Security Industry Regulatory Authority, 2007 and 2009; Brogden and Nijhar, *Community Policing*, p. 154.

[22] D. de Lange, 'Call for Private Security to Fight Crime', *Cape Argus*, 20 May 2008; Brogden and Nijhar, *Community Policing*, p. 154.

in 2006, which saw fierce clashes between trade unions and police, has also had an effect on the sector's relationship with public authorities.[23] Nevertheless, it is fair to say that the South African private security industry at the moment enjoys an unprecedented acceptance and endorsement of its contributions to safety and security. In part, this is due to the simple passage of time without the occurrence of any major criminal or political misconduct by the sector, making it difficult if not impossible to sustain arguments of conspiracy and threats to the state. Equally, the 2001 Private Security Industry Regulation Act is seen as providing a more tightly regulated sector with higher standards and better procedures and as weeding out many 'rogue' or 'cowboy' companies.[24] But, more than anything, it is South Africa's continuous 'crime wave' and the effort to reform the police that explain the current acceptability of the private security sector and its cooperation with the public police.

According to official statistics, most categories of crime increased dramatically in the period leading up to and immediately following the transition. From 1990 to 1996, serious assaults increased by 86 per cent, rape by 148 per cent and theft of motor vehicles by 42 per cent.[25] In the ten years from 1988 to 1997, the number of reported

---

[23] State of the Nation Address by the President of South Africa, Thabo Mbeki, Joint Sitting of Parliament, 9 February 2007. The strike took place from April to June 2006 and was highly conflictual and controversial. Fifty-seven security guards were killed, according to the Private Security Industry Provident Fund, because they wanted to return to work. The South African Transport and Allied Worker's Union is suing the Ministry of Safety and Security following a march in Cape Town, where the police fired shots and used teargas against demonstrators. See *Mail & Guardian*, 'At Long Last, Security Strike Is over', 22 June 2006, and *Mail & Guardian*, 'Provident Fund: 57 Guards Killed During Strike', 19 June 2006.

[24] This is of course not to say that the South African PSC sector is immune from criminal involvement or professional neglect.

[25] Shaw and Shearing, 'Reshaping Security', p. 5. South Africa's crime statistics are notoriously difficult to evaluate, and, more than anywhere else, the definition of 'crime' is highly political. The State of Emergency between 1985 and 1990 almost certainly suppressed crime levels, and fear and distrust of the police among the black population led to a significant under-reporting of crime during the apartheid era (see Shaw, *Crime and Policing*). Such uncertainties aside, it seems clear that most categories of crime increased significantly in the decade after 1994.

murders and rapes is said to have increased two and a half times.[26] The major urban areas, in particular, experienced a dramatic rise in crime. In the Johannesburg police area, the average resident in the year 2000 was over three times more likely to become a victim of a recorded crime than the average South African citizen.[27] Over a ten-year period, South Africa averaged 20,000 murders and 50,000 reported rapes and attempted rapes annually.[28] In 1998, fifty-nine murders were recorded per 100,000 population. By comparison, Brazil had twenty-one murders per 100,000, and Norway two.[29] According to statistics from the Medical Research Council, in the three years

[26] Schönteich 'Fighting Crime with Private Muscle'; Karina Landman and Martin Schönteich, 'Urban Fortresses: Gated Communities as a Reaction to Crime', *African Security Review*, 11 (4) (2002): 71–85; p. 74.

[27] Landman and Schönteich, 'Urban Fortresses', p. 74; see also Jo Beal, *The People behind the Walls: Insecurity, Identity and Gated Communities in Johannesburg*, London: London School of Economics, 2002.

[28] Gary Kynoch, 'Crime, Conflict and Politics in Transition-Era South Africa', *African Affairs*, 104 (416) (2005): 493–514.

[29] Landman and Schönteich, 'Urban Fortresses', p. 76. Any causal explanation of the rise of crime and violence would have to take into account a complex mix of social, political and economic factors that pre-dates the transition, but that may have been accentuated by rapid political reform. Decades of repressive racial policing and social conflict appears to have created a deeply entrenched culture of violence. As Graeme Simpson argues, the apartheid struggle saw both the criminalization of political activity and the politicization of crime, leading to a blurring of the dividing line between politics and crime. The liberation movements encouraged violence and self-defence as part of the opposition to apartheid, and many groups and individuals could not be easily pacified and disarmed following the advent of democracy. The apartheid state similarly armed vigilante groups and was closely involved in criminal activities, such as the smuggling of ivory, precious stones and drugs. The absence of adequate policing in the townships during apartheid also provided fertile ground for criminal networks, as well as vigilante protection, which in turn have facilitated a continuation of violence and organized crime. See Marlene Burger and Chandre Gould, *Secrets and Lies: Wouter Basson and South Africa's Chemical and Biological Warfare Programme*, Johannesburg: Zebra, 2002; Graeme Simpson, '"A Snake Gives Birth to a Snake": Politics and Crime in the Transition to Democracy in South Africa', in Bill Dixon and Elrena van der Spuy (eds.), *Justice Gained? Crime and Crime Control in South Africa's Transition*, Cape Town: University of Cape Town Press, 2004, pp. 1–28; Kynoch, 'Crime, Conflict and Politics'; Stephen Ellis, 'The New Frontiers of Crime in South Africa', in Jean-François Bayart, Stephen Ellis and Beatrice Hibou (eds.), *The Criminalization of the State in Africa*, Oxford: James Currey Publishers, 1999; André Standing, 'Out of the Mainstream: Critical Reflections on Organised Crime in the Western Cape', in Dixon and van der

from 2001 to 2003, more people were murdered than were killed in road accidents. The statistics show a clear racial division; the leading cause of non-natural death amongst blacks and coloureds was murder, while amongst whites it was road accidents.[30] There are now signs that the overall crime situation may be improving, with reported contact crime declining by over 6 per cent in 2007–8.[31] Nevertheless, in the same year, the police recorded 18,487 murders in a population of 47.9 million, and Cape Town, one of the country's main tourist attractions, has the dubious honour of being dubbed one of the world's 'murder capitals': the city's murder rate increased by 2.7 per cent from 2006 to 2007, with an average of 5.9 murders a day.[32]

This high level of violent crime and its extensive media coverage resulted in a pervasive sense of insecurity, especially among the white elite. Fear of crime became (perhaps understandably) something of a national obsession, increasingly dominating public debate, people's lives and their choices. Surveys of public perceptions of security tell a clear story. In 1997, 47 per cent of those surveyed said they felt unsafe, compared with only 16 per cent in 1994.[33] Importantly, the level of fear among the various groups of the population does not correspond to their likelihood of becoming victims of crime and violence. Black and coloured people are the most common victims but are least likely to regard themselves as unsafe. White people, on the other hand, consider themselves more unsafe but are statistically less likely to experience crime.[34] The feeling of insecurity among the wealthy and the middle class may thus be linked to a broader sense of unease concerning the new political order and the transition to majority rule, as much as to any real experience of crime. In this way, what Caldeira in the context of Brazil calls the 'talk of crime' is expressive not only

Spuy, *Justice Gained?*, pp. 29–57; Jonny Steinberg, *Crime Wave: The South African Underworld and Its Foes*, Johannesburg: Witswaterand University Press, 2001.

[30] Rob Turrell, 'Murder and Capital Punishment after Apartheid', in Dixon and van der Spuy, *Justice Gained?*, pp. 83–113.

[31] Statistics available at www.saps.gov.za.

[32] 'The List: Murder Capitals of the World', *Foreign Policy*, September 2008.

[33] Schönteich, 'Fighting Crime with Private Muscle'. For full surveys of crime rates and attitudes towards them, see the ongoing studies of the ISS project on crime, funded – interestingly – by one of South Africa's largest financial institutions, Nedbank.

[34] Shaw, *Crime and Policing*, p. 92.

of very real fears but also of a general disquiet relating to other social changes. Crime, as she argues, supplies a generative symbolism for talking about other issues that are perceived as wrong or bad but for which there is no consensus of interpretation or acceptable vocabulary. It offers a symbolism for expressing other kinds of loss, such as downward mobility and the erosion of status and privileges, and in the South African context may provide a way of making sense of the transformations associated with the end of apartheid.[35]

In this setting of rising fear and crime, 'doing something' about crime became crucial to the political legitimacy and support of the ANC-led Government of National Unity, and, as early as February 1995, President Nelson Mandela's speech to the opening of Parliament decried the 'crime wave' that was engulfing the country.[36] The police, however, were under tremendous pressure as resources previously used to protect a small minority now had to be stretched to meet the demands of over 40 million people, and there was a growing recognition that the SAPS could not adequately secure and protect South Africans. As the public police plainly lacked both the capacity and the resources to tackle the situation, a concerted effort to curtail the services of PSCs seemed not only politically misplaced but also practically potentially counterproductive and probably unenforceable given the widespread reliance on private services among the wealthier sections of the population. Such a move would also have been at odds with dominant transnational discourses of police reform that stressed the virtues of plural policing and that had a significant impact as the police became the focus of extensive international assistance to transform and democratize its operations and services.[37]

---

[35] Caldeira, *City of Walls*, p. 34.

[36] The President stated that 'the situation cannot be tolerated in which our country continues to be engulfed by the crime wave which includes murder, crimes against women and children, drug trafficking, armed robbery and theft. We must take the war to the criminals and no longer allow the situation in which we are mere sitting ducks of those in our society who, for whatever reason, are bent to engage in criminal and anti-social behaviour'. 'Address of President Nelson Mandela on the Occasion of the Opening of the Second Session of the Democratic Parliament', Cape Town, 17 February 1995.

[37] As part of this reform process, the SAP was re-branded as the South African Police Service (SAPS).

That the (old) SAP needed radical reform is beyond doubt. The new
South Africa inherited a dysfunctional but reasonably well resourced
police force, primarily committed to public order and regime maintenance rather than to crime fighting. In the words of Elrena van der
Spuy, the SAP had become 'totally committed to the fight against
those organizations and people who were committed to ending apartheid … it was an inefficient and ineffective police force, which had
lost the confidence of the South African public.'[38] In line with global trends, community policing was the key buzzword of the initial
reform strategy, intended both to increase community control over
the police and to make it more legitimate in the eyes of previously dis-
enfranchised groups such as township dwellers.[39] Thus, the National
Crime Prevention Strategy, launched in 1996, identified community
policing and the creation of partnerships with citizens and other non-
state actors as the 'first pillar' of the new democratic police force.[40]

At the same time, rising crime, dwindling resources and demands
for improvement in service delivery led the SAPS to investigate various
possibilities for outsourcing, privatization and contracting of specialist services.[41] Notably, the National Crime Prevention Strategy was
launched in the same year as the ANC abandoned its welfare-oriented
Reconstruction and Development Programme (RDP) in favour of the
neo-liberal-inspired GEAR plan.[42] It also paralleled a wider promotion of private involvement in urban management in the region by

---

[38] Quoted in Brogden and Nijhar, *Community Policing*, p. 136.

[39] According to Brogden and Nijhar, the British Government alone provided
$9.4 billion for community policing projects in South Africa; *Community
Policing*, p. 158. The transnationalization of criminal justice policies, and,
in particular, the more or less universal spread of Western and especially US
approaches to criminality, has been well documented, and South Africa is
no exception here. See Elrena van der Spuy, 'Foreign Donor Assistance and
Policing Reform in South Africa', *Policing and Society*, 10 (2000): 343–66;
Dixon, 'Globalising the Local'; and Bill Dixon and Janine Rauch, *Sector
Policing: Origins and Prospects*, Pretoria: Institute for Security Studies,
2004.

[40] Government of South Africa, *National Crime Prevention Strategy*,
Pretoria: Department of Safety and Security, 1996.

[41] Minaar, 'Crime Prevention, Partnership Policing'.

[42] For a useful evaluation of GEAR, see Hain Marais, *Limits to Change*,
London: Zed Books, 2001; for a discussion of the social implications, see
David McDonald and John Pape (eds.), *Cost Recovery and the Crisis of
Service Delivery in South Africa*, London: Zed Books, 2002, and Ashwin
Desai, *We Are the Poors*, New York: Monthly Review Press, 2002.

international organizations, such as the United Nations Development Programme's Urban Management Programme.[43] In much the same manner as GEAR has a stronger focus on private-sector growth, free trade and fiscal austerity, various forms of new public management strategies became intrinsic to South Africa's policing reform. As part of this shift, reform efforts moved away from the concern with police accountability to the community towards more managerial notions of accountability as service delivery. At the same time, community policing and the radical democratic imperatives that accompanied early reform initiatives were commonly seen to have failed and were largely abandoned in favour of a return to more hard-core and conventional crime-fighting methods, and a reliance on expert private-sector involvement.[44]

Elrena van der Spuy thus notes a second phase of foreign donor assistance to South African police reform, which abandoned the effort to legitimate the police in favour of an emphasis on building police capacity in the 'war against crime'.[45] Community involvement in this context takes on a different meaning; no longer primarily concerned with democratic accountability, it is primarily aimed at increasing police effectiveness and efficiency through harnessing the energies of various civil society actors as partners. In the words of the SAPS, there is a need for 'the police, the public, elected officials, government, business and other agencies to work in partnership to address crime and

[43] David A. McDonald and Laila Smith, 'Privatising Cape Town: From Apartheid to Neo-Liberalism in the Mother City', *Urban Studies*, 41 (8) (2004): 1461–84.

[44] Shaw and Shearing note with disappointment that community policing has 'rather become a mechanism to achieve better bandit catching, than a way of involving the police in wider strategies to enhance community involvement in crime prevention'. Shaw and Shearing 'Reshaping Security', pp. 8–9. For a review of community policing, more recently renamed sector policing in South Africa, see Brogden and Nijhar *Community Policing*, Chapter 6; Eric Pelser, *The Challenge of Community Policing in South Africa*, Pretoria: Institute for Security Studies, 1999; Eric Pelser and Antoinette Louw, 'Evaluating Community Safety Forums', in Eric Pelser (ed.), *Crime Prevention Partnerships*, Pretoria: Institute for Security Studies, 2002, 103–12. On the increasing role of private-sector consultants in urban decision-making, see McDonald and Smith, 'Privatising Cape Town'.

[45] She also identifies a third phase of Western donor assistance primarily concerned with tackling organized crime and its implications for Western countries: 'foreign donor assistance'. See also Shaw and Shearing, 'Reshaping Security'.

community safety'.[46] The Department of Community Safety similarly concluded that the 'SA [South African] Police Service can no longer be seen as the sole agency responsible for fighting crime ... other sectors of society with a force multiplying capacity must be called on to support the SA Police Service in their efforts.'[47] As the White Paper on Safety and Security puts it, it is necessary

to enhance the *spirit of voluntarism* in our country. There are many important partners in the fight against crime. These include, amongst others, organizations of civil society, particularly business and community organizations, citizens who volunteer for service as Police Reservists as well as the private security industry which performs a useful role. The role of such players is, in principle, one of *partnership with the State*. For this reason, greater attention will be paid to their role in the safety and security environment in future policy processes.[48]

As part of this transformation, some tasks have been specifically assigned as 'private' – police stations across South Africa are now, for example, guarded by PSCs in recognition that commercial guards are cheaper than police officers – while much day-to-day policing has been reframed as a partnership with a multiplicity of private actors and local communities.

Global security assemblages in Cape Town

South Africa's particular path of reform, combining transnational and local agendas for community policing with the managerialism of new policing models, has resulted in the emergence of a highly diverse security field and the development of a multiplicity of various public–private policing partnerships. The formation of community policing forums, for example, is constitutionally mandated, and various local

---

[46] Quoted in Julie Berg, 'Private Policing in South Africa: The Cape Town City Improvement District – Pluralisation in Practice', *Society in Transition*, 35 (2) (2004); 224–50; p. 227.

[47] Government of South Africa, *Provincial Government Western Cape: Strategic Plan 2003/04 to 2005/06*, Pretoria: Department of Community Safety, 2002, p. 6.

[48] Government of South Africa, *White Paper on Safety and Security: In the Service of Safety 1999–2004*, Pretoria: Department of Safety and Security, 1998, p. 7; emphasis added.

institutions and individuals are actively encouraged to join the police in identifying and solving local security issues.[49] The organization Business Against Crime estimates that there are currently more than 800 different models of how communities support the police throughout South Africa, including through sponsoring or paying for vehicles, fuel, buildings, communications technologies and so on. Rising crime and transnational policing trends have thus combined to encourage South Africa's highly diverse and in many ways 'hybrid' security sector, where public and private actors are increasingly interwoven in intricate networks of power and authority.

Perhaps the most extensive examples of such public–private policing networks are the Cape Town City Improvement Districts (CIDs), which also have significant global dimensions.[50] The idea of CIDs derives from international models for urban renewal and has numerous similarities with so-called 'business improvement districts' (BIDs) exemplified by the Metro Tech BID in Brooklyn, New York.[51] Like the BIDs, the CIDs are non-profit organizations established by property-owners in an area who agree to an additional tax on their property in order to finance and promote business and economic development. In common with the Metro Tech in New York, which has its own private security force, the primary concern of the CIDs has been security. At present there are about fifteen CIDs in and around Cape Town, including neighbourhoods and suburbs such as Sea Point, Orangekloof and Rondebosch. The largest, and perhaps most controversial, is the Central City Improvement District (CCID) focusing on downtown Cape Town and its central business district.

---

[49] Dixon and Rauch, *Sector Policing*; Millicent Maroga, 'Two Sides of the Same Coin? Sector Policing and Community Policing Forums', *SA Crime Quarterly*, (6) (2003): 13–16.

[50] Cape Town and the Western Cape region are of course not representative of all of South Africa, particularly in terms of party politics and the relative lack of dominance of the ANC.

[51] Richard Briffault, 'A Government for Our Time? Business Improvement Districts and Urban Governance', *Columbia Law Review*, 99 (2) (1999): 366–425; Tony Travers and Jeroen Weimar, *Business Improvement Districts: New York and London*, London: Corporation of London, 1996; Robert C. Davies, Christopher W. Ortiz, Sarah Dadush, Jenny Irish, Arturo Alvarado and Diane Davis, 'The Public Accountability of Private Police: Lessons from New York, Johannesburg, and Mexico City', *Policing and Society*, 13 (2) (2003): 197–210.

The CCID is an initiative of the Cape Town Partnership, a not-for-profit company founded in 1999 by the City Council and the local business community.[52] The main aim of the partnership is to reverse urban decay and to prevent capital flight from the city centre to surrounding suburbs and business parks. As part of this effort, the CCID was established in November 2000 after the majority of property-owners, or ratepayers, in the area agreed to the payment of an additional top-up levy on their council bill. Today, the Cape Town CCID collects about 15 million rand annually from the 1,200 ratepayers within the area. Of this amount, 51 per cent is allocated to security. The remainder is spent on the CCID's other four areas of responsibility: cleaning the city (22 per cent), marketing and communication (11 per cent), social development (3 per cent, a recent decline from 8 per cent) and administration (13 per cent).

The CCID is, in effect, a large-scale partnership policing effort aimed at making central Cape Town safe and secure, an international city and a first-class tourist destination.[53] G4S, trading in Cape Town as Securicor, has been contracted as the main security provider in the CCID, as well as in all the other CIDs in Cape Town. At the start of the initiative, the CCID security force consisted of only seven officers, but it has since expanded to a total of six patrol vehicles, ten horse-mounted officers and sixty foot-patrol officers providing a twenty-four hour (often armed) security presence in the city centre. At night, the city is patrolled by forty officers, supported by six vehicles. As a result, the presence of security personnel in the city has increased noticeably, and CCID vehicles and foot patrols are frequently encountered throughout Cape Town's relatively compact city centre.

[52] In recent years, the Board of Directors has included representatives from, amongst others, Business Against Crime, the Chamber of Commerce and Industry, the South African Property Owners Association and the City of Cape Town, as well as members from the arts and educational sectors (www.capetownpartnership.co.za); see also Berg, 'Private Policing'. Similar metropolitan crime-prevention areas exist in Johannesburg and Durban's Ethekwini municipality; see Cheryl Goodenough and Jenny Irish, *Owning Safety: A Profile of Community Initiatives*, Durban: Independent Project Trust, 2002; also Richard Tomlinson, 'From Exclusion to Inclusion: Rethinking Johannesburg's Central City', *Environment and Planning A* 31 (1999): 1665–78; Anna-Marie Smith, 'South Africa: Mother City a Role Model', *Business Day*, 9 November 2007.

[53] See www.capetownpartnership. co.za.

To a significant extent, the security of central Cape Town has been devolved to the largest security company in the world. Unlike the more commonplace private guarding of 'public private spaces' such as shopping centres, in Cape Town a private company is involved in policing the public space of the city.[54] The visibility of Securicor's mounted, foot and mobile patrols far exceeds that of the police. Both the City Police and the SAPS concentrate their efforts in the poorer areas of town, where crime rates are highest, and the City Police has dedicated only two mobile patrols to the city centre.[55] Moreover, the police do not conduct foot patrols. Yet, it would be incorrect to perceive the police as absent from Cape Town's security arrangement. Instead, Securicor officers are closely networked with the police, especially the City Police, but also the SAPS, often in novel and surprising ways. The CCID/Securicor-branded patrol vehicles, for example, include a City Police officer, but there are no police markings on the car. The CCID security patrols are also linked to the City Police control room by radio. In addition, Securicor operates the Strategic Surveillance Unit (SSU), the control room that supervises Cape Town's 170 CCTVs.[56] The SSU is manned by around fifty Securicor officers, reinforced by eight City Police officers and is in direct contact with the SAPS as well as the City Police, thus facilitating mobile response to incidents. As part of the move towards community or sector policing, Securicor participates in weekly sector policing forums to identify potential problems, to share information and to coordinate the provision of security with the SAPS and the City Police. Securicor officers in the CCID also frequently provide support to police operations within the city, for example by providing perimeter security when the police are searching a building or an area. Because of this extensive and close collaboration (seen also in the other CIDs in Cape Town), Securicor managers in interviews often characterized the CIDs as a 'paradigm shift' in the provision of security.

---

[54] Shearing and Stenning, 'Modern Private Security'.

[55] The Cape Town City Police is a municipal police service established in December 2001. The main aim is visible policing, and they make arrests and issue fines for all types of offences but do not have investigative functions, which is the responsibility of the SAPS.

[56] In yet another example of partnership policing, the CCTV cameras were initially financed by the association Business Against Crime, and then donated to the city.

The CCID is a striking example of a global security assemblage and one illustration of the new forms of security governance emerging on the African continent. Within this security arrangement, power and authority cannot be fitted into the neat grid of the territorial nation-state or clear public–private distinctions. Instead, significant power and authority over domestic territory resides with a transnational PSC. Its material and symbolic capital is, in turn, linked in important ways to global discourses and practices. Market principles and economic capital exercise a particularly powerful influence, and the power of Securicor derives in large part from the company acting as the agent of the city's property owners, who fund and directly participate in overseeing a system with security at its core. The CCID is a contractual community between ratepayers, businesses and the City Council, and security is regarded as a service like any other – to be bought from the best qualified provider. The commodification of security enables the CCID to present itself as a consumer (as opposed to a client) of security, actively making choices about security provision within a marketplace where public authorities are only one possible provider. Transnational policing models of community policing and partnership, spearheaded by international advisers and financed by development budgets, have further encouraged this trend. In this sense, the CIDs are in part a consequence of the shift to neo-liberal GEAR policies and also reflect a more marketized approach to civic management.[57] Within this marketplace, the CCID's choice of Securicor/G4S was directly related to the company's extensive organizational and financial resources, its expertise, technical and managerial capabilities, as well as its global reputation and brand recognition. In short, the company's possession of material, symbolic and cultural capital allowed it to establish a central position in the creation and operation of a public–private, global–local security assemblage.

At the same time, it is clear that the security arrangements in the CCID are far from entirely private; the City Council makes up one-third of the Cape Town Partnership, and the public police plays an important role in security provision. The CCID derives considerable legitimacy precisely from its connection to the symbolic capital of the public and its incorporation into 'hybrid' security assemblages.

---

[57] Faranak Miraftab, 'Governing Post-Apartheid Spatiality: Implementing City Improvement Districts in Cape Town', *Antipode*, 39 (4) (2007): 602–26.

Security governance in Cape Town thus emerges out of a combination of the private and the public, and these public–private, global–local relations highlight the inadequacies of regarding private security as a straightforward threat to the sovereignty of the state or as 'illicit' authority. The power and authority of private security actors in Cape Town emerges in large part from their endorsement by and cooperation with public authorities. In other words, its legality and relationship to law and order maintenance bestows considerable symbolic and cultural capital on private security, but not necessarily at the expense of the state. In South Africa, it seems that PSCs have to an important extent helped secure the authority of the state by allowing for the presence of a much greater security capacity than the state alone could have provided, thus generating important material and symbolic resources for combating post-transition insecurity, urban blight and capital flight. In brief, the utilization of private security resources has made it easier for the government to claim that it is 'doing something about crime'. In this way, the public has, to a significant extent, been able to mobilize the economic capital of the private to strengthen its own symbolic position, both nationally and internationally.

In terms of a reduction of insecurity, the exact achievements of the CCID are difficult to assess, given the South African moratorium on the release on local crime statistics and the lack of independent evaluations.[58] Some sources claim a 60 per cent drop in crime in the city, particularly in the most common forms of offence, such as pickpocketing, mugging and theft from cars. Research in 2002 showed that 52 per cent of respondents felt safe in the city centre, compared to only 17 per cent only two years earlier.[59] Urban capital flight also appears to have been reversed, and the four-year period from 2001 to 2004 saw new investment of about 8 billion rand in the CCID.[60] Clearly, not all of this is the result of security arrangements alone, much less the sole achievement of a global PSC. However, advocates of the CCID are quick to point to its perceived successes and its links

[58] Ingrid Palmary, 'Shifting Agendas: Crime Prevention in the Major Cities', in Pelser, *Crime Prevention Partnerships.*

[59] Sylvester E. Sylvester, 'It's Official: Cape Town Is Clean and Safe', *Cape Argus*, 6 March 2002.

[60] Derek Bock, 'Cape Town Central City: An Urban Renewal Success Story', public Powerpoint presentation, 2005; Smith, 'South Africa: Mother City a Role Model'.

to other positive indicators. To the extent that the South African state relies upon income from foreign investment and tourism, not to mention the status of Cape Town as a 'world-class' city, the involvement of G4S can be seen as crucial to its continued authority and legitimacy, especially in the international arena.

This is not to say that private security everywhere acts to support the legitimacy and authority of the state or that this is a permanent or static relationship in South Africa. In part, the country's transnational security networks have emerged at the instigation of the state and are part of a state-led policy to maximize security and efficiency. In part, they reflect broader social, economic and political transformations in global governance and are a reaction to global market pressures and demands from 'customers' empowered by the commodification of security. Importantly, these transformations lie outside the control of any one state, and, as we discussed in Chapter 3, attempts to rein in and limit external involvement in the sector by parts of the South African government failed in 2001. Thus, while South African official documents stress again and again that the role of private security actors is 'one of partnership with the State', this assigned role of subservience may well depend on circumstances outside the state's direct control.[61] Because the capital and authority of private actors arise not only from the state but also from global practices and discourses, it cannot be assumed that the state will always and inevitably be in a position of control – or even of obvious primacy – in such security assemblages. Sovereign state power, in other words, is not static in these global structures of governance but is a contingent outcome of political struggles and negotiations in the security field.[62]

Private security and public policing relations are certainly not without tensions, whether at the level of everyday practice or symbolic struggles within the field. While the private is integrated into the public to a previously unprecedented degree, this is not a uniform structure of policing and social control. The field, in other words, remains structured by the public–private relationship, even though its articulation and political significance has changed since the early to mid-1990s. As our focus on the CCID shows, the underlying paradox (and, to some degree, the lesson) of the South African situation

---

[61] Government of South Africa, *White Paper on Safety and Security*, p. 7.
[62] On this broad analytic point, see Johnston, *Policing Britain*, p. 162.

is that the monopoly of legitimate violence claimed by the state is not seen as directly undermined by private security, even in a situation where its presence is by any standards extensive and its armed capacity substantial.

Governing through crime

The mobilization of private security actors as part of broader public initiatives and strategies not only allows the state to say that something is being done about crime, it can also be seen as a way of governing through crime. The responsibilization of individuals, corporations, neighbourhoods and various other groups leads to significant transfers of the burden of 'fighting crime' onto the individual and simultaneously makes certain forms of behaviour acceptable while others are deemed undesirable or criminal. The discourses of community and community policing are instructive in this regard, since they entail more pluralized approaches to government that seek to mobilize allegiance to particular communities of morality and identity and attempt to govern behaviour through these vectors of identity and belonging. In this way, what Nikolas Rose refers to as 'governing through community' successfully combines the individualism of neoliberal political discourses with the more left-wing ideals of empowerment, self-reliance and active citizenship.[63]

The language of community invokes the image of a more intimate and natural relationship, less remote and aloof than the traditional state–society division of political governance. In the same way that a degree of romanticism permeates so many discourses of community, community policing is also predicated on a 'conception of community as the embodiment, or potential embodiment, of collective sentiments'.[64] Yet communities, and particularly today's urban communities, are often heterogeneous, with limited consensus or shared

---

[63] Nikolas Rose, 'The Death of the Social? Re-Figuring the Territory of Government', *Economy and Society*, 23 (5) (1996a): 327–56. A critique of how 'progressive' theories of late modernity (such as those of Beck and Giddens) that stress processes of individuation and responsibilization within a broader context of globalization can actually end up supporting neo-liberal social and political strategies, is provided in Mitchell Dean, *Governing Societies*, Maidenhead: Open University Press, 2007.

[64] Johnston, *Policing Britain*, p. 195.

norms regarding crime and punishment. To the extent that such consensus exists, it is often a product of political and social domination rather than some natural, inherent sentiment shared equally by all community members. As Les Johnston incisively argues, these are less 'communities of collective sentiments' than they are 'communities of risk'. In other words, their defining characteristic is not that they are at risk from some external threat but rather that they are 'increasingly defined, oriented, organized and governed around matters of risk'.[65] Risk is internal to the communities themselves, constituted in their everyday experiences.

Importantly, this experience is mediated through the commodification of security, which itself leads to the increased demand for security and provides the conditions for the pluralization of policing. In this sense, communities of risk are not necessarily spatially or geographically defined, or limited to local neighbourhoods, but stretch across national boundaries to the global level. In South Africa and Cape Town, for example, communities of risk may include transnational actors such as tourists and corporate capital, and rely on the consumption of global technologies and knowledge.

This form of community (or partnership) policing has significant implications in terms of who gets secured and how. In the CCID, those who pay are also able to play a powerful role in determining the security agenda or to speak on behalf of or represent the 'community'. In Cape Town this has led to a focus on 'cleaning up the city', and there are more than faint echoes of the neo-conservative 'broken windows' thesis in the public discourse of the CCID.[66] In the words of the Provincial Development Council of the Western Cape: 'In order to become a "world class city" … we must vanquish "crime and grime" … and remove the "undesirable elements".'[67] While this has resulted in an impressive twenty-four-hour cleaning service, it has also generated a security effort focused on order maintenance and on reducing what are often described as 'minor nuisances' such as beggars, vagrants, informal parking assistants and street children. Securicor officers are instructed to 'move along' beggars congregating

---

[65] Johnston, *Policing Britain*, pp. 195 and 201.

[66] James Q. Wilson and George L. Kelling, 'Broken Windows: The Police and Neighbourhood Safety', in Irwin Stelzer (ed.), *Neoconservatism*, New York: Atlantic Books, 2004, pp. 151–66.

[67] Quoted in Berg, 'Private Policing', p. 242.

at intersections. For 'undesirable elements', such as street children and vagrants, the CCID has meant increased harassment and more frequent arrest. Street children are regarded as a special problem, allegedly perceived by Capetonians and tourists alike as both a nuisance and as responsible for the majority of petty crime.[68] Securicor officers frequently transport street children to so-called safe houses, in order to get them off the street, in full knowledge that they will be back the next day. A number of by-laws have also been passed to facilitate the clean-up of Cape Town, including prohibition of begging that inhibits or obstructs the public, begging within six metres of an ATM or cash point, as well as washing and drying clothes on city streets.[69]

There can be little doubt as to who is excluded from Cape Town's city centre by these practices and by-laws. For sections of the population, the altered politics of 'community' and the forms of protection brought about by the CCID are experienced as an increasing restriction of access. A combination of public by-laws and private enforcement serves to prevent the poor and the homeless from utilizing the city's public spaces, where they frequently make their livings through various forms of informal trading. The comparison to the apartheid era is obvious, but now these dividing practices are continued through the mobilization of 'community', public–private partnerships and the incorporation of active, responsible citizens of all races. And, unlike apartheid proper, it is sustained by global trends in economics and politics and facilitated by global as well as local PSCs.

It would be both wrong and insincere to suggest that the CCID, the police or the private security sector are unaware of these issues. All these actors are acutely aware of the potential divisiveness of 'community', as well as the relative power of different sections of the population to make use of available (including private) resources to improve their security.[70] For the police, partnership and community

---

[68] See Sylvester, 'It's Official'.
[69] See www.capetown.gov.za/by-laws. For a highly critical view of the CCID along these lines, see Tony Roshan Samara, 'State Security in Transition: The War on Crime in Post Apartheid South Africa', *Social Identities*, 9 (2) (2003): 277–312.
[70] As David Garland points out, this is representative of the 'political *ambivalence* which results from a state confronted by its own limitations'. 'Limits of the Sovereign State', p. 462.

policing is precisely a manner of extending their resources further, allowing more affluent communities to contribute to their own security while the police concentrate their efforts in less privileged areas. The Cape Town Partnership, and its security provider G4S, are also aware of the social implications and symbolic politics of their operations. The CCID recognizes that the causes of vagrancy and homelessness are social and cannot be solved by security measures alone and has appointed a social development officer and five street workers to help street children and homeless adults. In addition, the partnership sponsors one of the city's organizations providing shelter for the homeless. At 3 per cent of the CCID's total budget, social services nevertheless account for a relatively small amount of the CCID's expenditure. Securicor, in turn, openly acknowledges in interviews that 'We are not solving crime in the CCID, we are merely moving it along.' In this way, Securicor managers themselves draw parallels between the CIDs and gated communities, admitting the social costs and exclusionary implications of this type of security solution. The articulation of public–private and global–local that has emerged in Cape Town thus facilitates specific forms of security provision that strengthen aspects of the public good and the state, at the same time as it increases power differentials, disempowers already marginalized individuals or groups and renders the security provided by both public and private agents a distinctly variable good.

Nairobi: security for whom?

In Nairobi, private security has become both increasingly indispensable and highly controversial. Here, too, private security is central to the politics of protection, but, unlike in Cape Town and South Africa more generally, security governance and networks are less formalized and less regulated. Although the private security sector is unarmed, there is considerable controversy regarding the relationship between the police and private providers as well as within the private sector itself. The security field in Nairobi is highly fractured along the lines of public–private as well as global–local. Transnational practices and discourses play a key influencing role, and the manner of the partial disassembly of the Kenyan state lends a particular salience to the symbolic struggles over the public that is crucial to an understanding of the operations of global assemblages in the security field.

Partial state disassembly and private security

At the heart of Kenya's and Nairobi's security anguish is a political regime that over many years has privatized public violence (and appropriated much private violence) in order to secure its own survival at the expense of its citizens.[71] So far, democratic developments have done little to remedy the situation. The electoral defeat of President Daniel arap Moi in 2002 marked the end of nearly forty years of unbroken rule by the Kenya Africa National Union (KANU), twenty-four of them with Moi residing in State House. While the Government of President Mwai Kibaki and the National Rainbow Coalition (NARC) initially showed greater interest in reforming the security sector, their ability or willingness to govern security for the public good left much to be desired. The violence surrounding the disputed December 2007 elections, including widespread brutality and human rights abuses by the police and the mobilization of rival militias by a number of political elites, further underscored the privatization of public violence.[72]

The Kenya Police Service (renamed from the Kenya Police as part of a broader orientation towards community policing in 2004) lacks public accountability and trust, while the vast private security sector remains almost entirely unregulated. Although no exact data exists, there may currently be as many as 2,000 PSCs in Kenya, and, according to one estimate, the private security sector has an annual turnover of $400 million.[73] By far the highest concentration of companies is in

---

[71] Musambayi Katumanga, 'A City under Siege: Banditry and Modes of Accumulation in Nairobi, 1991–2004', *Review of African Political Economy*, 32 (106) (2005): 505–20; Edwin E. Gimode, 'The Role of the Police in Kenya's Democratisation Process', in Godwin R. Murunga and Shadrack. W. Nasong'o (eds.), *Kenya: The Struggle for Democracy*, London and Dakar: Zed and Codesria Books, 2007, pp. 227–60.

[72] For accounts of the electoral violence, see Daniel Branch and Nic Cheeseman (eds.), 'Special Issue: Election Fever: Kenya's Crisis', *Journal of Eastern African Studies*, 2 (2) (2008). Daniel Branch and Nic Cheeseman, 'Democratization, Sequencing and State Failure: Lessons from Kenya', *African Affairs*, 108 (430) (2009): 1–26; and the Report of the Commission of Inquiry into Post-Election Violence, 15 October 2008, available online at www.dialoguekenya.org/docs/pev%20report.pdf, 24 July 2010.

[73] Wairagu *et al.*, *Private Security in Kenya*; John Kariuki, 'The Cost of Fear: Security Firms' Turnover Tops $400m', *The East African*, 25–31 October 2004. It is however important to emphasize that no exact statistics are available, as PSCs require no special license and are registered in the same way as other businesses. Many companies are not registered at all.

Nairobi, where there are believed to be more than 500 PSCs. Most companies, however, are relatively small, and the sector is dominated by approximately ten leading PSCs. The largest in terms of number of employees is G4S (trading in Kenya as Securicor), with nearly 10,000 employees and operations in over 100 different locations across the country. Other main players include KK Security with approximately 8,000 guards, Security Group with approximately 3,800 employees, as well as BM Security, Securex, Patriotic Guards and Ultimate Security. Most of these companies operate throughout the country, and some have a regional presence in East Africa. While the capital's more affluent population as well as the middle classes can afford to hire sophisticated private security firms, the majority of people rely on some type of private protection, whether in the form of relatively basic commercial services or neighbourhood watches. So-called vigilante groups, such as the Taliban, the Baghdad Boys and Mungiki, have also proliferated. Often formed by marginalized youth, these groups provide security in some neighbourhoods, prey on others and also occasionally 'subcontract' their violent services to politicians.[74]

In Kenya, the rise in crime and the growth of the private security sector go hand in hand with the erosion of state capacities and services that began in the late 1980s. For Kenya, as for so many other African countries, this was a period of declining economic prosperity.[75] State expenditure and investment were drastically reduced, often in line with international donor requirements for economic liberalization and structural adjustment. The result was a continuing deterioration of the capacity (and willingness) of government and municipal institutions to deliver services, including the provision of law and order, education and employment for its

---

[74] While central to the politics of protection, the growth of informal protection and vigilante groups is not the focus of this study. For interesting discussions of the political connections of such groups, see David Anderson, 'Vigilantes, Violence and the Politics of Public Order in Kenya', *African Affairs*, 101 (405) (2002): 531–55; Peter Kagwanja, 'Facing Mount Kenya or Facing Mecca? The Mungiki, Ethnic Violence and the Politics of the Moi Succession in Kenya, 1987–2002', *African Affairs*, 102 (406) (2003): 25–50.

[75] Godwin R. Murunga, 'Governance and the Politics of Structural Adjustment in Kenya', in Murunga and Nasong'o, *Kenya: The Struggle for Democracy*, pp. 263–300; Nicolas Van De Walle, *African Economies and the Politics of Permanent Crisis, 1979–1999*, Cambridge: Cambridge University Press, 2001.

citizens. At the same time as poverty and deprivation spread among Kenyans, the political elite showed little inclination to curtail its own appetite, and corruption and mismanagement of state assets continued unabated. Throughout the 1990s, the embattled Moi regime deftly complied with the minimum of external demands for economic and political liberalization, but instead of the predicted textbook result of good governance and democracy the outcome was further erosion of accountability, trust and authority. Regime survival took precedence over any notion of the public good, and President Moi and his KANU party emerged as the winners of both the 1992 and the 1997 elections. The latter in particular was won against a fractured opposition and allegations of intimidation and fraud, and Moi recaptured power with less than 30 per cent of the votes cast.[76] The privatization of power continued and, as in many other countries on the continent, external demands for the privatization of public enterprises and economic liberalization were turned into further sources of enrichment for the regime, resulting in some spectacular financial scams such as the Goldberg scandal when over \$769.2 million was siphoned out of the Central Bank.[77]

The landmark elections of 2002 saw the NARC Government elected on an anti-graft ticket and a promise to deliver a new political era of dialogue and power-sharing.[78] Disappointment quickly set in on both fronts. Assurances of power-sharing and curtailment of the extensive presidential powers were swiftly abandoned, and efforts to reform the constitution stalled.[79] Far from cleaning up politics, the NARC presided over continued high-level corruption, and any credibility

---

[76] See Rok Ajulu, 'Kenya's Democracy Experiment: The 1997 Elections', *Review of African Political Economy*, 25 (76) (1998): 275–85; Marcel Rutten and Alamin Mazrui (eds.), *Out for the Count: The 1997 General Elections and Prospects for Democracy in Kenya*, Kampala: Fountain Publishers, 2001.

[77] Peter Warutere, *The Goldberg Conspiracy: The Game of Paper Gold, Money and Power*, Pretoria: Institute for Security Studies, 2005; more generally, see Beatrice Hibou, 'The Social Capital of the State as an Agent of Deception, or the Ruses of Economic Intelligence', in Bayart *et al.*, *The Criminalization of the State in Africa*, pp. 69–112; Roger Tangri, *The Politics of Patronage in Africa: Parastatals, Privatization and Private Enterprise*, Oxford: James Currey, 1999.

[78] Murunga and Nasong'o, *Kenya: The Struggle for Democracy*.

[79] This in turn was an important contributing factor to the post-election violence in 2008.

the government might have established in this regard evaporated in 2005 when the Permanent Secretary for Ethics and Governance, John Githongo, fled to seek exile in Britain after exposing several ministers' involvement in the so-called Anglo Leasing affair, where government security contracts worth approximately $270 million were signed with a non-existent company.[80]

This personalization of power and the deterioration of state capacities has provided the setting for a highly criminalized and insecure environment. Today, Musambayi Katumanga refers to Nairobi as a 'city under siege', its citizens the prey of a pervasive and violent 'urban banditry' that includes elements of the political regime, the state and the economic elite, as well as the poor.[81] Accurate and reliable statistics are rare, but it is clear that crime in Kenya, and particularly in the capital, has risen sharply in the past decade, to the extent that Nairobi is now perceived as one of the most insecure cities in the world.[82] In 2002, about 37 per cent of Nairobi residents reported having been victims of robbery, and 22 per cent victims of theft.[83] In 2004, a victimization survey found that 66 per cent of individual respondents on the city streets had been victims of crime, while 86 per cent had witnessed crime within the city.[84] The survey also found that levels of insecurity were growing, and there was a clear sense among respondents that crime has become more violent, more ruthless and more organized. Carjackings, often at gunpoint, have become more frequent, as has the hijacking, robbery and even murder of *matatu* (minibus) passengers. As transit to and from places of work and leisure has come to be seen as risky and dangerous, the streets are increasingly deserted at nightfall.

---

[80] See John Githongo, 'John Githongo's Report on Kenyan Corruption'. Available online at http://news.bbc.co.uk/2/hi/africa/4697612.stm (accessed 24 June 2010); Michela Wrong, *It's Our Time to Eat: The Story of a Kenyan Whistleblower*, London, Harper Collins Publishers, 2009.

[81] Katumanga, 'A City Under Siege'.

[82] Commonwealth Human Rights Initiative, *The Police, the People, the Politics: Police Accountability in Kenya*, n.p.: Commonwealth Human Rights Initiative and Kenya Human Rights Commission, 2006, p. 9; Aki Stavrou, *Crime in Nairobi: Results of a Citywide Victim Survey*, Nairobi: UN-HABITAT, 2002.

[83] Stavrou, *Crime in Nairobi*.

[84] Rose Ngugi *et al.*, *Security Risk and Private Sector Growth in Kenya*, Nairobi: Kenya Institute for Public Policy Research and Analysis, 2004, p. 24.

As urbanization and urban unemployment have increased, so too has the so-called informal sector of the economy and Nairobi's informal settlements, or slums. Nairobi is home to Africa's largest slum, Kibera, where between 800,000 and 1 million people share 2.5 square kilometres. New slums are emerging, and urban migration continues, and by now at least half of Nairobi's 3.2 million inhabitants live in slums such as Kibera, Mathare and Soweto.[85] By 2002, urbanization and low employment had resulted in some 10,000 hawkers trying to earn a living on the streets of Nairobi, which in turn led more established businesses and shops to abandon the city centre and to retreat to highly secured enclaves in more suburban settings.[86] By 2004, an upscale shopping mall such as the Village Market was reported to spend $6,250 per month on security, an expenditure that had doubled in two years. The Sarit Centre, another shopping mall, reports a monthly cost of $10,000, while most tourist hotels employ an equal number of security guards and waiters.[87]

There is also a strong perception among Kenyans that criminals are collaborating more and more with law-enforcement agents.[88] In one survey, 36 per cent of respondents attributed all crime in Nairobi directly or indirectly to the police force.[89] Whatever the reliability of such figures, they reflect a deep and widespread distrust of the police and the extent to which they are regarded as part of the problem rather than the solution to crime and disorder. Even after recent

---

[85] Winnie Mittulah, 'Nairobi, Kenya: Understanding Slums', in *Global Report on Human Settlements 2003: The Challenges of Slums*, New York: UN-HABITAT, 2003, pp. 195–228. It is important to stress here that our argument is not one that links poverty and increased socio-economic inequality to rising crime in a direct causal mechanism. As Caldeira has observed in relation to São Paulo, a simple combination of economic crisis, urbanization and declining state expenditure on security cannot alone explain contemporary violence. Instead, the rise in crime is expressive of a complex combination of factors, at the heart of which stands a justice system that is highly politicized and lacks respect for the rights of the poor. In Kenya and Nairobi, the everyday practices of the police and the institutions of law and order, the continuing excessive use of force, the disrespect of civil rights, and the failure to reform the police along more democratic lines are key elements of any explanation of crime and insecurity. See Calderia, *City of Walls*.

[86] Katumanga, 'A City under Siege'.   [87] Kariuki, 'The Cost of Fear'.

[88] Ngugi, *Security Risk and Private Sector Growth*.

[89] Stavrou, *Crime in Nairobi*.

pay rises, the police are underfunded and poorly remunerated and continue to suffer from a lack of infrastructure and institutional capacity, poor leadership and 'favouritism, nepotism and corruption' in relation to recruitment, deployment and promotion.[90] Low morale is thus a continuing feature of the Kenyan police, a difficulty further compounded when in 2000 the National Security Intelligence Service was created by recruiting the best police officers from existing units, leaving the remainder with low pay and lack of promotion opportunities.[91] In part for these reasons, elements of the Kenyan police often resort to extortion and corruption in order to subsidize their wages. The Kenya Bribery Index 2008 found the police were the most corrupt public agency, with 93 per cent of its clients reporting demands for bribes.[92]

The Kenyan police also has a history of frequent implication in political intimidation and violence. At independence, the police enjoyed little public trust, primarily because of its extensive and repressive role on behalf of the colonial authorities during the Mau Mau rebellion and the nationalist resistance.[93] The early Kenyan police has thus been described as 'a punitive citizen containment squad', a legacy that has proved depressingly resilient.[94] The Kenyatta era saw the gradual politicization of the police force,

---

[90] In January 2004, pay for the lowest-ranking officers rose from 4,645 Kenya Shillings per month to 10,000 Kenya Shillings (about $140 per month). However, living conditions have not improved, and the force is reported to have an estimated deficit of 63,326 housing units. There are reportedly 8,891 housing units to accommodate 32,361 junior officers, which means three officers, plus their families, to every room. Commonwealth Human Rights Initiative, *The Police, the People*, pp. 16, 17. Katumanga, 'A City under Siege'; Alice Hills, 'Police Commissioners, Presidents and the Governance of Security', *Journal of Modern African Studies*, 45 (3) (2007): 403–23.

[91] Gimode, 'The Role of the Police'; Katumanga, 'A City under Siege'.

[92] Transparency International Kenya, *Kenya Bribery Index 2008*, available online at www.tikenya.org.

[93] See David Throup, 'Crime, Politics and the Police in Colonial Kenya, 1939–63', in David M. Anderson and David Killingray (eds.), *Policing and Decolonisation: Politics, Nationalism and the Police, 1917–65*, Manchester: Manchester University Press, 1992, pp. 127–57; David Anderson, *Histories of the Hanged: The Dirty War in Kenya and the End of Empire*, New York: Norton, 2005. As noted in Chapter 1, the first police force in Kenya was established by the East Africa Trading Company in 1896; see Clayton and Killingray, *Khaki and Blue*.

[94] Ruteere and Pommerolle, 'Democratizing Security or Decentralizing Repression?'

while the twenty-four-year-long autocratic rule of President Moi was marked by the extensive and brutal use of the police for political purposes, including detentions, torture and assassinations of political opponents.[95]

Acknowledging that in 'the last two decades the Kenya public security system deteriorated to the point where the government was unable to guarantee its citizens personal security, and that of their property', the NARC government blamed the situation on 'low morale in the police force, low professionalism, inadequate allocation of required resources, and endemic corruption in the force'.[96] Controversially, President Kibaki in 2004 appointed a senior military officer, Brigadier (now Major-General) Hussein Ali to the position of Police Commissioner, a move that was interpreted as signalling a lack of trust in the higher ranks of the police.[97] A Police Reforms Task Force was set up, and, in line with international policing trends, community policing was adopted as a means of making the police more accountable and democratic.[98] So far, however, there are few signs that public confidence and trust in the police have improved, or that police reforms have significantly increased the accountability of the police. The President retains the power to appoint and remove the Police Commissioner, which gives him direct influence over policy and operational decisions. As the Commonwealth Human Rights Initiative observes, the 'President's authority over the Commissioner of Police is absolute' and 'illegitimate political interference is entrenched in both law and habit.'[99] Police brutality also appears to have continued unabated. Prior to the post-election violence of 2007–8, the Kenya National Commission on Human Rights accused the police of execution-style killings of as many as 500 people suspected of

---

[95] Gimode, 'The Role of the Police'; Human Rights Watch, *Divide and Rule: State Sponsored Ethnic Violence in Kenya*, New York: Human Rights Watch, 1993. Kenya Human Rights Commission, *Killing the Vote: State-Sponsored Violence and the Flawed Elections in Kenya*, Nairobi: Kenya Human Rights Commission, 1998.

[96] Government of Kenya, *Economic Recovery Strategy for Wealth and Employment Creation 2003–2007*, Nairobi: Government Printer, 2003, p. 10.

[97] Commonwealth Human Rights Initiative, *The Police, the People*.

[98] Gimode, 'The Role of the Police'; Ruteere and Pommerolle, 'Democratizing Security'.

[99] Commonwealth Human Rights Initiative, *The Police, the People*, p. 27.

involvement with the banned Mungiki sect.[100] The Kenya Human Rights Commission had previously estimated that every month the police killed at least three people aged between fifteen and twenty-five in the slums of Korogocho for questioning their arrest. Similarly, the report of the Commission of Inquiry into Post-election Violence details a disturbing series of failings and abuse by the police, including rape and execution-style killings.[101] A special UN investigation also called for the President to dismiss the Chief of Police and the Attorney General following an inquiry into the alleged killing of 1,000 gang members, petty criminals and political protestors since 2007. According to the investigator, the 'Kenyan police are a law unto themselves. They kill often, with impunity.'[102]

In Nairobi, the privatization of public security for the purpose of regime survival has thus contributed to high crime rates and increased fear, which is in turn a key driving force in the expansion of private security. Fear of international terrorism is another prominent factor that merits a brief mention. Following the attack on the US Embassy in 1998, which killed 232 people and injured over 5,000, and the hotel bombing and failed missile attack on an Israeli airliner in Mombasa in 2002, the demand for private security services has escalated, especially among international organizations and personnel. The US State Department still warns against the high risk of both crime and international terrorism in Nairobi, as does the UK Foreign and Commonwealth Office. The security arrangements at the new US Embassy, the second-largest on the African continent, involve 750 private security guards, in addition to the Embassy's own in-house security staff. Nairobi is also home to a number of international organizations, national embassies and the regional headquarters of the UN. Reluctant to place the security of their personnel and assets in the hands of the police, international clients provide a substantial and particularly lucrative market for PSCs in Nairobi, with all

---

[100] Kenya National Commission on Human Rights, *Preliminary Report on Alleged Executions of Persons between June and October 2007*, Nairobi: Kenya Human Rights Commission, 2007. Excessive force extends to the cells, and the UN Human Rights Committee estimates that 3,400 people died in custody in Kenya in 2004; quoted in Commonwealth Human Rights Initiative, *The Police, the People*.

[101] The full 529-page report is available at www.dialoguekenya.org/docs/pev%20report.pdf.

[102] Xan Rice, 'UN Condemns Executions Carried Out by Kenyan Police', *The Guardian*, 25 February 2009, p. 14.

internationally recruited UN employees entitled to the services of a PSC. In a telling indictment of the police, the UN's guide to living and working in Kenya informs its staff that 'in the event of a security breach at your home, you should always call your own security firm first, which will provide the fastest response.'[103]

Global security assemblages in Nairobi

The often ineffective and predatory nature of public security, combined with the 'moral discredit' of the state, plays a crucial structuring role in Nairobi's security field.[104] The public generally distrusts the police; the state has proven unable or unwilling to regulate both the police and the private security sector; and the various actors – public and private, global and local – while networked to some extent, often stand in an intensely competitive relationship to each other. In principle, the city has a UN-HABITAT Safer City programme, coordinated by the City Council of Nairobi, which has developed a citywide crime-prevention and urban-safety strategy, adopted by the City Council in March 2005.[105] As articulated by UN-HABITAT and the United Nations Development Programme, the strategy endorses a partnership model of policing, in line with transnational models:

Today, crime is a common responsibility for all citizens – and not just for the police. The challenges that face Nairobi in addressing this scourge transcend sectoral interests. It is beyond the power of any single stakeholder to address on its own. Progress in the years ahead will require unprecedented levels of co-operation and collaboration among different stakeholders, including both the public and private sectors, matatu owners, hawkers, NGOs, women and youth groups, just to mention a few. Only a collective effort is capable of meeting the challenges that the citywide crime prevention strategy presents.[106]

[103] UN Office of Nairobi, 'Karibu Kenya: An Orientation Guide for United Nations Staff Working in Kenya'. see www.unon.org/karibukenya (accessed 24 June 2010). The instruction also illustrates how deeply embedded private security has become in the everyday life of a certain class of international employees; it is simply business as usual, as we discussed in Chapter 1.

[104] Lemarchand, 'Uncivil States'.

[105] *Nairobi Salama Newsletter*, No. 1, February 2006 Nairobi: City Council of Nairobi.

[106] City Council of Nairobi, 'Safer Nairobi Initiative: Making Nairobi Safer – Together We Can'. Available online at www.unhabitat.org/programmes/safercities/documents/convention/safercitiesbrochure.pdf (accessed 10 March 2008).

Despite such endorsements of partnerships and cooperation, in practice there is little coordination between the numerous PSCs and the police in Nairobi. Unlike in Cape Town, what cooperation exists is haphazard, personalized and negotiated on an individual basis. The result is a highly fractured and intensely competitive security field, with profound implications in terms of equality of protection and access to security. The relationship between the police and PSCs is best described as one of mutual suspicion and at times even outright hostility. Private security providers are quick to point to police collusion with criminals while the police are similarly inclined to dismiss security guards as compulsive lawbreakers. Media reports, anecdotal evidence and victimization surveys indicate that both are all too frequently accurate. The private security sector itself is also divided, with the smaller local companies pitted against the larger international companies, each drawing on different forms of capital in their struggle for position within the security field.

The forms of capital possessed by PSCs in this setting, and their relationship to the police and public authorities, are significantly different from those operating in Cape Town. In particular, the political economy of the sector is entwined with a struggle over symbolic and cultural capital structured by a global–local divide and linked to the strained legitimacy of the Kenyan state in terms of its (in)ability to provide reliable security. Commercial security is by definition a domain of economic market competition. However, in Kenya – and in Nairobi in particular – competition in a capitalist security market is inextricable from its connections to competition in the symbolic market of security.

One of the best illustrations of this field of struggle is found within the private security industry itself, where the development of two competing industry associations illustrates some of the key dynamics in the field. The larger PSCs in Nairobi argue that private security is an essential part of everyday security in the city, but that to make a positive contribution the sector needs to conform to high standards and international best practice. Without such standards, these companies maintain, the sector is likely to be ineffective and even potentially dangerous. A poorly regulated private security industry, they argue, will only contribute to Nairobi's security predicament through ineffectiveness, random violence and collusion with criminals. Conversely, a properly structured and well-resourced sector can contribute to the public good, freeing the police to take on the most important tasks and potentially assisting them in their duties. Accordingly, the larger PSCs have, through the Kenya Security Industry Association (KSIA), actively worked for better self-regulation and lobbied for higher standards, including better training requirements and proper vetting of personnel – often drawing inspiration from private security associations in South Africa and the UK, amongst others. The KSIA also instituted membership criteria that exclude companies that fail to meet what it presents as internationally validated standards. Importantly, as we discuss below, KSIA strongly supported the government's extension of minimum wage standards to the security industry in 2003.

For Nairobi's smaller security companies, which provide mainly low-tech labour-intensive manned guarding and not the more capital-intensive services such as alarms and alarmed response, regulation means higher barriers to entry, less profit and possible bankruptcy. Mobilizing against the prospect of regulation, the local companies deployed two closely connected arguments. The first was a nationalist discourse of white imperialism against domestic capital. In this argument, the KSIA companies are presented as multinationals, or 'white' expatriate companies, and the quest for regulation is presented as an attempt by these companies to displace local firms and to gain a competitive advantage, especially vis-à-vis international clients such as embassies and aid organizations. The smaller companies also argue that the KSIA plays on a widespread perception in Kenya that anything 'white' or 'foreign' is superior to local goods or services, thus making it difficult for local companies to succeed. The international and the local occupy particular positions here, as many of the larger PSCs are indeed Kenyan companies, but with expatriate or 'settler' capital, management, origins and ownership structures. By contrast, the smaller companies present themselves as 'indigenous' and unfairly disadvantaged by their lack of access to international capital and by the biased preference of many larger clients towards hiring 'foreign' firms. While such conflicts clearly need to be understood as part of the broader commercial competition within the sector, they also reflect the manner in which the private security industry is often linked to sensitive political issues and struggles, and the forms of cultural capital that actors attempt to mobilize in struggles in the field.

The second part of the smaller companies' argument was that a more regulated private security sector would effectively make private security available only to the rich and, hence, would further cement Nairobi's existing socio-economic inequalities. Local businesses and organizations, as well as many private homes, are unable to pay as much for their security services as international investors, organizations and embassies. A consequence of tighter regulation and higher standards, the smaller companies argued, would be to leave less-advantaged parts of the population without the additional protection of private services. The struggle within the security sector came to a head in May 2003 when the Government, in an effort to deal with the level of exploitation in the industry, introduced a minimum wage Bill.[107] The debates around the Bill provide a useful way of illustrating the various forms of power and capital employed by the various actors in Nairobi's fractured security field.

Including monthly housing and other allowances, the new legislation brought the minimum wage for a guard to 9,469 Kenyan shillings. This represented an increase of 12.5 per cent, significantly adding to the salary costs of PSCs. The KSIA quickly endorsed the Bill and made payment of the minimum wage a condition of membership in the association. For these companies, regulation in terms of minimum wages and minimum training standards represented a sign of legitimacy and acceptance. As such, regulation was something that would add to their symbolic capital while at the same time undercutting a key economic advantage of their lower-paying competitors. Tellingly, all the largest international clients in Nairobi, such as the US Embassy, the UN and international organizations, make payment of the minimum wage a requirement for contracts. In this way, such international institutions are able to influence the security field to the commercial advantage of the biggest PSCs.

A number of the smaller security companies, however, refused to accept the government's wage regulation and in protest formed a new security association: the Protective Services Industry Association (PSIA). The PSIA, which has a membership of approximately thirty companies, argued that the new minimum wage would make security available only to the wealthy and would force a number of smaller security companies out of business. In fact, the PSIA regarded the wage legislation

---

[107] Government of Kenya, *Legal Notice No. 53*, '*The Regulation of Wages (Protective Security Services) (Amendment) Order, 2003*', Nairobi: Government Printer, May 2003.

as a product of direct lobbying by the companies represented by KSIA and hence as an effort to squeeze smaller companies out of the market. Rather than a uniform minimum wage, the Chairman of the PSIA argued for a differentiated salary structure, where the top-tier companies providing highly trained security guards and integrated security solutions would pay a substantially higher wage than the lower-tier companies, who offer less intensive security consisting predominantly of static guarding. The PSIA rejected notions of exploiting the labour force by paying below the minimum wage, arguing that there are 'plenty of people on the street' willing to work for the wages on offer. PSIA members have openly stated that they will not comply with the minimum wage requirement, and to date there are no signs that the government will attempt to enforce the regulation. On the contrary, the Minister for Planning and National Development at the time the legislation was introduced, Professor Peter Anyang'Nyong'o, was present at the launch of the PSIA, endorsing its contributions to Kenyan security. Despite openly breaking the law, the PSIA companies also continue to sign new contracts with government agencies and parastatals.

The competition between the memberships of the two security associations in Kenya demonstrates how the political economy of private security cannot be read out of pure 'market' forces. There is a powerful temptation to see global PSCs as yet another form of global capital constantly in search of the lowest possible wage labour in what is already a notoriously long-hour, low-wage industry where exploitation of the workforce is often rife. Yet although there is no doubt that global security firms are driven by profit, to automatically see them as akin to predatory forms of capital constantly in search of the lowest costs misunderstands the specific political economy of security. Here, effective market competition does not always come from low price, and global PSCs often attempt to maximize their competitive position by reversing conventional economic logic and arguing that a 'race to the bottom' actually results in a dangerous diminishment of security. As we have shown, this need not be seen in altruistic terms – it can privilege the position of global firms and give them an advantage through their organizational and material capacities relative to smaller competitors.[108] But neither are such claims spurious: they reflect instead the

---

[108] More narrowly, this is also seen in the tendency of firms to replace humans with technology (alarms, surveillance, centralized response, etc), as a means

peculiar nature of security as a service and the symbolic and cultural forms of capital to which it is connected.

Kenya's fractured security field is also evident in the relationship of private security to the police. From the police's point of view, the public's increased reliance on private providers is a threat to their status and position. There is little doubt that the police are in part jealously guarding their position against the security companies, especially the international firms and the larger Kenyan PSCs, whose economic capital exceeds that of the police and whose access to technology enables them to provide forms of protection to their clients that the police are unable to match. On the other hand, the police are the only security actors that are legally armed.[109] PSCs thus depend on the police and require their cooperation and backup when responding to dangerous situations and, of course, when arrests are to be made.[110] Most PSCs report that the number of armed incidents in Nairobi has increased significantly in recent years, with many companies referring to more than five incidents a week involving firearms. This poses a serious challenge: simply responding with unarmed guards provides limited security for clients, while simultaneously placing guards in significant danger. Guards are instructed to withdraw and wait for police assistance in the case of any serious incident, and PSCs will frequently send a vehicle to pick up police in order to ensure a more rapid response. In the case of alarmed response services, current practice in many

of reducing labour costs – an area where large global firms again possess significant competitive advantages.

[109] A few private security companies in Nairobi appear to have acquired an armed capacity by obtaining individual gun licences for security guards. Companies are not, however, licensed to provide armed protection and this practice is not legal.

[110] Cooperation with the division known as the Administration Police is perhaps the most straightforward, in that they act as an armed force for hire to clients, including embassies, banks, supermarkets and PSCs. The Administration Police is also hired by PSCs for cash in transit, at the cost of approximately $3 per officer per hour. The high costs of the Administration Police make this an unaffordable arrangement for many companies, thus acting as a marker of differentiation within the sector. Personnel from the paramilitary General Service Unit (GSU) are also stationed at many embassies and particular high-risk sites and cooperate with PSCs in these instances. The GSU was formed during the emergency in the 1950s as part of the colonial state's effort to suppress the Mau Mau Rebellion; see Throup, 'Crime, Politics and the Police'.

companies is to send one vehicle to the incident and another to the nearest police station to transport the required number of police officers to the scene. This not only potentially delays effective response time but also carries the risk that there may be no available police officers at the station.

One consequence of this situation is that private guards are placed in an intolerably dangerous position. In a region awash with small arms, Kenyan guards are typically issued only with a whistle and a baton. Attacks and violence towards security guards are common, and sources within the industry estimate that within greater Nairobi and Mombasa combined, between five and ten security guards are killed every month. One leading company interviewed had lost fifteen guards in the first ten months of 2004, whereas many other PSCs reported frequent violent incidents towards guards.[111] In this context, many companies express concerns that police regulations make it difficult to issue guards with body armour, which requires a firearms certificate. Despite this high incidence of violence, no nation- or industry-wide statistics detailing guards hurt or killed on duty appear to exist, and the issue has received surprisingly little public attention.

Another consequence of the lack of public–private coordination is the reduction in security for the clients of PSCs, and for this reason the KSIA has lobbied for the reinstatement of a previous pilot arrangement, whereby individual PSCs had primary responsibility for patrolling and responding to alarms in various residential areas and the police provided two officers per PSC vehicle – a system somewhat akin to the arrangements in Cape Town, albeit at a much less extensive and formalized level. According to the PSCs involved in the pilot project, the scheme was beneficial not only for their clients but also for Nairobi's citizens in general. The police and PSCs, they argue, have a common interest in preventing crime, and whereas the police are short on transport and resources, the PSCs have approximately 200 alarm response vehicles stationed at strategic locations around Nairobi at any one time. In making this argument, the larger companies point simultaneously to their considerable material capabilities

---

[111] By comparison, the *Daily Nation* reported that fifty police officers were killed and another thirty-seven maimed while on duty in the two-year period from January 2003; Stephen Muiruri, 'How 50 Crimebusters Died in the Line of Duty', *Daily Nation* (Nairobi), 8 November 2004.

and expertise while seeking to gain important symbolic capital and coercive capacity from a closer cooperation with the police. On the other hand, since the police have the security of all citizens as their stated objective, and since the arrangement predominantly increased security to residential customers who could afford to pay for private services and was only in operation in a few wealthy areas of the capital, it could be seen as a privatization of scarce public resources. There are also reports that individual police officers objected to being assigned to private security duties, regarding this as a misuse of their skills and resources.[112] While the private security vehicles purportedly also responded to incidents involving non-paying clients or members of the public, it is unclear precisely how the division of public and private responsibilities and priorities was determined or how effective it was for those outside the contractual relationship.

The arrangement was terminated by the new Provincial Police Officer in 2004, and the relationship between private security providers and the police is now largely informal, depending to a large extent on the personal relationships between company directors, high-level police officials and individual station commanders. Whereas some companies have succeeded in hiring police officers on their patrol vehicles through ad hoc arrangements, the majority patrol without police or any armed support.

In Nairobi's fractured security field, global practices and discourses and their connections to international clients and transnational PSCs play significant roles in the distributions of power between security actors. Yet this is also a localized struggle, where specific structures and historical trajectories have important impacts on the ways that global security assemblages interact with local settings. The political economy of security as a market intersects with a symbolic economy that reflects the ambivalent place of security as a global commodity.

The political economy of Nairobi's insecurity

Nairobi has been substantially transformed from the ideal of the city as an open public sphere famously described and defended by Jane

---

[112] 'CID Officers "Embedded" to Private Security Firms Disapprove New Role', *The Nation* (Nairobi), 17 April 2005. This reluctance again demonstrates the practical significance of the public–private divide as a symbolic marker and resource and as a dimension of the identity and *habitus* of actors within the security field.

Jacobs in 1961; the public space of the street has to a significant extent become a place of danger.[113] While insecurity is a feature of life for almost all citizens in Kenya, it affects people differently. Kenya is one of the ten most unequal countries in the world, and, according to the Government's own figures, 56 per cent of the population (or 17 million people) live in poverty, while a small elite of 10 per cent control 42 per cent of all wealth.[114] To a significant extent, crime and insecurity follow the lines of wealth, and surveys show that the feeling of insecurity varies greatly according to income. In short, the poorer Kenyans are, the more they suffer from both the fear and the real experience of crime.[115] Money buys (some) security in contemporary Kenya, whereas the expanding shanty towns and slums suffer from pervasive insecurity. The operation of a security market means that economic inequality is compounded by inequitable access to security, and while it can be argued that this is the case virtually by definition wherever private security exists, under conditions where public provision is low or lacking, its effects are even more significant.

This situation is by no means limited to Kenya; it holds for numerous African countries experiencing high levels of crime and low levels of public law enforcement. The provision of security is thus at the heart of the social and political order. Strategies such as the use of public police as an integrated part of private security clearly raise difficult questions. It is easy to see them as providing yet more protection to paying clients while taking away public resources from those unable to afford private security. Yet, at the same time, it is important to acknowledge the attractions that such arrangements can hold in these situations – attractions that do not apply only to the wealthy. Public policing is desperately inadequate for the poorer sections of the population in Kenya. The police-to-population ratio has become worse over time, from one police officer per 711 people in 1991, to 1:875 in 2001 and 1:1,150 in 2004.[116] Thus, it is clear that even if one leaves aside the question of the police's priorities and commitments, its resources are likely to remain severely overstretched for the foreseeable future. In such a setting, thinking through the interactions

---

[113] Jacobs, *Death and Life of American Cities*.

[114] Government of Kenya, *Economic Recovery Strategy*, p. 1; *Daily Nation* (Nairobi), 'Our Unequal Kenya', 27 October 2004.

[115] Ngugi *et al.*, *Security, Risk and Private Sector Growth*.

[116] Commonwealth Human Rights Initiative, *The Police, the People*, p. 14.

between public and private security is essential. However, this cannot take place in the abstract. It requires an appreciation of the specific security field and its dynamics of contestation and competition. In Nairobi, and elsewhere in the country, individuals, businesses and organizations will have few options but to continue to rely to a large extent on private providers. This cannot be approached solely as an ideological or normative question of whether or not security should be a public good – it is also an inescapable reflection of the material resources and political position of the present Kenyan state.

Where private security is so central, its political economy matters more than ever in terms of who gets secured. It is clear that security provision in Nairobi is both deeply privatized and transnational, and Nairobi also demonstrates with particular clarity that global security assemblages are by definition local; while global actors (such as global PSCs) and discourses (such as community policing, public–private partnerships or models of private security regulation) have a significant influence, the global is produced in action, and actions are by definition localized.[117] Transnational private security actors do not dominate, and commercial security does not operate according to the 'pure' logic of a commodified market. Instead, the 'economy' of security is much more complex, constituting a *political* economy in the fullest sense of the term in that it reflects the distribution of different and often competing forms of capital and the specific historical trajectories of the Kenyan state and its public security forces. In Nairobi, the position of the state is paradoxical and is marked by its simultaneous symbolic centrality and weakness, its retention of the monopoly of armed force and justice and yet its incapacity (and sometimes unwillingness) to deliver security. The strictly monetary market of security is, as everywhere, crucial; yet this plays out against a symbolic economy in which the right of access to security for all (even if in the questionable form of cheap, exploitative security services) matters and where the symbolic capital of the national–global divide is constantly mobilized in commercial struggles.

The significance of private security in Kenya has recently been more clearly recognized, and the Government has begun consultations over draft legislation to regulate the sector. In part this has been influenced by the lobbying efforts of the leading security companies, who have

---

[117] Strathern, *Shifting Contexts*.

also been involved in consultations regarding the new regulation. The first result was the announcement that training of security guards will be standardized and regularized, with all guards required to undertake a minimum of 119 hours of training.[118] This is undoubtedly an important development, given that the sector has been almost entirely unregulated and little or no attention has been paid to its role and functions. But while the move towards regulation is to be welcomed, it is clear that the private security sector should not be approached simply in terms of regulation, quality control and wages. Instead, private security needs to be regarded as part of a wider network of security provision located within a field of struggle and connected to fundamental political and economic questions.

Conclusion

Our purpose in this chapter has not been to compare directly the impact of security privatization in Cape Town and Nairobi, or to present one as an optimal fusion of public and private and the other as dysfunctional. Instead, we have attempted to capture the central role that private security plays in both these urban settings and to demonstrate its complex relations to public forces and state power. Both Cape Town and Nairobi point towards the growing role of private security actors in urban areas but caution against an automatic, blanket assumption that private security solutions will always and everywhere have the same effects. Private security certainly follows the lines of wealth, but this fact needs to serve as the starting point – rather than the conclusion – for an analysis of the much more complex political economy of security in contemporary global assemblages.

Although a systematic comparison of the two cities has not been the intention (and would indeed require a different conceptual and empirical framework), one inescapable conclusion that emerges from this discussion is that state capacity plays a crucial role in determining the role and impact of private security. Yet it needs to be stressed that this relationship is in some ways counter-intuitive and runs contrary to many common assumptions about the relationship between state strength and security privatization. In particular, it contradicts the

---

[118] Kabura Mugambi, 'With Training, Govt Hopes to Regulate Private Security', *The Nation* (Nairobi), 21 July 2007.

view that private security will be more pervasive and have a freer rein in 'weak' states and that its growth and adoption of armed, coercive capacities inevitably weakens the state by undermining one of the central components of sovereignty.

In Cape Town, where the state is clearly more capable than in Kenya, and where the sector is highly regulated, private security is, if anything, more pervasive than it is in Nairobi. It is also generally armed, and often heavily so, in contrast to an unarmed Kenyan security industry. Extensive and intensive security privatization cannot, therefore, be automatically related to relative state weakness. Moreover, a strong case could be made that a pervasive private security sector may well have supported the legitimacy of the South African state through its ability to assist the state in meeting one of its most pressing challenges: the provision of security. As we have shown, this situation is not without tensions, conflicts and inequities – dynamics that are crucial in understanding public–private relations in the security field. But it is equally apparent that there is no automatic relationship between the growth of security privatization and state weakness or straightforward delegitimization. These reflections point towards the variably constitutive nature of security – its place in the relationship between the governance of behaviour and the exercise of coercion. This relationship is one of the key themes of our final chapter.

6 | Security, politics and global assemblages

Globalization, it is frequently noted, has eroded traditional understandings of state sovereignty. In the words of David Held and Anthony McGrew, it has 'unbundled' the relationship between sovereignty, territory and political power and made the 'proper locus of politics and the articulation of the public interest ... a puzzling matter'.[1] Today, this is also the case in the field of security. While frequently seen as the last secure bastion of sovereignty in a rapidly globalizing world, the state's much-vaunted monopoly of legitimate force is increasingly enmeshed in networks and relations that cannot be contained within the boundaries of the national state. Across the globe, from megacities to isolated resource production facilities, security provision and governance take place within assemblages that are deterritorialized in terms of actors, technologies, norms and discourses and are embedded in a complex transnational architecture that defies the conventional distinctions of public–private and global–local. Security, in other words, is increasingly beyond the state.

As part of transformations in global governance and shifting social forces, private security has become integral to contemporary power and politics. The key issue is no longer the familiar one of whether or not the state is losing power and sovereignty in a zero-sum game with non-state actors. As we have shown, the new geographies of power cannot be reduced to a simple question of more or less state power or weakened domestic government, in the manner of so much early scholarship on globalization and security privatization. Instead, they demand an investigation of the production of new modalities of power through which the very categories of public–private and global–local are reconstituted and reconfigured.

---

[1] David Held and Anthony McGrew, *Globalization/Anti-Globalization*, Cambridge: Polity, 2002, pp. 127, 129.

The emergence of global security assemblages has important implications for the conditions and context of the politics of protection,
as it too is 'unbundled' and stretched across national boundaries,
involving a multiplicity of actors and forms of capital in transnational
networks of power. In this sense, global security assemblages are
boundary fields in that they are neither private, nor public, neither
local, nor global but mark analytical spaces that lie between these
common distinctions and require their own empirical investigation.
In this concluding chapter we turn to the issue of security politics in
global assemblages, focusing in particular on security governance and
the possibilities and conditions of political struggles.

Global security governance

To open up the issue of private security in contemporary global governance, it is useful to return to our point of departure: the historically constituted character of the public and the private, the global
and the local. Situating the growth and globalization of private security within transformations in governance at the national and international levels, we have shown its connections to broader processes
of restructuring within states and to the expanding security agenda
and predominant social attitudes and mores associated with late
modernity and risk society. Through these varied trends and developments, private logics have become lodged within key institutions
and practices of the competitive state, as well as within a range of
international organizations that act to promote and defend globalization and privatization. In the case of security, the result has been
the empowerment of private actors, who, by virtue of their growing
economic and symbolic power, have become able to play prominent
roles in security provision and governance, contributing to the formulation and enforcement of collective norms and agendas. Security
privatization, approached in this manner, is not simply a question of
a transfer of previously public functions to private actors but indicates
a more fundamental rearticulation of the public–private and global–
local relationship.

For the study of global security governance, two points follow.
First, analysis requires the abandonment of the public–private and the
inside–outside dichotomies, in favour of a perspective on world politics and governance as one analytical field connected by a multitude

of mutually constitutive relationships. Second, power has to be placed at the centre of analysis. To say that the world is interconnected does not mean that it is uniform, that states are irrelevant, or that the same processes or the same actors have the same effects regardless of time and place. Instead, the assembled nature of contemporary governance demands attention to the manner in which the field is assembled in particular locations and how the actors' various forms of capital can be realized in specific fields.

In global security assemblages, the existence of the global in the local is evident in numerous ways and underscores the importance of escaping the 'territorial trap' in theorizing about world polit-ics.[2] It is, for example, clear that shifts in security governance in the North have given rise to conceptualizations and technologies of security with global impacts – whether as powerful discourses in themselves or in combination with other social logics (and institu-tions) such as free trade or risk-based knowledge. Transnational corporations, international development organizations, NGOs and tourists, to mention but a few, are vehicles for the global transpor-tation of such technologies, discourses and practices, which inev-itably also have their local origins and inflections. Similarly, PSCs have been empowered by transformations in security governance in advanced liberal societies and have as a consequence of their acquired capital and capacities been able to enter and influence security fields in the South. As we have shown, this has important effects on security in multiple diverse settings on the African con-tinent. At the same time, most countries in Africa (and elsewhere in the South) have also been significantly impacted by the discourses and practices of neo-liberalism, and the processes of partial state disassembly and reassembly, albeit in different ways and with dif-fering outcomes, are central aspects of the recent history and rela-tionship between the North and the South. In other words, security politics and policies on the African continent cannot be understood with reference to its domestic politics alone, but require instead careful attention to shifts in the international political economy and global discourses and normativities.

---

[2] John Agnew, 'The Territorial Trap: The Geographic Assumptions of International Relations Theory', *Review of International Political Economy*, 1 (1) (1994): 53–80.

Importantly, however, our emphasis on interconnectedness is not to be understood as the emergence of a uniform logic of global policing, nor is there a single rationality driving these developments.[3] The global is not simply the domestic writ large, nor is the power and impact of private security the same in all parts of the world. Put differently, the global circulation of discursive rationalities and technologies of rule should not be mistaken for, or reduced to, a singular seamless web of power, to be read from the pages of public documents or field manuals. Instead, as our empirical investigations show, global security assemblages are influenced by specific struggles within the field of practice and what has emerged are complex fields of interaction, structured by specific modalities of power. As such, capturing global security governance requires at the same time attention to the global and to the point where the global is inserted and translated into the local. At these points, different actors, capacities and discourses can coalesce to make an assemblage and a structure of security governance possible and powerful.

Within these assemblages, the public and the private, the global and the local are neither fixed, nor irrelevant, but constitute instead forms of capital that actors can mobilize within the security field. This in turn speaks to an important set of debates in current studies of global governance, namely the relationship between coercion and what is variously called governmentality, productive power, soft power or simply norms in the constructivist International Relations literature.[4] While more liberal studies of governance frequently ignore the question of power and security in favour of an emphasis on collective governance outcomes and the spread of liberal norms, more Foucauldian-inspired approaches in social theory and global governmentality have highlighted the importance of strategies of rule at a distance focused on the creation of self-governing, disciplined and responsible subjects. While the latter approaches have insightfully

---

[3] For a recent critique of the application of global governmentality to security privatization along these lines, see Jonathan Joseph 'The Limits of Governmentality: Social Theory and the International', *European Journal of International Relations*, 16 (2) (2010): 223–46.

[4] For contributions to the debate, see, for example, Michael Barnett and Raymond Duvall, 'Power in International Politics', *International Organization*, 59 (1) (2005). Neumann and Sending, 'The "International" as Governmentality'; Wendy Larner and William Walters (eds.), *Global Governmentality*, London and New York: Routledge, 2005.

emphasized the diverse forms of power at work in global governance, they have tended to stress its disciplinary and productive dimensions at the expense of the material and coercive power traditionally associated with modern sovereignty. As Mitchell Dean comments, in 'most social and political narratives, sovereign power is being undermined, decentred, flattened, deterritorialized, pluralized, and conceptually displaced', and, as a result, it appears as 'a second-order phenomenon, even as an archaism or survival of absolutist or monarchical power'.[5] Yet coercive power remains central in the global order – not just in the obvious sense of the continuing importance of military might, but also in its relationship to disciplinary and productive power in structures of governance. In Dean's incisive words: 'Governing society might be about the construction and deployment of freedom, but it is also about the deployment of barbed wire and the construction of detention facilities.'[6]

Taking private security seriously, and looking at it in detail in concrete locations, places the question of the relationship between compulsory power (the direct, often coercive, capacity to control the actions of others) and productive power (the constitution of specific types of actors capable of effective action within a given social domain) inescapably at the centre of analysis of global governance. One reason why private security is so interesting is precisely because it is not simply an instrument of coercion or a singular neo-liberal technique for the production of self-governing, responsible subjects: it is both – in complex, simultaneous and often paradoxical ways. Through its various practices and interventions, and its connections to the symbolic and material power of the public, private security illustrates with particular clarity how, in Barnett and Duvall's words, 'productive power makes some instances of compulsory power possible and legitimate, and, in turn, ... compulsory power shapes the terms of meaning that influence how actors see what is possible and desirable'.[7]

Seen in this light, PSCs are simultaneously a result or effect of productive power and agents of productive power in specific sites. Their presence and growth is intimately linked to shifts in security

---

[5] Mitchell Dean, *Governing Societies*, Maidenhead: Open University Press, 2007, p. 133.
[6] *Ibid.*, p. 6.
[7] Barnett and Duvall, 'Power in International Politics', p. 44.

governance, and what we have referred to as their symbolic power arises in large part from their embeddedness in broader legitimated structures, norms and discourses such as free trade and property rights, as well as their cooperation with public actors and security forces. But they are also agents that act to produce forms of security governance through their ability (or attempts) to influence how other security actors 'see what is possible and desirable'. The widespread use of risk-based security technologies, for example, has direct implications for how security practices are constructed and also for the production of 'safe' and 'unsafe' spaces. The security technologies of alarms, security fencing, CCTV and so on are now found across the globe, with PSCs as important vectors for the production of particular forms of subjectivities and responsibilized security behaviour.

At the same time, their power is also coercive, sometimes by virtue of their own capacities and technologies, and sometimes as a result of their (albeit uneasy) cooperation with public forces. Here commercial private security differs in important ways from the neo-mercenary activities of the 1990s, as do its implications for global security governance. PSCs generally do not wield lethal violence, and they usually lack the capacity to engage in armed conflict. They remain tied to the coercive and judicial institutions of the state in ways that the PMCs of that earlier period (and in some places still today) often were not. Even in resource enclaves, where security operations may seem to bear the closest resemblances to PMCs, the integration of private security with the state and structures of legitimation changes the dynamics of its interventions. Unlike the privatized military, commercial PSCs have generally escaped becoming subjects of intense international concern or condemnation. The activities of global commercial security are usually treated as private issues, so long as they do not challenge the symbolic pre-eminence of the state in the security field.[8] Alternatively, they are regarded as a matter requiring proper management and regulation, where regulation may in turn serve to further empower and entrench the private within the public. The manner in which PSCs frequently work with and within the bureaucratic state raises the

---

[8] Clearly, material power also matters in this context, as the diversity of national policies concerning firearms in the private security sector illustrates. In South Africa, PSCs with semi-automatic weapons may be seen on public streets, whereas in Nigeria they are by law unarmed. It is not arms alone, but their place within specific security fields that is crucial.

possibility that they may strengthen the structures of the formal legal-rational state instead of the private networks of the shadow state. This is, of course, not to say that private security will act as the midwife of a centralized – and much less a democratic and egalitarian – state. It may strengthen the coercive capacities of the already executive-dominated African state, but the key point is that the manner in which the private is linked to the public through legitimated structures and forms of coercion and power means that there can be no automatic assumption that commercial private security encourages a deliberate undermining or weakening of formal state institutions. Instead, global private security is a key illustration of James Ferguson's observation that an important effect of the new forms of transnational power is not so much to make states 'weak' or 'strong' as to reconfigure the way in which they are able to spatialize their authority and to stake their claims to superior generality and universality.[9] If the state is perceived not merely as a formal institution of power, but as the effect of a wider range of dispersed forms of power, then PSCs can be seen to help produce and enact the state in the eyes of its inhabitants, making the state more real and tangible in everyday practices.[10] In this way, the impact of commercial security on social power may be more enduring and socially embedded than the generally fraught and episodic interventions of private military contractors in the 1990s, even though its effects on both coercive and governmental strategies often go unnoticed due to its connections to legitimated structures.

In contemporary Africa, the reconfiguration of the public and the private, the global and the local, can be seen as intrinsic to the manner in which the state is able to enact its power, whether coercive or governmental. The Niger Delta provides a telling illustration. As we showed in Chapter 4, PSCs are integrated into global security assemblages that not only facilitate the operations of multinational oil companies (in this case, those of Chevron Nigeria Ltd), but also interact with and enhance the public security organizations of the Nigerian state. As such, private security is central to the

---

[9] Ferguson, *Global Shadows*, p. 112.
[10] See Timothy Mitchell, 'Society, Economy and the State Effect', in Steinmetz (ed.), *State/Culture: State Formation after the Cultural Turn*, NY: Cornell University Press, pp. 76–97; Thomas Blom Hansen and Finn Stepputat (eds.), *States of Imagination: Ethnographic Explorations of the Postcolonial State*, Durham NC: Duke University Press, 2001.

maintenance of Nigeria's highly unequal and coercive social and political order, as well as to the continuation of resource extraction from 'Afrique utile'.[11]

This is not, however, a simple process whereby private security only serves to enhance the coercive capacity of the state – more governmental and productive forms of power are simultaneously at work. In a setting where participation in internationally developed frameworks such as the Voluntary Principles on Security and Human Rights and the UN's Global Compact have become a mark of a socially responsible firm (something that is in part the result of broader international pressures) and where the oil companies are seeking new strategies in response to the failure of past security policies, PSCs may become important actors in attempts to transform security governance.[12] The symbolic and material power of global private security firms, combined with that of their clients, and the significant role of both in the reproduction of political power in Nigeria, mean that as parts of global security assemblages private actors may have the potential to influence practices within assemblages in significant and novel ways. Global PSCs provide the oil companies with expert agents directly involved in day-to-day security practices with state forces and may be capable of shaping and modifying the behaviour of those forces by embedding them in norms and routines of internationally sanctioned standards and guidelines. Importantly, however, the adoption of such international standards and guidelines can simultaneously make possible and legitimate certain forms of coercion and exclusionary practices, thus exposing the inherent limits and contradictions of governmental power.

While the power of corporate social responsibility in global security governance should not be exaggerated, and it is crucial to keep in mind that it does not change or challenge the underlying economic

---

[11] Reno, 'Order and Commerce in Turbulent Areas'.
[12] On business and human rights, see Andrew Clapham, *Human Rights Obligations of Non-State Actors*, Oxford: Oxford University Press, 2006; on changing corporate strategies, including those in the oil industry, see Deborah Avant and Virginia Haufler, 'Private Security Strategies and Their Public Consequences: Transnational Organizations in Historical Perspective', paper presented at the workshop on 'Public/Private Interaction and the Transformation of Global Governance'. University of Ottawa, Canada, 5–6 June 2009; and Deborah Avant, 'NGOs, Corporations and Security Transformations in Africa', *International Relations*, 21 (2) (2007): 143–61.

and political order (and may in fact serve to secure it), it does draw attention to the possibility that private security actors may in certain settings contribute towards a less directly coercive environment.[13] Of course, for both the oil companies and PSCs, any concern for socially responsible behaviour remains linked to the logics of capital and profitability. Nevertheless, the power of private actors to shape security practices goes beyond the external pressure that private firms might be able to bring to bear (or be forced to bring to bear) on the Nigerian state. It extends to the ability to influence practices along a continuum from strategic planning, to the provision of certain kinds of material capabilities, to efforts to mould the subjectivities of state security actors and how they and other security actors 'see what is possible and desirable'. In this way, the study of private security provides an important window on what Mitchell Dean refers to as the 'core conundrum of the present' – the complex relationship between productive and coercive, or governmental and sovereign, power.[14] In the case of global security governance, private security actors are central to unravelling these relationships, both globally and locally.

Private security and the (global) public

The assembled nature of the contemporary security field, consisting of a multitude of public–private, global–local actors with different forms of capital, may also alter the conditions of security politics. While the state by no means disappears as an actor or a locus of politics, it is located within networks that cut across and through it, and where public and private, global and local intersections and connections provide multiple sites for political engagement. As a wide variety of appraisals have demonstrated, the global era is changing the conditions and possibilities of politics and political struggles.[15] Whereas in the past, broad-based demands for rights, equality, welfare and security were targeted at and achieved primarily through the

---

[13] For a cautionary note on the limits of corporate social responsibility as a means of fundamental change, see Lipschutz, *Globalization, Governmentality, and Global Politics*, pp. 130–70.

[14] Dean, *Governing Societies*, p. 6.

[15] In a huge literature, see M. Keck and K. Sikkink, *Activists beyond Borders: Advocacy Networks in International Politics*, Icatha, NY: Cornell University Press. Max Kirsch (ed.), *Inclusion and Exclusion in the World Economy*, London and New York: Routledge, 2006.

national state, the shrinking welfare state and changing conceptions of public provision not only limits the range of citizens' entitlements and interactions with their states, but also means that to be effective, political struggles must be broader. Today, interest groups, activists and individuals increasingly find that their demands require engagement with more distant organizations, institutions and discourses of rights. The global era has also to a certain extent altered the politics of identification, leading to translocal loyalties and global solidarities where people establish and maintain affective and political connections in the context of a growing transnational civil society or global public.[16] Not exclusively the preserve of the rich and the educated, transnational networks can also include more disadvantaged and marginalized groups whose capacity for political voice and presence can be strengthened through political processes that escape the boundaries of the nation-state.[17]

The implications of global assemblages for these dimensions of security politics are, however, far from straightforward. On one level, global assemblages can mark a narrowing of politics since they represent particular constellations of actors and empower PSCs, their clients and other actors who generally regard security as a depoliticized service. Such specialized assemblages, as Sassen points out, 'constitute particularized "normative" orders internal to each assembly which easily amount to mere utility logics'.[18] Within global security assemblages actors may be able to mobilize private resources and technified security logics to secure private interests in ways that are to some extent beyond the purview of wider normative debates and political procedures. The incorporation of these logics within the state via public–private collaboration and regulation furthers the tendency of these assemblages to insulate themselves

---

[16] See, in what is again a vast body of analysis, Helmut Anheier, Mariles Glasius and Mary Kaldor (eds.), *Global Civil Society: 2004/05*, London: Sage 2004; Appudarai, *Modernity at Large*; Richard Falk, 'The Making of Global Citizenship', in Jeremy Brecher, John Brown Childs and Jill Cutler (eds.), *Global Visions: Beyond the New World Order*, Montreal: Black Rose Books, 1992, pp. 39–52.

[17] For an engaging and relevant analysis, see Obi, 'Global, State and Local Interactions'.

[18] Saskia Sassen, 'Neither Global Nor National: Novel Assemblages of Territory, Authority and Rights', *Ethics and Global Politics*, 1 (1–2) (2008): 62.

from broader political considerations and democratic accountability and for norm-making to be in the interest of the few rather than the many. As we saw in the case of the Cape Town CCID, for example, the internal utility logics of such assemblies – in this case, particular visions of crime and insecurity, and strategies for countering them – can yield powerful and effective concentrations of resources in the pursuit of clearly defined security goals. Judged on its own terms, the CCID can be deemed relatively successful, yet it is also a constellation that systematically empowers some actors, disempowers others and marginalizes wider considerations and constituencies – simultaneously making political debate over security more difficult and unlikely.

At the same time, assemblages are not hermetically sealed. Their internal logic is always susceptible to challenges from the outside, as new actors seek to enter the assemblages and thereby change the forms and distribution of capital operating within them. In global security assemblages, this is particularly the case due to the symbolic position of security as a public (and in principle universal) and national good. Actors thus continually struggle to maintain a security assemblage reduced to narrow security logics in the face of others who challenge it, with greater or lesser success, depending on their capital and strategies. Normative narrowing, in other words, is a continual practical achievement and a practice of power, not a fixed characteristic of security assemblages. The various trajectories of these assemblages cannot therefore be predicted a priori but require a careful investigation of the structures and dominant positions and forms of capital underpinning their likely stability or fragility.

A transnational labour campaign against G4S, the world's largest security company, provides an intriguing window on this new deterritorialized political space and struggles against normative narrowing within the security field. Private security is traditionally a notoriously low-paid occupation, and with the merger of Group4 and Securicor in 2004, labour unions became increasingly concerned about the ability of this global giant to drive down wages and labour standards. Arguing that both companies were poor employers (particularly in the USA), the Service Employees International Union (SEIU) mounted a legal challenge to the merger. When this proved unsuccessful, the SEIU, together with the Geneva-based Union Network International (UNI), a federation of more than 900 unions in the service sector, spearheaded a global campaign to allow union rights and improve wages and working conditions for over 500,000 G4S employees.

The campaign led to the formation of the Alliance for Justice at G4S and brought together workers at G4S and their unions across the globe in a demand for living wages, social protection and freedom to organize.[19] The campaign turned the spotlight on a series of unfair dismissals, denials of union rights and failures to comply with national minimum wage conditions. In 2006, it published an alternative annual report – *The High Costs of the Low Road* – detailing the abuses of employees' human rights in the USA, Indonesia, India, Uganda, Malawi and Mozambique, amongst others.[20] In Malawi, the report argued, workers had been granted no leave for five years; in Indonesia, employees had been fired for attempting to organize unions; while in Mozambique wages were so low that guards were unable to afford basic food, let alone school fees for their children. Generally, G4S's workers in Africa were described as 'underpaid, overworked and abused'.[21] During its 'global day of action to end human rights abuses by G4S', the campaign on 12 December 2006 delivered an official complaint to the Organisation for Economic Co-operation and Development (OECD), maintaining that the company was guilty of serious violations of the organization's *Guidelines for Multinational Enterprises*.

Throughout the campaign, the unions stressed G4S's failure to live up to its corporate social responsibility and also contrasted it unfavourably with its main competitor, Securitas. Initially, G4S's

---

[19] All documents and press releases by UNI Global Union were previously available at www.union-network.org/unipropertyn.nsf/eng4s?openpage&start=1 and last accessed 16 December 2008.

[20] Focus on G4S, *The High Costs of the Low Road: Alternative Annual Report*. The report was previously available on the campaign's website www.focusong4s.com, which is no longer active (last accessed 12 August 2006). See also Peter Rosenblum and Catriona Drew, 'The Human Rights of Private Security Firm G4S' (no date or place of publication). Available online at www.norwatch.no/images/stories/NW_dokumenter/g4s-rapport_2008.pdf (accessed 24 June 2010).

[21] UNI Global Union, 'G4S: African Workers – Underpaid, Overworked and Abused'. The use of the language of human rights is instructive here, as is its power; for a series of analyses, see Thomas Risse, Steven C. Ropp and Kathryn Sikkink (eds.), *The Power of Human Rights*, Cambridge: Cambridge University Press, 1999.

response was consistently that these were individual cases requiring attention at the country level. The campaigners, on the other hand, maintained the need for a global solution and global pressure. As part of its strategy, the campaign targeted high-profile actors, including the organizing committees of South Africa's 2010 Football World Cup and the 2012 London Olympics, reminding potential clients of their moral obligations and the risks to their image posed by being involved with a company that, for example, kept '130,000 Indian security workers in poverty'.[22] In June 2008, the Norwegian Pension Fund KLP divested its holdings in G4S, citing concerns over the company's ethical standards.[23] The OECD pursued the SEIU complaint in relation to four countries (Nepal, Congo, Mozambique and Malawi), and, in December 2008, G4S reached a settlement with the OECD's appointed mediator. Shortly afterwards, the company signed a global agreement with UNI Property Services, bringing the campaign to an end. The agreement makes clear that all G4S employees, in over 100 countries, have the right to organize unions in a free and fair atmosphere. The agreement also states that G4S will follow international and national labour laws in its relations with workers.[24]

The campaign of the Alliance for Justice at G4S draws attention to the potentiality of a global political space, where the possibilities of intervention and political action transcend the immediate national locality. In this case, local security guards were able to draw on the resources of a global union network to appeal to international standards of legitimate behaviour, to norms set by international organizations such as the OECD and to mobilize investors such as a Norwegian pension fund in order to influence the actions of a global private security firm. It is highly unlikely that workers in individual countries could have achieved these results in isolation, and their organization into the global federation of UNI, which represents more than 900 unions with over 15.5 million members, clearly provided resources that would

[22] UNI Global Union, 'G4S Keeps Its 130,000 Indian Security Workers in Poverty', 28 May 2008.
[23] KLP, 'KLP Excludes Security Service Provider', 6 March 2008. Available online at www.klpinsurance.com/web/kplno.nsf.doc (accessed 8 March 2008).
[24] UNI Global Union, 'G4S & UNI Sign Global Agreement', 16 December 2008.

not otherwise have been available. It is equally unlikely that this kind of campaign would have been mounted against a national company; G4S's transnational status is precisely what allows local actors to 'extravert' in order to gain influence and to realize their aims.[25] As a global actor, G4S derives significant symbolic capital from being seen to live up to standards of corporate social responsibility and is both more vulnerable and potentially more responsive to such campaigns than smaller, local firms. By virtue of its multiple countries of operations, the company is not only susceptible to pressures from numerous national settings, but disputes and transgressions in any single market can have global repercussions in terms of damage to its international brand recognition and, ultimately, profitability.

The campaign illustrates how, within global assemblages, excluded and marginalized groups may gain political voice by drawing on global networks and forms of symbolic capital (e.g., human rights, corporate social responsibility) that play powerfully in distant locales.[26] In this case, poorly paid local employees were able to utilize a deterritorialized political space to gain global visibility and political voice. Even though their local political marginalization might well persist, this shows how global civil society is often rooted in local practices of daily life and how individual actions centred on concrete localities and struggles can gain force from their ability to engage global audiences and to utilize global discourses and forms of capital. While there should be no illusions that labour rights and minimum wages solve the issue of exploitation and injustice once and for all, it would be similarly naive to deny that the agreement, in the words of UNI,

paves the way for improvements in the lives of hundreds of thousands of workers, including many in the Global South. Improvements in employment conditions and wages negotiated by local unions pursuant to this agreement will have a positive effect not only on the company's employees

[25] Bayart, 'Africa in the World'.
[26] There are affinities here to the processes discussed in Margaret Keck and Katherine Sikkink, *Activists beyond Borders*, though our theoretical approach differs from theirs. For wider analyses, see Robert O'Brien, Anne Marie Goetz, Jan Aart Scholte and Marc Williams (eds.), *Contesting Global Governance: Multilateral Economic Institutions and Global Social Movements*, Cambridge: Cambridge University Press, 2000; Neumann and Sending, '"The International" as Governmentality', p. 698.

but on the security sector overall, on the workers' families, and on the communities in which they live and work.[27]

In this respect, it is instructive that G4S has sought to turn its concessions to the unions into a victory – to transform the issue of labour rights into a form of symbolic capital. The agreement signed in December 2008 is the first global framework agreement signed between a global union and a UK corporation. In the words of Philip Jennings, General Secretary of UNI: 'A global company working with a global union is the way forward for a sustainable business model. Global agreements are an integral part of a genuine corporate social responsibility policy and enable us grow the "triple bottom line" together.'[28] For G4S, this new-found labour harmony and the praise lavished on it by unions can translate into a potential competitive advantage, adding to its symbolic capital vis-à-vis many of its rivals. In many countries, G4S is already the market leader, and the ability to enhance its cultural and symbolic capital as a globally legitimated actor may further strengthen its position, particularly in relation to local companies, which – as we have seen in the case of Kenya – may not be able to live up to the same standards of pay and conditions.[29] Moreover, since the company often serves global clients whose own reputations for corporate social responsibility are potentially at risk from their security arrangements, the agreement provides G4S with important symbolic capital when attempting to secure these, often most lucrative, contracts.

This is not then simply a nice liberal story of spreading global norms, or a neutral process of benign corporate social responsibility. Instead, power is central to an understanding of the campaign, highlighting how certain actors occupy positions within the

---

[27] UNI Global Union, 'G4S & UNI Sign Global Agreement'.
[28] *Ibid.*
[29] As Ronnie Lipschutz has warned, national-level policies remain crucial, and 'projects, campaigns, and codes that do not address the political context within which violations of labor regulations are taking place in specific jurisdictions are likely to have limited effects.' Lipschutz, *Globalization, Governmentality, and Global Politics*, p. 79. As we discussed in Chapter 5 in the context of Nairobi, the question of wages can be a key issue, with many locally based security companies unwilling even to accede to national minimum wage legislation.

field from where they may attempt to assert authoritatively what is appropriate, legitimate and effective. It cannot of course be taken for granted that global political struggles or global 'publics' will emerge, and the ability of actors to act globally and to mobilize capital in a more deterritorialized political landscape remains highly unequal. More powerful actors may be able to utilize global security assemblages as a means of narrowing the political space, defining the terms of engagement within the utility logics of security. Nevertheless, the global public domain remains a field of possibility where claims can be made about the nature of rights, community and political agendas, and global security assemblages can potentially provide the opportunity to use diverse national spheres to impact practices in other jurisdictions. The transnational labour campaign against G4S is an illustration of how productive power operates through distant social relationships and works to 'structure the possible field of action of others' by setting standards of appropriate, effective and legitimate action for states, companies, groups and individuals.[30] Since global private security actors draw part of their power from their legitimacy, they must constantly work to maintain and solidify this symbolic capital in a field where it is rendered particularly ambiguous and potentially fragile due to its contrasting relationship to public authority and the symbolic power of security as a public good. In the case of the campaign, a global PSC was susceptible to strategies and forms of power that targeted precisely that legitimacy and challenged the narrow security logics of the assemblages. It is not inconceivable that similar struggles for increased security could be mobilized, especially in cases where the involvement of global private actors has exclusionary effects. In the case of the Niger Delta, for example, Cyril Obi has observed how the ability to appeal to international audiences has on occasion strengthened the voice of local communities vis-à-vis the state and the oil companies, and, in the present situation, it is clear that PSCs are very much aware of the potential risks to their involvement in this politically difficult environment.[31]

---

[30] Michel Foucault, 'The Subject and Power', in Michel Foucault, 'The Subject and Power', in *Michel Foucault: Beyond Structuralism and Hermeneutics*, edited by Hubert L. Dreyfus and Paul Rabinow, University of Chicago Press, 1983, pp. 208–228.
[31] Obi, 'Global, State and Local Interactions'.

The public good in global assemblages

The idea of the state's monopoly of legitimate violence, and of security as a quintessentially public good, is deeply ingrained in the modern political imagination, and its eventual achievement has become part of almost teleological visions of state formation, state-building and development in the West and beyond.[32] Against this backdrop, the contemporary resurgence of private security can seem inescapably fragmenting, an intrinsic erosion of the social and political order leading to increased polarization between rich and poor. This is a powerful narrative in current debates, where the power of concepts and categories tightly tied to the symbolic power of the modern state support the seemingly obvious view that since security is a – if not the – core function of the state, its privatization is both a symbol and a cause of decreased social cohesion and governmental legitimacy. From this perspective, security privatization is part of a 'downward spiral' and even an indicator (or cause) of incipient state failure.[33]

These are important concerns, and they are not to be dismissed lightly. The security implications of predatory warlord politics or the violent entrepreneurship of mafias and gangs provide clear warnings of the possible dangers accompanying privatization, and the ease with which initiatives of order and crime control can transmogrify into new forms of violence and predation cannot be ignored.[34] Nor should it be forgotten that commercial security follows the lines of wealth and can solidify and produce socio-economic divisions. Recognizing the assembled nature of the security field, however, complicates any straightforward causal logic from privatization to fragmentation and social disintegration and requires instead a nuanced and careful analysis of the relationship between security and the state, as well as a recognition that the social and the public may be differently assembled in different settings.

An important step in this direction has been provided by Ian Loader and Neil Walker.[35] Loader and Walker reject any naive identification

---

[32] David Slansky, 'Private Police and Democracy'.
[33] For an instructive example, see *Human Security for an Urban Century*, p. 26.
[34] For a recent study of these dynamics, see Kristof Titeca, 'The "Masai" and Miraa: Public Authority, Vigilance and Criminality in a Ugandan Border Town', *Journal of Modern African Studies*, 47 (2) (2009): 291–317.
[35] Loader and Walker, *Civilizing Security*.

of security with the state – as they note, any realistic assessment of contemporary security must recognize the substantial, real and potential threats posed to populations by their own governments in the name of 'security'. Nonetheless, they argue, it is equally essential to acknowledge that security is important not just as an entitlement or a right of citizenship, but as a constitutive good. A common sense of security as a public good is, they maintain, part of the 'structure of feeling' through which members of a community perceive their security as mutual. As such, security is an essential element of political community and social solidarity, and the general provision of security to all as a public good is not simply an instrument of order – it is a constitutive dimension (and value) of a viable social order. Without the 'civilizing' role played by public security, these constitutive features of a political community are undermined and, with them, both social cohesion and the substantial provision of security itself. In this view, various types of private security may have roles to play within a broadly pluralized structure of provision, but this must be an 'anchored pluralism' with the state and public authorities at its core, so as not to undermine social stability, institutional legitimacy and political community.

The global security assemblages examined in this book demonstrate both the complexity of the constitutive role of security and the challenges presented by private security in settings where liberal-democratic structures may be either absent or differently practised. In countries where the state is frequently predatory or ineffective, the symbolic position of the public and its relationship to security is necessarily part of a complex field whose functioning cannot be posited a priori. The anchoring role of public security actors is premised upon their symbolic power – upon their *recognized* status as agents of a non-discriminatory public good. One of the merits of seeing security as a field constituted by different relations of capital and forms of recognition, however, is that it captures the possibility that in some settings public security actors may not be recognized as agents of the public good.[36] In countries where state security has often been very

---

[36] As we argued in Chapter 3, public agents must continually reproduce their status as recognized agents of the public good and thereby mobilize the power connected to it. This issue is not by any means specific to developing societies, even though the institutional trajectories obviously differ.

limited in its reach, and oppressive in its actions, people may not see the 'public' provision of security, or the lack thereof, in the way suggested by an ideal-typical model of state–sovereignty–security.

This is not to say that many people might not wish that public provision was better, or that they might not prefer it to privatized solutions – if such an ideal state existed.[37] It does, however, indicate the possibility of different relationships between security, the social and 'structures of feeling'. As Bruno Latour has forcefully argued, 'the social' is not something we can assume to exist, either as a cause or as some pre-existing entity to be solidified or eroded.[38] Instead, the social is assembled through practices – including security practices, and the challenge is to see how this takes place within specific fields in specific settings.

Where the legitimacy of the state in the security field is already under question, the provision of security by private actors need not necessarily be socially corrosive. Instead, it can be stabilizing and conservative, preserving the existing social and political order. Clearly, this is far from an unmitigated blessing. While it may provide security to some otherwise vulnerable parts of the population, it can also contribute directly and indirectly to continuing inequality and exploitation, allowing elites to continue to disregard the provision of public security in part because their own security and economic reproduction is bolstered by private force and because the lack of effective public security does not yield rampant insecurity in society as a whole, its inadequacies being to some degree compensated for by private provision.[39] Deeply entrenched social divisions, however politically and morally troubling, need not lead automatically to ever-increasing state delegitimation and social fragmentation, and social forces can

---

[37] Although, for a different suggestion, see Baker, *Multi-Choice Policing*.

[38] Bruno Latour, *Reassembling the Social*, Oxford: Oxford University Press, 2005; for an interesting discussion of the relationship between Latour's form of network theory and different approaches to global governmentality, see Kendall, 'Global Networks, International Networks, Actor Networks'.

[39] It is frequently assumed that the increased presence of private security will lead to a decrease in support for public policing (and taxation to fund it). As a general empirical claim this requires further investigation. In the four countries discussed in this book, we encountered no clear and unequivocal signs of decreased pressure to strengthen and improve the police. Within these global assemblages, civil society, international development donors and human rights activists continue to demand a more effective and democratic police, and, if anything, with the merger of development and security, these pressures have escalated in recent years.

be balanced in such a way as to prevent a 'downward spiral' from privatization, to fragmentation, to state collapse.

As we have argued, the emergence of global security assemblages represents a reconfiguration of the relationship between the public and the private, and the abilities of actors to mobilize diverse forms of capital produces a more deterritorialized political space. The ability of both state and other social actors to engage the capacities of global private security providers may well alter power relations, and hence the strategies and outcomes of struggles in the security field, with wider political implications. Some of the most astute analyses of PMCs in Africa have, for example, stressed how state actors have sometimes been able to draw on external private military support in order to bolster their positions and gain a degree of autonomy from domestic structures and competitors.[40] The pervasive growth of commercial security holds a similarly intriguing, yet potentially quite different, set of possibilities. Here, the embedding of private security in the social makes this process of 'extraversion' available to a wide variety of actors, public and private. This may strengthen neo-patrimonial state elites, but it may also shift the relationship between the state and other elements of society as the latter are able to loosen the role of the state in security provision. Importantly, this does not happen outside the structures of the state: it is embedded in the social and the legal and may well involve the participation of elements of the public security forces. But it nonetheless shifts the relative positions of actors within the security field, altering the context of political contestation. The rationalities of rule and coercion and the possible sociologies and trajectories of state formation are thus more diverse than can be captured in a too-linear logic from privatization to state collapse.

Like so much in the realm of security privatization, these issues raise difficult challenges, and the complex imbrication of global and local, public and private in contemporary security assemblages requires analytic attention and political engagement. As the best dialogues on these questions exhibit, this means resisting too easy a retreat to the safe and cosy language of condemnation, to assumptions about the virtues of public security and to abstract moralizing.[41] Making cogent

---

[40] Reno, *Warlord Politics*.
[41] Again, see the engaged critique of Johnston and Shearing in Loader and Walker, *Civilizing Security*.

judgements about the consequences of global security assemblages in concrete settings is difficult. It requires challenging many of the constitutive analytic and evaluative categories through which social life has traditionally been understood and demands that we explore the complex ways in which private security is connected to social, economic and political structures and dynamics that cross conventional analytic, ethical and political boundaries. Even if the neo-liberal state may seem to be on the retreat in the face of recent crises, private security continues to expand – its logics firmly entrenched in social, individual and global practices and discourses. The question of security and security politics beyond the state is thus likely to be of ever-greater significance in years to come.

Bibliography

Abdulla, Ibrahim (1997) 'Bush Path to Destruction: The Origin and Character of the Revolutionary United Front (RUF-SL)', *Africa Development*, 22 (3/4): 45–76.

Abrahamsen, Rita (2000) *Disciplining Democracy*, London: Zed Books.

(2005) 'Blair's Africa: The Politics of Securitization and Fear', *Alternatives*, 30 (1): 55–80.

Abrahamsen, Rita and Michael C. Williams (2004) *The Globalisation of Private Security: Country Report: Sierra Leone*, Aberystwyth: University of Wales, Aberystwyth. Available online at http://users.aber. ac.uk/rbh/privatesecurity/index.html.

(2005) *The Globalisation of Private Security: Country Report: Kenya*, Aberystwyth: University of Wales, Aberystwyth. Available online at http://users.aber.ac.uk/rbh/privatesecurity/index.html.

(2005) *The Globalisation of Private Security: Country Report: Nigeria*, Aberystwyth: University of Wales, Aberystwyth. Available online at http://users.aber.ac.uk/rbh/privatesecurity/index.html.

(2006) 'Privatisation, Globalisation and the Politics of Protection in South Africa', in Jef Huysmans, Andrew Dobson and Raia Prokhovnik (eds.), *The Politics of Protection: Sites of Insecurity and Political Agency*, London and New York: Routledge, pp. 34–47.

(2006) 'Security Sector Reform: Bringing the Private In', *Conflict, Security and Development* 6 (1): 1–23.

Abrahamsen, Rita, Don Hubert and Michael C. Williams (eds.) (2009) 'Special Issue on Urban Insecurities ', *Security Dialogue*, 40 (4/5).

Agnew, John (1994) 'The Territorial Trap: The Geographical Assumptions of International Relations Theory', *Review of International Political Economy*, 1 (1): 53–80.

Agnotti, Thomas (1997) 'A Metropolis of Enclaves: Image and Reality in Urban North America', *Urbana* 22: 13–24.

Aiyetan, Dayo (2004) 'And the Navy Lied', *Tell magazine*, 39: 12–15.

Ajulu, Rok (1998) 'Kenya's Democracy Experiment: The 1997 Elections', *Review of African Political Economy*, 25 (76): 275–85.

Akinyele, Rufus T. (2001) 'Ethnic Militancy and National Stability in Nigeria: A Case Study of the Oodua People's Congress', *African Affairs*, 100 (401): 623–40.

Albert, D. (2004) 'New Security Company Identifies Niche Market', *Security Focus*, 22 (1): 56.

Alie, Joe (2005) 'The Kamajor Militia in Sierra Leone: Liberators or Nihilists?' in David Francis (ed.), *Civil Militia: Africa's Intractable Security Menance?* London: Ashgate, pp. 51–70.

Allen, F. A. (1981) *The Decline of the Rehabilitative Ideal: Penal Policy and Social Purpose*, New Haven, Conn.: Yale University Press.

Amnesty International (2008) *Nigeria: Amnesty International Report 2008*, New York: Amnesty International.

(2008) 'Nigeria: Pragmatic Policing through Extra-Judicial Executions and Torture', New York: Amnesty International.

Amoore, Louise and Marieke de Goede (2005) 'Governance, Risk and Dataveillance in the War on Terror', *Crime, Law and Social Change*, 43 (2): 149–73.

Amuta, Chidi (2009) 'Nigeria: A Case for Private Prisons', *This Day* (Lagos), 19 February.

Anderson, David M. (2002) 'Vigilantes, Violence and the Politics of Public Order in Kenya', *African Affairs*, 101 (405): 531–55.

(2005) *Histories of the Hanged: The Dirty War in Kenya and the End of Empire*, New York: Norton.

Anderson, David and David Killingray (eds.) (1991) *Policing the Empire: Government, Authority and Control, 1830–1940*, Manchester: Manchester University Press.

Anderson, D. C. (1995) *Crime and the Politics of Hysteria: How the Willie Horton Story Changed American Justice*, New York: Times Books.

Anderson, Perry (1974) *Lineages of the Absolutist State*, London: Verso.

Andreas, Peter (1997) 'The Rise of the American Crimefare State', *World Policy Journal*, 14 (3): 37–45.

(2000) *Border Games: Policing the US–Mexican Border*, Ithaca, NY: Cornell University Press.

Andreas, Peter and Ethan Nadelmann (2006) *Policing the Globe*, Oxford: Oxford University Press.

Andreas, Peter and Richard Price (2001) 'From War Fighting to Crime Fighting: Transforming the American National Security State', *International Studies Review*, 3 (3): 31–52.

Anheier, Helmut, Mariles Glasius and Mary Kaldor (eds.) (2004) *Global Civil Society: 2004/05*, London: Sage.

Aning, Kwesi, Thomas Jaye and Samuel Ayobi (2008) 'The Role of Private Military Companies in US–African Policy', *Review of African Political Economy*, 35 (118): 613–228.

Appadurai, Arjun (1996) *Modernity at Large*, Minneapolis, Minn.: University of Minnesota Press.

Armstrong, Stephen (2008) *War PLC: The Rise of the New Corporate Mercenary*, London: Faber and Faber.

Arnold, Guy (1999) *Mercenaries: Scourge of the Third World*, London: Palgrave.

Ashcroft, James (2007) *Making a Killing: The Explosive Story of a Hired Gun in Iraq*, London: Virgin Books.

Avant, Deborah (2004) 'Conserving Nature in the State of Nature: The Politics of INGO Policy Implementation', *Review of International Studies*, 30: 361–82.

(2005) *The Market for Force*, Cambridge: Cambridge University Press.

(2007) 'NGOs, Corporations and Security Transformation in Africa', *International Relations*, 21 (2): 143–61.

Avant, Deborah and Virginia Haufler (2009) 'Private Security Strategies and Their Public Consequences: Transnational Organizations in Historical Perspective', paper presented at the workshop on 'Public/ Private Interaction and the Transformation of Global Governance, University of Ottawa, Canada, 5–6 June.

Baker, Bruce (2008) 'Beyond the Tarmac Road: Local Forms of Policing in Sierra Leone and Rwanda', *Review of African Political Economy*, 35 (118): 555–70.

(2008) *Multi-Choice Policing in Africa*, Uppsala: Nordiska Afrikainstitutet.

Barkawi, Tarak (2006) *Globalization and War*, Oxford: Rowman & Littlefield.

Barkawi, Tarak and Mark Laffey (2006) 'The Postcolonial Moment in Security Studies', *Review of International Studies*, 32 (2): 329–52.

Barnett, Michael (2001) 'Authority, Intervention, and the Outer Limits of International Relations Theory', in Thomas Callaghy, Ronald Kassimir and Robert Latham (eds.), *Intervention and Transnationalism in Africa*, Cambridge: Cambridge University Press, pp. 47–65.

Barnett, Michael and Raymond Duvall (2005) *Power and Global Governance*, Cambridge: Cambridge University Press.

(2005) 'Power in International Politics', *International Organization*, 59 (1): 39–75.

Barry, Andrew, Thomas Osborne and Nikolas Rose (eds.) (1996) *Foucault and Political Reason*, London: UCL Press.

Bartelson, Jens (1995) *A Genealogy of Sovereignty*, Cambridge: Cambridge University Press.

Bauman, Zygmunt (1998) *Globalization: The Human Consequences*, Cambridge: Polity.

(2000) *Liquid Modernity*, Cambridge: Polity Press.

Bayart, Jean-François (2000) 'Africa in the World: A History of Extraversion' *African Affairs*, 395 (99): 217–67.

Beal, Jo (2002) *The People behind the Walls: Insecurity, Identity and Gated Communities in Johannesburg*, London: London School of Economics.

Bearpark, Andy and Sabrina Schultz (2007) 'The Private Security Challenge in Africa: Problems and Options for Regulation', in Sabelo Gumedze (ed.), *Private Security in Africa: Manifestations, Challenges and Regulation*, ISS Monograph No. 139, Pretoria: Institute of Security Studies, pp. 73–88.

Beck, Ulrich (1992) *Risk Society: Towards a New Modernity*, London: Sage.

Beckett, Katherine (1997) *Making Crime Pay: Law and Order in Contemporary American Politics*, Oxford: Oxford University Press.

Bennett, Jody Ray (2009) 'India's Private Security Metamorphosis', *ISN Security Watch*, 27 November.

Berg, Julie (2004) 'Private Policing in South Africa: The Cape Town City Improvement District – Pluralisation in Practice', *Society in Transition*, 35 (2): 224–50.

Bernstein, Nina (2010) 'Officials Obscured Truth of Migrant Deaths in Jail: Evidence of Mistreatment Was Routinely Covered Up, Documents Show', *New York Times*, 10 January, p. A1.

Bigo, Didier (2000) 'When Two Become One: Internal and External Securitizations in Europe', in Morten Kelstrup and Michael C. Williams (eds.), *International Relations Theory and the Politics of European Integration*, London and New York: Routledge, pp. 171–204.

(2008) 'Globalised (In)security: The Field and the Ban-Opticon', in Didier Bigo and Anastassia Tsoukala (eds.), *Terror, Insecurity and Liberty: Illiberal Practices of Liberal Regimes after 9/11*, London and New York: Routledge, pp. 5–49.

Blom Hansen, Thomas and Finn Stepputat (eds.) (2001) *States of Imagination: Ethnographic Explorations of the Postcolonial State*, Durham, NC: Duke University Press.

Blundo, Giorgio and Jean-Pierre Olivier De Sardan (eds.) (2006) *Everyday Corruption and the State: Citizens and Public Officials in Africa*, London: Zed Books.

Bock, Derek (2005) 'Cape Town Central City: An Urban Renewal Success Story', Cape Town: Public Powerpoint Presentation.

Börzel, Tanja A. and Thomas Risse (2005) 'Public-Private Partnerships: Effective and Legitimate Tools of Transnational Governance', in Edgar Grande and Louis Pauly (eds.), *Complex Sovereignty* (Toronto: University of Toronto Press), pp. 195–216.

Bourdieu, Pierre (1987) *In Other Words: Essays toward a Reflexive Sociology*, Palo Alto, Calif.: Stanford University Press.

(1991) *Language and Symbolic Power*, edited by John Thompson, Cambridge, Mass.: Harvard University Press.

(1992) *The Logic of Practice*, Cambridge: Polity.

(1999) 'Rethinking the State: Genesis and Structure of the Bureaucratic Field', in George Steinmetz (ed.), *State/Culture: State-Formation after the Cultural Turn*, Ithaca, NY: Cornell University Press, pp. 53–75.

Boutellier, Hans (2000) *Crime and Morality*, Amsterdam: Kluwer Academic Publishers.

Braithwaite, John (2000) 'The New Regulatory State and the Transformation of Criminology', *British Journal of Criminology*, 40 (2): 222–38.

Branch, Daniel and Nic Cheeseman (eds.) (2008) 'Special Issue: Election Fever: Kenya's Crisis', *Journal of Eastern African Studies* 2 (2).

(2009) 'Democratization, Sequencing and State Failure: Lessons from Kenya', *African Affairs*, 108 (430): 1–26.

Briffault, Richard (1999) 'A Government for Our Time? Business Improvement Districts and Urban Governance', *Columbia Law Review*, 99 (2): 366–425.

Brogden, Mike (2003) 'Democratizing Security or Decentralizing Repression? The Ambiguities of Community Policing in Kenya', *African Affairs*, 102 (409): 1–18.

Brogden, Mike and Preeti Nijhar (2005) *Community Policing: National and International Models and Approaches*, London: Willan.

Brogden, Mike and Clifford Shearing (1993) *Policing for a New South Africa*, London and New York: Routledge.

Bryant, G. J. (2000) 'Indigenous Mercenaries in the Service of European Imperialists: The Case of the Sepoys in the Early British Indian Army, 1750–1800', *War in History*, 7 (1): 2–28.

Bryden, Alan (2007) 'Approaching the Privatization of Security from a Security Governance Perspective', in Alan Bryden and Marina Caparini (eds.), *Private Actors and Security Governance*, Berlin: Lit Verlag, pp. 3–22.

Bryden, Alan and Marina Caparini (eds.) (2007) *Private Actors and Security Governance*, Berlin: Lit Verlag.

Buckley, Cara (2007) 'New York Plans Surveillance Veil for Downtown', *New York Times*, 9 July, p. 3.

Burchell, Graham, Colin Gordon and Peter Miller (eds.) (1991) *The Foucault Effect: Studies in Governmentality*, Chicago, Ill.: University of Chicago Press.

Burchett, Wilfred and Derek Roebuck (1977) The *Whores of War: Mercenaries Today*, New York: Penguin Books.

Burger, Marlene and Chandra Gould (2002) *Secrets and Lies: Wouter Basson and South Africa's Chemical and Biological Warfare Programme*, Johannesburg: Zebra.

Burke, Pamela L. (1999) 'Embedded Private Authority: Multinational Enterprises and the Amazonian Indigenous Peoples Movement in Ecuador', in A.Claire Cutler, Virginia Haufler and Tony Porter (eds.), *Private Authority and International Affairs*, Albany, NY: State University of New York Press, pp. 223–56.

Button, Mark (2002) *Private Policing*, London: Willan.

Buur, Lars (2008) 'Democracy and Its Discontents: Vigilantism, Sovereignty and Human Rights in South Africa', *Review of African Political Economy*, 35 (118): 571–84.

Cain, Maureen (2000) 'Orientalism, Occidentalism and the Sociology of Crime', *British Journal of Criminology*, 40 (2): 139–60.

Caldeira, Teresa (2001) *City of Walls: Crime, Segregation and Citizenship in São Paulo*, Berkeley, Calif.: University of California Press.

Callaghy, Thomas, Ronald Kassimir and Robert Latham (eds.) (2001) *Intervention and Transnationalism in Africa*, Cambridge: Cambridge University Press.

Campbell, David (1998) *Writing Security: United States Foreign Policy and the Politics of Identity*, Minneapolis, Minn.: University of Minnesota Press.

Campbell, Greg (2002) *Blood Diamonds*, Boulder, Col.: Westview.

Cauvin, Henri E. (2001) 'Homegrown Guards', *New York Times*, 9 October, p. B3.

Chesterman, Simon and Chia Lenhardt (eds.) (2007) *From Mercenaries to Market: The Rise and Regulation of Private Military Companies*, Oxford: Oxford University Press.

Christensen, Maya and Mats Utas (2008) 'Mercenaries of Democracy: The "Politricks" of Remobilized Combatants in the 2007 General Elections, Sierra Leone', *African Affairs*, 107 (429): 515–39.

Chuang, Jimmy (2007) 'Police Agency Blames Security Company for Heist', *Taipei Times*, 5 January.

Cilliers, Jackie and Peggy Mason (eds.) (1999) *Peace, Profit or Plunder?* Pretoria: Institute of Security Studies.

City Council of Nairobi (n.d.) 'Safer Nairobi Initiative: Making Nairobi Safer – Together We Can', Nairobi: Safer Nairobi Secretariat (Safer Cities brochure).

Clapham, Andrew (2006) *Human Rights Obligations of Non-State Actors*, Oxford: Oxford University Press.

Clark, S. J. G. (1968) *The Congo Mercenary*, Johannesburg: South African Institute of International Affairs, University of Witswatersrand.

Clayton, Anthony and David Killingray (1989) *Khaki and Blue: Military and Police in British Colonial Africa*, Athens, OH: Ohio University Press.

Cockayne, James (2009) 'Regulating Private Military and Security Companies', *Journal of Conflict and Security Law*, 13 (3): 401–28.

Confederation of European Security Services and Institut National de Haute Étude de Sécurité (2008) *Private Security and Its Role in European Security*. White Paper, December. Available online at www. coess.org/pdf/coess-inhes_white_paper-private_security.pdf (accessed 9 April 2009).

Commonwealth Human Rights Initiative (2006) *The Police, the People, the Politics: Police Accountability in Kenya*, n.p.: Commonwealth Human Rights Initiative and Kenya Human Rights Commission.

Cornia, Giovanni Andrea, Richard Jolly and Francis Stewart (eds.) (1987) *Adjustment with a Human Face*, Oxford: Clarendon Press.

Cox, Robert (1981) 'Social Forces, States and World Orders: Beyond International Relations Theory', *Millennium*, 10 (2): 126–55.

Coyle, Andrew (2008) 'Prison Privatization in the African Context', *Review of African Political Economy*, 35 (118): 660–5.

Credit Suisse/First Boston (2001) *Review of the South African Private Security Industry*, Boston, 7 February.

Crooks, Ed (2009) 'Shell to Lend Nigeria $3 Billion', *Financial Times*, 20 February.

Cutler, A. Claire (1997) 'Artifice, Ideology and Paradox: The Public/Private Distinction in International Law', *Review of International Political Economy*, 4 (2): 261–85.

    (2003) *Private Power and Global Authority*, Cambridge: Cambridge University Press.

Cutler, A. Claire, Virginia Haufler and Tony Porter (eds.) (1999) *Private Authority and International Affairs*, Albany, NY: State University of New York Press.

Daily Nation (2004) 'Our Unequal Kenya', 27 October.

Dandeker, Christopher (1990) *Surveillance, Power and Modernity: Bureaucracy and Discipline from 1700 to the Present Day*, Cambridge: Polity Press.

Davies, Robert C., Christopher W. Ortiz, Sarah Dadush, Jenny Irish, Arturo Alvarado and Diane Davis (2003) 'The Public Accountability of Private Police: Lessons from New York, Johannesburg, and Mexico City', *Policing and Society*, 13 (2): 197–210.

Davis, Mike (1990) *City of Quartz: Excavating the Future in Los Angeles*, London: Verso.

(2006) *Planet of Slums*, London: Verso.

De Lange, D. (2008) 'Call for Private Security to Fight Crime', *Cape Argus*, 20 May.

De Parle, Jason (2007) 'The American Prison Nightmare', *New York Review of Books*, 12 April, pp. 33–6.

De St Jorre, John (1972) *The Nigerian Civil War*, London: Hodder & Stoughton.

De Silva, N., P., Cowell, T. Chow, and P. Worthington, (2006) 'Prison Population Projection, 2006–2013, England and Wales', *Home Office Statistical Bulletin*, July.

Dean, Mitchell (1999) *Governmentality: Power and Rule in Modern Society*, London: Sage.

(2007) *Governing Societies*, Maidenhead: Open University Press.

Denis, Eric (2006) 'Cairo as Neo-Liberal Capital? From Walled City to Gated Community', in Diane Singerman and Paul Amar (eds.), *Cairo Cosmopolitan: Politics, Culture, and Urban Spaces in the New Middle East*, Cairo: American University in Cairo Press, pp. 47–71.

Desai, Ashwin (2002) *We Are the Poors*, New York: Monthly Review Press.

Dillon, Michael (1996) *The Politics of Security*, London and New York: Routledge.

Dippenaar, Marius De Witt (1988) *The History of the South African Police, 1913–1988*, Pretoria: Promedia.

Dixon, Bill (2007) 'Globalising the Local: A Genealogy of Sector Policing in South Africa', *International Relations*, 21 (2): 163–82.

Dixon, Bill and Janine Rauch (2004) *Sector Policing: Origins and Prospects*, Pretoria: Institute for Security Studies.

Dixon, Bill and Elrena van der Spuy (eds.), *Justice Gained? Crime and Crime Control in South Africa's Transition*, Cape Town: University of Cape Town Press.

Donahue, John D. (1989) *The Privatization Decision: Public Ends, Private Means*, New York: Basic Books.

Donziger, Steven (1996) *The Real War on Crime*, New York: Basic Books.

Douglas, Ian (1999) 'Fighting for Diamonds: Private Military Companies in Sierra Leone', in Jackie Cilliers and Peggy Mason (eds.), *Peace, Profit, or Plunder?* Pretoria: Institute of Security Studies, pp. 175–200.

Douglas, Mary (1994) *Risk and Blame: Essays in Cultural Theory*, London and New York: Routledge.

Drohan, Madelaine (2003) *Making a Killing: How and Why Corporations Use Armed Force to Do Business*, Toronto: Random House.

Duffield, Mark (2001) *Global Governance and the New Wars*, London: Zed Books.

(2007) *Development, Security and Unending War: Governing the World of Peoples*, Cambridge: Polity.

Dupont, Benoît (2004) 'Security in the Age of Networks', *Policing and Society*, 14 (1): 76–91.

(2006) 'Power Struggles in the Field of Security: Implications for Democratic Transformation', in Jennifer Wood and Benoît Dupont (eds.), *Democracy, Society and the Governance of Security*, Cambridge: Cambridge University Press, pp. 86–110.

Elliot, Andrea (2003) 'Stores Fight Shoplifting with Private Security', *New York Times*, 17 June.

Ellis, Stephen (1999) 'The New Frontiers of Crime in South Africa', in Jean-François Bayart, Stephen Ellis and Beatrice Hibou (eds.), *The Criminalization of the State in Africa*, Oxford: James Currey Publishers, pp. 49–68.

Englund, Harri (2006) *Prisoners of Freedom: Human Rights and the African Poor*, Berkeley, Calif.: University of California Press.

Ericson, Richard and Kevin Haggerty (1997) *Policing the Risk Society*, Oxford: Oxford University Press.

Evans, Stephen (2004) 'Private Wars Need New Laws', *BBC News*, 10 May.

Falk, Richard (1992) 'The Making of Global Citizenship', in Jeremy Brecher, John Brown Childs and Jill Cutler (eds.), *Global Visions: Beyond the New World Order*, Montreal: Black Rose Books, pp. 39–52.

Falkner, Robert (2003) 'Private Environmental Governance and International Relations: Exploring the Links', *Global Environmental Politics*, 3 (2): 72–87.

Fanthorpe, Richard (2001) 'Neither Citizen Nor Subject? "Lumpen" Agency and the Legacy of Native Administration in Sierra Leone', *African Affairs*, 100 (400): 363–86.

Fanthorpe, Richard and Ray Maconachie (2010) 'Beyond the "Crisis of Youth": Mining, Farming and Civil Society in Post-War Sierra Leone', *African Affairs*, 109 (435) 251–72.

FDI Magazine (2001) 'South African Security Sector Wins Bill Reprieve', 2 November.

Ferguson, James (2006) *Global Shadows: Africa in the Neoliberal World Order*, Durham, NC: Duke University Press.

Ferguson, James and Akil Gupta (2002) 'Spatializing States: Towards an Ethnography of Neoliberal Governmentality', *American Ethnologist*, 29 (4): 981–1002.

Fickling, David (2009) 'G4S Leapfrogs Rival on Revenue', *Financial Times*, 10 March.

Fofana, Lansana (2008) 'Sierra Leone: Activists Cry Foul over Mining Policy', *Inter Press Service*, 26 August. Available online at http:// ipsnews.net/africa/nota.asp?idnews=43679 (accessed 24 June 2010).

Foreign Policy (2008) 'The List: Murder Capitals of the World', September.

Foucault, Michel (1970) *The Order of Things: An Archaeology of the Human Sciences*, New York: Pantheon.

    (1983) 'The Subject and Power', in Michel Foucault: Beyond Structuralism and Hermeneutics, edited by Hubert L. Dreyfus and Paul Rabinow: University of Chicago Press, pp. 208–228.

    (1991) 'Governmentality', in The Foucault Effect: Studies in Governmentality, edited by Graham Burchell, Colin Gordon and Peter Miller: University of Chicago Press, pp. 87–104.

Frynas, Jedrzej George (2000) *Oil in Nigeria: Conflict and Litigation between Oil Companies and Village Communities*, Berlin: Lit Verlag.

    (2001) 'Corporate and State Responses to Anti-Oil Protests in the Niger Delta', *African Affairs*, 100 (398): 27–54.

Gamble, Andrew (1988) *The Free Economy and the Strong State: The Politics of Thatcherism*, Basingstoke: Macmillan.

Garland, David (1990) *Punishment and Modern Society*, Oxford: Clarendon Press.

    (1996) 'The Limits of the Sovereign State: Strategies of Crime Control in Contemporary Society', *British Journal of Criminology*, 36 (4): 445–71.

    (2001) *The Culture of Control: Crime and Social Order in Contemporary Society*, Oxford: Oxford University Press.

Gberie, Lansana (2005) *A Dirty War in West Africa: The RUF and the Destruction of Sierra Leone*, Indianapolis, Ind.: Indiana University Press.

Germain, Randall D. (ed.) (2000) *Globalization and Its Critics: Perspectives from Political Economy*, Basingstoke: Palgrave Macmillan.

Gerth, H. H. and C. Wright Mills (eds.) (1958) *From Max Weber: Essays in Sociology*, Oxford: Oxford University Press.

Giddens, Anthony (1990) *Consequences of Modernity*, Cambridge: Polity.

Gie, Janet and Craig Haskins (2007) *Crime in Cape Town, 2001–7*, Cape Town: Strategic Information Branch.

Gill, Steven (2003) 'Globalization, Market Civilization and Disciplinary Neo-Liberalism', in Steven Gill (ed.), *Power and Resistance in the New World Order*, Basingstoke: Macmillan, pp. 116–42.

Gimode, Edwin E. (2007) 'The Role of the Police in Kenya's Democratisation Process', in Godwin R. Murunga and Shadrack Wanjala Nasong'o (eds.), *Kenya: The Struggle for Democracy*, London: Zed Books, pp. 227–60.

Githongo, John (2005) 'Report on Kenyan Corruption', available online at http://news.bbc.co.uk/2/hi/africa/4697612.stm (accessed 24 June 2010).

Goldsmith, Stephen and William D. Eggers (2004) *Governing by Network: The New Shape of the Public Sector*, Washington, DC: Brookings Institution.

Goodenough, Cheryl and Jenny Irish (2002) *Owning Safety: A Profile of Community Initiatives*, Durban: Independent Project Trust.

Gordenker, Leon and Thomas G. Weiss (1996) 'Pluralizing Global Governance: Analytical Approaches and Developments', in Leon Gordenker and Thomas G. Weiss (eds.), *NGOs, the UN and Global Governance*, Boulder, Col.: Lynne Reinner, pp. 17–47.

Gore, Charles and David Pratten (2003) 'The Politics of Plunder: The Rhetoric of Order and Disorder in Southern Nigeria', *African Affairs*, 102 (407): 211–40.

Gould, Jeremy (ed.) (2006) *The New Conditionality: The Politics of Poverty Reduction Strategies*, London: Zed Books.

Gounev, Philip (2006) 'Bulgaria's Private Security Industry', in Alan Bryden and Marina Caparini (eds.), *Private Actors in Security Governance*, Berlin: Lit Verlag, pp. 109–28.

Graham, Stephen (ed.) (2004) *Cities, War, and Terrorism*, Oxford: Blackwell.

Grande, Edgar and Louis W. Pauly (eds.) (2006) *Complex Sovereignty*, Toronto: University of Toronto Press.

Greenwood, Gavin (2008) 'The Thin Black Line', *G4S International*, June, pp. 17–20.

Group4Securicor (2008) *Annual Report and Accounts 2008: Securing Your World*, London: Group4Securicor.

Guild, Elspeth and Joanne Van Selm (eds.) (2005) *International Migration and Security: Opportunities and Challenges*, London and New York: Routledge.

Gunn, J. A. W. (1969) *Politics and the Public Interest in the Seventeenth Century*, London: Routledge & Kegan Paul.

Guyer, Jane I. (1992) 'Representation without Taxation: An Essay on Democracy in Rural Nigeria, 1952–1990', *African Studies Review*, 35 (1): 41–80.

Hacking, Ian (1990) *The Taming of Chance*, Cambridge: Cambridge University Press.

Haggerty, Kevin D. and Richard V. Ericson, 'The Surveillant Assemblage', *British Journal of Sociology* 51 (4) (2000): 605–22.

Hall, Rodney B. and Thomas Bierstecker (eds.) (2002) *The Emergence of Private Authority in Global Governance*, Cambridge: Cambridge University Press.

(2002) 'The Emergence of Private Authority in the International System', in Rodney B. Hall and Thomas Bierstecker (eds.), *The Emergence of Private Authority in Global Governance*, Cambridge: Cambridge University Press, pp. 1–21.

(2002) 'Private Authority as Global Governance', in Rodney B. Hall and Thomas Bierstecker (eds.), *The Emergence of Private Authority in Global Governance*, Cambridge: Cambridge University Press, pp. 203–22.

Harrison, Graham (2004) *The World Bank and Africa: The Construction of Governance States*, London and New York: Routledge.

Held, David and Anthony McGrew (2002) *Globalization/Anti-Globalization*, Cambridge: Polity.

(2002) 'Introduction', in David Held and Anthony McGrew (eds.), *Governing Globalization: Power, Authority, and Global Governance*, Cambridge: Polity, pp. 1–22.

Henry, Leroy, Giles Mohan and Helen Yanacopulos (2004) 'Networks as Transnational Agents of Development', *Third World Quarterly*, 25 (5): 839–55.

Hibou, Beatrice (1999) 'The Social Capital of the State as an Agent of Deception, or the Ruses of Economic Intelligence', in Jean-François Bayart, Stephen Ellis and Beatrice Hibou (eds.), *The Criminalization of the State in Africa*, Cambridge: James Currey Publishers, pp. 69–112.

Higgott, Richard, Geoffrey Underhill and Andreas Bieler (eds.) (2000) *Non-State Actors and Authority in the Global System*, London and New York: Routledge.

Hills, Alice (2000) *Policing Africa: Internal Security and the Limits of Liberalization*, Boulder, Col.: Lynne Reinner.

(2007) 'Police Commissioners, Presidents and the Governance of Security', *Journal of Modern African Studies*, 45 (3): 403–23.

Hindess, Barry (1998) 'Neoliberalism and the National Economy', in Mitchell Dean and Barry Hindess (eds.), *Governing Australia: Studies in Contemporary Rationalities of Government*, Cambridge: Cambridge University Press, pp. 126–7.

Hirst, Paul and Grahame Thompson (1996) *Globalization in Question*, Cambridge: Polity Press.

Hoffman, Danny (2007) 'The Meaning of a Militia: Understanding the Civil Defence Forces in Sierra Leone', *African Affairs*, 126 (425): 639–62.

Hönke, Jana (forthcoming) 'Transnationalised Pockets of Territoriality: Western Mining Companies and Security Governance in Katanga (DRC)', *Politique Africaine*.

Hough, Mike (2002) 'Private and Public Security in the RSA: Competition or Cooperation?' *Strategic Review for Southern Africa*, 24 (2): 78–96.

Howe, Herbert M. (2001) *Ambiguous Order: Military Forces in African States*, Boulder, Col.: Lynne Rienner Publishers.

Hsu, Spencer S. and Sylvia Moreno (2007) 'US: Border Policy's Success Strains Resources: Tent City in Texas among Immigrant Holding Sites Drawing Criticism', *Washington Post*, 2 February.

Human Rights Watch (1993) *Divide and Rule: State Sponsored Ethnic Violence in Kenya*, New York: Human Rights Watch.

  (1999) *The Price of Oil: Corporate Responsibility and Human Rights Violations in Nigeria's Oil Producing Communities*, New York: Human Rights Watch.

  (2004) *Nigeria's 2003 Elections: The Unacknowledged Violence*, New York: Human Rights Watch.

Humansecurity-Cities.org (2007) *Human Security for an Urban Century*. Available online at www.interpeace.org/pdfs/Publications_(PDF)/ Current_Reports/Human-Security-for-an-Urban-Century.pdf (accessed 24 June 2010).

Huysmans, Jef (2006) *The Politics of Insecurity*, London and New York: Routledge.

International Crisis Group (2008) *Sierra Leone: A New Era of Reform?* Africa Report 143. Abuja, Dakar and Brussels: International Crisis Group, 31 July.

  (2009) *Nigeria: Seizing the Moment in the Niger Delta*, Africa Briefing No. 60, Abuja, Dakar and Brussels: International Crisis Group, 30 April.

Irish, Jenny (1999) *Policing for Profit: The Future of South Africa's Private Security Industry*, Pretoria: Institute for Security Studies.

Isenberg, David (2008) *Shadow Force: Private Security Contractors in Iraq*, New York: Praeger.

Jacobs, Jane (1961) *The Death and Life of Great American Cities*, New York: Modern Library.

Jensen, Steffen (2001) 'The Battlefield and the Prize: ANC's Bid to Reform the South African State', in Thomas Blom Hansen and Finn Stepputat (eds.), *States of Imagination: Ethnographic Explorations of the Postcolonial State* (Durham, NC: Duke University Press), pp. 97–122.

Johnston, Les (1992) *The Rebirth of Private Policing*, London and New York: Routledge.

  (2000) *Policing Britain: Risk, Security and Governance*, Harlow: Longman.

(2000) 'Transnational Private Policing', in J. W. E. Sheptycki (ed.), *Issues in Transnational Policing*, London and New York: Routledge, pp. 21–42.

(2006) 'Transnational Security Governance', in Jennifer Wood and Benoît Dupont (eds.), *Democracy, Society and the Governance of Security*, Cambridge: Cambridge University Press, pp. 33–51.

(2008) 'Glocal Heroes: Transnational Commercial Security Companies in the 21st Century', paper presented at the workshop on 'New Economies of Security', Merton College, Oxford, 3–4 July.

Johnston, Les and Clifford Shearing (2005) *Governing Security*, London and New York: Routledge.

Jones, Trevor and Tim Newburn (1998) *Private Security and Public Policing*, Oxford: Clarendon Press.

(eds.) (2006) *Plural Policing: A Comparative Perspective*, London and New York: Routledge.

Joseph, Jonathan (2010) 'The Limits of Governmentality: Social Theory and the International', *European Journal of International Relations*, 16 (2): 223–46.

Joseph, Richard A. (1983) 'Class, State, and Prebendal Politics in Nigeria', *Journal of Commonwealth and Comparative Politics*, 21 (3): 21–38.

(1987) *Democracy and Prebendal Politics in Nigeria: The Rise and Fall of the Second Republic*, Cambridge: Cambridge University Press.

Kagwanja, Peter (2003) 'Facing Mount Kenya or Facing Mecca? The Mungiki, Ethnic Violence and the Politics of the Moi Succession in Kenya, 1987–2002', *African Affairs*, 102 (406): 25–50.

Kamensy, John M. and Thomas J. Burlin (2004) *Collaboration: Using Networks and Partnerships*, Lanham, Md.: Rowman & Littlefield.

Kariuki, John (2004) 'The Cost of Fear: Security Firms' Turnover Tops $400m', *The East African*, 25–31 October.

Karl, Terry Lynn (1997) *The Paradox of Plenty: Oil Booms and Petro-States*, Berkeley, Calif.: University of California Press.

(1999) 'The Perils of the Petro-State: Reflections on the Paradox of Plenty', *Journal of International Affairs*, 53 (1): 31–48.

Katumanga, Musambayi (2005) 'A City under Siege: Banditry and Modes of Accumulation in Nairobi, 1991–2004', *Review of African Political Economy*, 32 (106): 505–20.

Katz, Menachem, Ulrich Bartsch, Harinder Malothra and Milan Cuc (2004) *Lifting the Oil Curse: Improving Petroleum Revenue Management in Sub-Saharan Africa*, Washington, DC: International Monetary Fund.

Keck, Margaret and Katherine Sikkink (1998) *Activists beyond Borders: Advocacy Networks in International Politics*, Ithaca, NY: Cornell University Press.

Keku, Patrick and Tunde Akinbade (2003) *Industrial Security in Nigeria*, Lagos: Authorhouse.

Kemedi, Dimieari Von (2003) 'The Changing Predatory Styles of International Oil Companies in Nigeria', *Review of African Political Economy*, 30 (95): 134–9.

Kendall, Gavin (2004) 'Global Networks, International Networks, Actor Networks', in Wendy Larner and William Walters (eds.), *Global Governmentality: Governing International Spaces*, London and New York: Routledge, pp. 59–75.

Kenya Human Rights Commission (1998) *Killing the Vote: State-Sponsored Violence and the Flawed Elections in Kenya*, Nairobi: Kenya Human Rights Commission.

Kenya National Commission on Human Rights (2007) *Preliminary Report on Alleged Executions of Persons between June and October 2007*, Nairobi: Kenya National Commission on Human Rights.

Kettl, Donald F. (1993) *Sharing Power: Public Governance and Private Markets*, Washington, DC: Brookings.

—— (2000) *The Global Public Management Revolution: A Report on the Transformation of Governance*, Washington, DC: Brookings.

Kiernan, Victor (1998) *Colonial Empires and Armies: 1815–1960*, Stroud: Sutton.

Kinsey, Christopher (2006) *Corporate Soldiers and International Security*, London and New York: Routledge.

Kipling, Rudyard (1990) 'Recessional', in *The Complete Verse*, London: Kyle Cathie Limited. First published 1897.

Kirsch, Max (ed.) (2006) *Inclusion and Exclusion in the World Economy*, London and New York: Routledge.

Knight, James and Katrina Mason (2007) 'Interview: Sierra Rutile to Be No. 1 in Three Years', *Reuters Business and Finance*, 4 April.

Kohli, Atul (2004) *State-Directed Development: Political Power and Industrialization in the Global Periphery*, Princeton, NJ: Princeton University Press.

Krahmann, Elke (2003) 'Conceptualizing Security Governance', *Cooperation and Conflict*, 38 (1): 5–26.

—— (2005) 'From State to Non-State Actors: The Emergence of Security Governance', in Elke Krahmann (ed.), *New Threats and New Actors in International Security*, Basingstoke: Palgrave Macmillan, pp. 1–21.

Kynoch, Gary (2005) 'Crime, Conflict and Politics in Transition-Era South Africa', *African Affairs*, 104 (416): 493–514.

Landman, Karina and Martin Schönteich (2002) 'Urban Fortresses: Gated Communities as a Reaction to Crime', *African Security Review*, 11 (4): 71–85.

Larner, Wendy and Richard Le Heron (2004) 'Global Benchmarking: Participating "at a Distance" in the Globalizing Economy', in Wendy Larner and William Walters (eds.), *Global Governmentality*, London and New York: Routledge, pp. 212–32.

Larner, Wendy and William Walters (eds.) (2005) *Global Governmentality*, London and New York: Routledge.

Latour, Bruno (2005) *Reassembling the Social*, Oxford: Oxford University Press.

Leander, Anna (2005) 'The Power to Construct International Security: On the Significance of Private Military Companies', *Millennium: Journal of International Studies*, 33 (3): 803–26.

Leander, Anna and Rens Van Munster (2007) 'Private Security Contractors in the Debate about Darfur: Reflecting and Reinforcing Neo-Liberal Governmentality', *International Relations*, 21 (2): 201–16.

Leishman, Frank, Barry Loveday and Steven Savage (eds.) (2000) *Core Issues in Policing*, New York: Longman.

Lemanski, Charlotte (2004) 'A New Apartheid? The Spatial Implications of Fear of Crime in Cape Town, South Africa', *Environment and Urbanization*, 16 (2): 101–11.

Lemarchand, René (1992) 'Uncivil States and Civil Societies: How Illusion Became Reality', *Journal of Modern African Studies*, 30 (2): 177–91.

Lewis, Peter (2007) *Growing Apart: Oil, Politics and Economic Change in Indonesia and Nigeria*, Ann Arbor, Mich.: University of Michigan Press.

Lipschutz, Ronnie (2005) *Globalization, Governmentality and Global Politics*, London and New York: Routledge.

Loader, Ian (1997) 'Policing and the Social: Questions of Symbolic Power', *British Journal of Sociology*, 48 (1): 1–18.

(1997) 'Private Security and the Demand for Protection in Contemporary Britain', *Policing and Society*, 7 (3): 143–62.

(1999) 'Consumer Culture and the Commodification of Policing and Security', *Sociology*, 33 (2): 373–92.

(2000) 'Plural Policing and Democratic Governance', *Social and Legal Studies*, 9 (3): 323–45.

Loader, Ian and Neil Walker (2007) *Civilizing Security: Policing and Political Community in a Global Era*, Cambridge: Cambridge University Press.

Lock, Peter (1999) 'Africa, Military Downsizing and Growth in the Security Industry', in Jakkie Cilliers and Peggy Mason (eds.), *Peace, Profit, or Plunder? The Privatization of Security in War-Torn African Societies*, Pretoria: Institute of Security Studies, pp. 11–36.

Low, Setha (2003) *Behind the Gates: Life, Security, and the Pursuit of Happiness in Fortress America*, London and New York: Routledge.

Lubeck, Paul M., Michael J. Watts and Ronnie Lipschutz (2007) *Convergent Interests: US Energy Security and the 'Securing' of Nigerian Democracy*, Washington, DC: Centre for International Policy.

Lyon, David (ed.) (2002) *Surveillance as Social Sorting*, London and New York: Routledge.

Mail & Guardian (Johannesburg) (2006) 'At Long Last, Security Strike Is Over', 22 June.

—— (2006) 'Provident Fund: 57 Guards Killed during Strike', 19 June.

Malan, Mark and Jakkie Cilliers (1997) *Mercenaries and Mischief: The Regulation of Foreign Military Assistance Bill*, Pretoria: Institute for Security Studies.

Malan, Mark, Sarah Meek, Thokozani Thusi, Jeremy Ginifer, and Patrick Coker (2003) *Sierra Leone: Building the Road to Recovery*, Pretoria: Institute for Security Studies.

Mancini, Francesco (2006) *In Good Company: The Role of Business in Security Sector Reform*, London: Demos.

Mandela, Nelson (1995) 'Address of President Nelson Mandela on the Occasion of the Opening of the Second Session of the Democratic Parliament', Cape Town, 17 February.

Mandel, Robert (2002) *Armies without States: The Privatization of Security*, Boulder, Col.: Lynne Reinner.

Manning, Peter K. (2006) 'The United States of America', in Trevor Jones and Tim Newburn (eds.), *Plural Policing: A Comparative Perspective*, London and New York: Routledge, pp. 98–125.

Marais, Hain (2001) *Limits to Change*, London: Zed Books.

Maroga, Millicent (2003) 'Two Sides of the Same Coin? Sector Policing and Community Policing Forums', *SA Crime Quarterly*, 6: 13–16.

Mazerolle, Lorraine, and Janet Ransley (2005) *Third Party Policing*, Cambridge: Cambridge University Press.

Mbeki, Thabo (2007) 'State of the Nation Address by the President of South Africa', 9 February.

Mbembe, Achille (2001) *On the Postcolony*, Berkeley, Calif.: University of California.

McCaskie, Tom (2008) 'The United States, Ghana and Oil: Global and Local Perspectives', *African Affairs*, 107 (428): 313–32.

McDonald, David A. and John Pape (eds.) (2002) *Cost Recovery and the Crisis of Service Delivery in South Africa*, London: Zed Books.

McDonald, David A. and Laila Smith (2004) 'Privatising Cape Town: From Apartheid to Neo-Liberalism in the Mother City', *Urban Studies*, 41 (8): 1461–84.

McFate, Sean (2008) 'Briefing: US Africa Command – Next Step or Next Stumble?' *African Affairs*, 107 (426): 111–20.

(2008) 'Outsourcing the Making of Militaries: Dyncorp International as Sovereign Agent', *Review of African Political Economy*, 35 (118): 645–54.

McKenzie, Evan (1994) *Privatopia*, New Haven, Conn.: Yale University Press.

McNeil, William H. (1982) *The Pursuit of Power: Technology, Armed Force and Society since A.D. 1000*, Chicago, Ill.: University of Chicago Press.

Meier, Karl (2004) 'Shell "Feeds" Nigeria Conflict, May End Onshore Work', *Bloomberg News Service*, 10 June.

Mills, Greg and John J. Stremlau (eds.) (1999) *The Privatization of Security in Africa*, Pretoria: South African Institute of International Affairs.

Minaar, Anthony (2004) 'Crime Prevention, Partnership Policing and the Growth of Private Security: The South African Experience', paper presented at Policing in Central and Eastern Europe: Dilemmas of Contemporary Criminal Justice, Ljubljana, Slovenia, 23–5 September.

Miraftab, Faranak (2007) 'Governing Post-Apartheid Spatiality: Implementing City Improvement Districts in Cape Town', *Antipode*, 39 (4): 602–26.

Mitchell, Timothy (1999) 'Economy and the State Effect', in George Steinmetz (ed.), *State/Culture: State-Formation after the Cultural Turn*, Ithaca, NY: Cornell University Press, pp. 76–97.

Mittulah, Winnie (2003) 'Nairobi, Kenya: Understanding Slums', in *Global Report on Human Settlements 2003: The Challenges of Slums*, New York: UN-HABITAT, pp. 195–228.

Mockler, Anthony (1969) *The Mercenaries*, New York: Macmillan.

Morn, Frank (1982) *The Eye that Never Sleeps: A History of the Pinkerton National Detective Agency*, Bloomington, Ind.: Indiana University Press.

Mudimbe, Valentin (1988) *The Invention of Africa: Gnosis, Philosophy and the Order of Knowledge*, Bloomington, Ind.: University of Indiana Press.

Mugambi, Kaburu (2007) 'With Training, Govt Hopes to Regulate Private Security', *The Nation* (Nairobi), 21 July.

Muiruri, Stephen (2004) 'How 50 Crimebusters Died in the Line of Duty', *Daily Nation* (Nairobi), 8 November.

Murunga, Godwin R. (2007) 'Governance and the Politics of Structural Adjustment in Kenya', in Godwin Murunga and Shadrack W. Nasong'o (eds.), *Kenya: The Struggle for Democracy*, London: Zed Books, pp. 263–300.

Murunga, Godwin R. and Shadrack W. Nasong'o (eds.) (2007) *Kenya: The Struggle for Democracy*, London: Zed Books.

Musah, Abdel-Fatau (2000) 'A Country under Siege: State Decay and Corporate Military Intervention in Sierra Leone', in Abdel-Fatau Musah and J. Kayode Fayemi (eds.), *Mercenaries: An African Security Dilemma*, London: Pluto, pp. 76–116.

— (2002) 'Privatization of Security, Arms Proliferation and the Process of State Collapse in Africa', *Development and Change*, 33 (5): 911–33.

Musah, Abdel-Fatau and J. Kayode Fayemi (eds.) (2000) *Mercenaries: An African Security Dilemma*, London: Pluto.

Mutheun, Bernadette and Ian Taylor (2002) 'Return of the Dogs of War? The Privatization of Security in Africa', in Rodney B. Hall and Thomas Bierstecker (eds.), *The Emergence of Private Authority in Global Governance*, Cambridge: Cambridge University Press, pp. 183–99.

Nairobi Salama Newsletter (2006) No. 1, February. Nairobi: City Council of Nairobi/Safer Cities Programme.

Nation, the (Nairobi) (2005) 'CID Officers "Embedded" to Private Security Firms Disapprove New Role', 17 April.

National Offender Management Service (2007) 'Prison Population and Accommodation Briefing for 15 June 2007', available online at www.hmprisonservice.gov.uk (accessed 30 June 2007).

Ndlovu-Gatsheni, Sabelo J. (2007) 'Weak States and the Growth of the Private Security Sector in Africa: Whither the African State', in Sabelo Gumedze (ed.), *Private Security in Africa*, Pretoria: Institute of Security Studies, pp. 17–38.

Neocleous, Mark (2008) *Critique of Security*, Edinburgh: Edinburgh University Press.

Neumann, Iver B. and Ole Jacob Sending (2007) '"The International" as Governmentality', *Millennium: Journal of International Studies*, 35 (3): 677–701.

Ngugi, Rose *et al.* (2004) *Security, Risk and Private Sector Growth in Kenya*, Nairobi: Kenya Institute for Public Policy Research and Analysis.

Norton, Richard J. (2003) 'Feral Cities: The New Strategic Environment', *Naval War College Review*, 56 (4): 2–15.

O'Brien, Cyrus (2008) 'The Dynamics of Private Security in Senegal', *Review of African Political Economy*, 35 (118): 655–9.

O'Brien, Robert, Anne Marie Goetz, Jan Aart Scholte and Marc Williams (eds.) (2000) *Contesting Global Governance: Multilateral Economic Institutions and Global Social Movements*, Cambridge: Cambridge University Press.

Obi, Cyril (2001) 'Global, State and Local Interactions: Power, Authority and Conflict in the Niger Delta Oil Communities', in Thomas Callaghy, Ronald Kassimir and Robert Latham (eds.), *Intervention and Transnationalism in Africa*, Cambridge: Cambridge University Press, pp. 173–95.

O'Doherty, J. (2008) 'G4S Hopes to Push the Boat Out More', *Financial Times*, 28 August.

Ogashe, Eghosa E. (1998) *Crippled Giant: Nigeria since Independence*, Bloomington, Ind.: Indiana University Press.

Okonta, Ike and Oronto Douglas (2003) *Where Vultures Feast: Shell, Human Rights and Oil*, London: Verso.

O'Malley, Pat (1992) 'Risk, Power and Crime Prevention', *Economy and Society*, 21 (3): 252–75.

O'Malley, Pat and Darren Palmer (1996) 'Post-Keynesian Policing', *Economy and Society*, 25 (2): 137–55.

Omeje, Kenneth (2006) *High Stakes and Stakeholders: Oil, Conflict and Security in Nigeria*, Aldershot: Ashgate.

Ong, Aihwa and Stephen J. Collier (eds.) (2005) *Global Assemblages: Technology, Politics and Ethics as Anthropological Problems*, Oxford: Blackwell.

Osborne, David and Ted Gaebler (1992) *Reinventing Government*, New York: Addison-Wesley.

Ouko, Otieno (2004) *Research Report on Police Excesses*, Nairobi: Kenya Human Rights Commission.

Owens, Patricia (2008) 'Distinctions, Distinctions: Public and Private Force', *International Affairs*, 85 (5): 977–90.

Palmary, Ingrid (2002) 'Shifting Agendas: Crime Prevention in the Major Cities', in Eric Pelser (ed.), *Crime Prevention Partnerships: Lessons from Practice*, Pretoria: Institute for Security Studies.

Partnership Africa Canada (2004) *Diamond Industry Annual Review, 2004: Sierra Leone 2004*, Ottawa and Freetown: Partnership Africa Canada and Network Movement for Justice and Development.

(2005) *Diamond Industry Annual Review, 2005: Sierra Leone 2005*, Ottawa and Freetown: Partnership Africa Canada and Network Movement for Justice and Development.

(2006) *Diamond Industry Annual Review, 2006: Sierra Leone 2006*, Ottawa and Freetown: Partnership Africa Canada and Network Movement for Justice and Development.

(2008) *Diamonds and Human Security: Annual Review 2008*, Ottawa: Partnership Africa Canada.

Pech, Khareen (1999) 'Executive Outcomes: A Corporate Conquest', in Jakkie Cilliers and Peggy Mason (eds.), *Peace, Profit or Plunder?* Pretoria: Institute of Security Studies, pp. 81–109.

Pelser, Eric (1999) *The Challenge of Community Policing in South Africa*, Pretoria: Institute for Security Studies.

Pelser, Eric and Annette Louw (2002) 'Evaluating Community Safety Forums', in Eric Pelser (ed.), *Crime Prevention Partnerships: Lessons from Practice*, Pretoria: Institute for Security Studies, pp. 103–12.

People's Daily Online (2006) 'China to Beef Up Security Guard Services for Beijing Olympics'. Available online at http://english.peopledaily.com.cn, 20 September 2006.

(2006) 'Security Service Market Ready to Open to Private, Foreign Investors'. Available online at http://english.peopledaily.com.cn, 21 September 2006.

Percy, Sarah (2007) *Mercenaries: History of a Norm in International Relations*, Oxford: Oxford University Press.

(2007) 'Mercenaries: Strong Norm, Weak Law', *International Organization*, 61 (2): 367–97.

Petrie, Ann (2008) 'Top Security', *Business Voice*, April, pp. 34–8.

Pignal, Stanley (2008) 'G4S Hungry for More Buys', *Financial Times*, 13 May.

Polanyi, Karl (1991) *The Great Transformation*, Boston, Mass.: Beacon Press. First published 1944.

Power, Michael (1997) *The Audit Society: Rituals of Verification*, Oxford: Oxford University Press.

Pratten, David (2006) 'The Politics of Vigilance in South-Eastern Nigeria', in Christian Lund (ed.), *Twilight Institutions: Public Authority and Local Politics in Africa*, New York: Wiley, pp. 33–60.

Pratten, David and Atreyee Sen (eds.) (2007) *Global Vigilantes*, Cambridge: Hurst.

Private Security Industry Regulatory Authority of South Africa (2007) *Annual Report 2006/2007*, Pretoria: Private Security Industry Regulatory Authority.

(2009) *Annual Report 2008/2009*, Pretoria: Private Security Industry Regulatory Authority.

Quinlan, J. Michael, Charles W. Thomas and Sherril Gautreaux (2001) 'The Privatization of Correctional Facilities', in Deborah Ballati (ed.), *Privatizing Governmental Functions*, New York: Law Journal Press.

Rasmussen, Jacob (2007) 'Struggling for the City: Evictions in Inner-City Johannesburg', in Lars Buur, Steffen Jensen and Finn Stepputat (eds.), *The Security-Development Nexus: Expressions of Sovereignty and Securitization in Southern Africa*, Uppsala: Nordiska Afrikainstitutet.

Rasmussen, Mikkel (2005) *The Risk Society at War*, Cambridge: Cambridge University Press.

Rawlence, Ben and Chris Albin-Lackey (2007) 'Briefing: Nigeria's 2007 Elections: Democracy in Retreat', *African Affairs*, 106 (424): 497–506.

Reno, William (1995) *Corruption and State Politics in Sierra Leone*, Cambridge: Cambridge University Press.

—— (1996) 'Ironies of Post-Cold War Structural Adjustment in Sierra Leone', *Review of African Political Economy*, 23 (67): 7–18.

—— (1999) *Warlord Politics and African States*, Boulder, Col.: Lynne Rienner.

—— (2004) 'Order and Commerce in Turbulent Areas: 19th Century Lessons, 21st Century Practice', *Third World Quarterly*, 25 (4): 607–25.

Rice, Xan (2009) 'UN Condemns Executions Carried Out by Kenyan Police', *The Guardian*, 25 February, p. 14.

Richards, Paul (1996) *Fighting for the Rainforest: War, Youth and Resources in Sierra Leone*, Oxford: James Currey.

—— (2005) 'To Fight or to Farm? Agrarian Dimensions of the Mano River Conflicts (Liberia and Sierra Leone)', *African Affairs*, 104 (417): 571–90.

Richards, Paul, Steven Archibald, Khadiga Bah and James Vincent (2003) 'Where Have All the Young People Gone? Transitioning Ex-Combatants toward Community Reconstruction after the War in Sierra Leone', unpublished report submitted to the National Commission for Disarmament, Demobilization, and Reintegration, Government of Sierra Leone, February.

Risse, Thomas, Steven C. Ropp and Katheryn Sikkink (eds.) (1999) *The Power of Human Rights*, Cambridge: Cambridge University Press.

Roberts, Adam (2007) *The Wonga Coup: Guns, Thugs, and a Ruthless Determination to Create Mayhem in an Oil-Rich Corner of Africa*, Washington, DC: Public Affairs Publishers.

Ronit, Karsten and Volker Schneider (eds.) (2000) *Private Organizations in Global Politics*, London and New York: Routledge.

Rose, Nikolas (1996) 'The Death of the Social? Re-Figuring the Territory of Government', *Economy and Society*, 23 (5): 327–56.

—— (1996) 'Governing "Advanced" Liberal Democracies', in Andrew Barry, Thomas Osborne and Nikolas Rose (eds.), *Foucault and Political Reason*, London: UCL Press.

Rose, Nikolas and Peter Miller (1992) 'Political Power beyond the State: Problematics of Government', *British Journal of Sociology*, 43 (2): 173–205.

Rosenau, James N. and Ernst Otto Czempiel (eds.) (1992) *Governance without Government: Order and Change in World Politics*, Cambridge: Cambridge University Press.

Rosenblum, Peter and Catriona Drew (n.d.) 'The Human Rights of Private Security Firm G4S'. Available online at www.norwatch.no/images/stories/NW_dokumenter/g4s-rapport_2008.pdf (accessed 24 June 2010).

Ruteere, Mutuma and Marie-Emmanuelle Pommerolle (2003) 'Democratizing Security or Decentralizing Repression? The Ambiguities of Community Policing in Kenya', *African Affairs*, 102 (409): 587–604.

Rutten, Marcel and Alamin Mazrui (eds.) (2001) *Out for the Count: The 1997 General Elections and Prospects for Democracy in Kenya*, Kampala: Fountain Publishers.

Said, Edward (1978) *Orientalism*, New York: Vintage.

Samara, Tony Roshan (2003) 'State Security in Transition: The War on Crime in Post-Apartheid South Africa', *Social Identities*, 9 (2): 277–312.

Sarre, Rick (1994) 'The Legal Basis for the Authority of Private Police and an Examination of Their Relationship with the Public Police', in David Biles and Julia Vernon (eds.), *Private Sector and Community Involvement in the Criminal Justice System*, Canberra: Australian Institute of Criminology, pp. 167–82.

Sassen, Saskia (ed.) (2002) *Global Networks, Linked Cities*, London and New York: Routledge.

(2006) *Territory, Authority, Rights: From Medieval to Global Assemblages*, Princeton, NJ: Princeton University Press.

(2008) 'Neither Global Nor National: Novel Assemblages of Territory, Authority and Rights', *Ethics and Global Politics*, 1 (1–2): 61–79.

Scahill, Jeremy (2007) *Blackwater: The Rise of the World's Most Powerful Mercenary Army*, New York: Nation Books.

Schalkwyk, P. J. (1987) 'Security and the Defense Force: The National Key Points Experience', in R. L. Jackson (ed.), *Security: A National Strategy – The Integration of Security in the Public and Private Sector*, Cape Town: Lex Patria.

Schmitt, Waldemar, Gordon Adler and Els Van Weering (2003) *Winning at Service*, New York: Wiley.

Schönteich, Martin (1999) 'Fighting Crime with Private Muscle: The Private Sector and Crime Prevention', *African Security Review*, 8 (5): 65–75.

(2002) '2001 Crime Trends: A Turning Point?' *SA Crime Quarterly*, 1 July.

(2002) 'South Africa's Private Security Industry', *ERA's Corporate Intelligence Review*, 18 July.

Securicor (2004) 'Focus on Nigeria', *Securicor Magazine*, May, pp. 38–42.

Securitas (2006) *Annual Report*, Stockholm: Securitas.

(2007) *Annual Report*, Stockholm: Securitas.

(2008) *Annual Report*, Stockholm: Securitas.

(2009) *Securitas AB Full Year Report, January–December*, Stockholm: Securitas.

Sending, Ole Jacob and Iver B. Neumann (2006) 'Governance to Governmentality: Analyzing NGOs, States, and Power', *International Studies Quarterly*, 50 (3): 651–72.

Shaw, Mark (2002) *Crime and Policing in Post-Apartheid South Africa*, Bloomington, Ind.: Indiana University Press.

Shaw, Mark and Clifford Shearing (1998) 'Reshaping Security: An Examination of the Governance of Security in South Africa', *African Security Review*, 7 (3): 3–12.

Shearer, David (1998) *Private Armies and Military Intervention*, Oxford: Oxford University Press.

Shearing, Clifford (1992) 'The Relation between Public and Private Policing', in Michael Tonry and Norval Morris (eds.), *Modern Policing*, Chicago, Ill.: University of Chicago Press, pp. 399–434.

Shearing, Clifford and Michael Kempa (2001) 'The Role of "Private Security" in Transitional Democracies', in Mark Shaw (ed.), *Crime and Policing in Political Transition*, Johannesburg: South African Institute of International Affairs, pp. 205–14.

Shearing, Clifford and Phillip Stenning (1981) 'Modern Private Security: Its Growth and Implications', in Michael Tonry and Norval Morris (eds.), *Crime and Justice: An Annual Review of Research*, Chicago, Ill.: University of Chicago Press, pp. 193–245.

Shearing, Clifford and Jennifer Wood (2003) 'Governing Security for Common Goods', *International Journal of the Sociology of Law*, 31 (3): 205–25.

(2003) 'Nodal Governance, Democracy and the New "Denizens"', *Journal of Law and Society*, 30 (3): 400–19.

Shell Petroleum Development Corporation (2002) *2001: People and the Environment – Annual Report*, Lagos: Shell Petroleum Development Corporation.

(2003) *2002: People and the Environment – Annual Report*, Lagos: Shell Petroleum Development Corporation.

Shepherd, Bob (2008) *The Circuit: An Ex-SAS Soldier's True Account of One of the Most Powerful and Secretive Industries Spawned by the War on Terror*, Basingstoke: Macmillan.

Shichor, David (1995) *Punishment for Profit: Private Prisons/Public Concerns*, Thousand Oaks, Calif.: Sage.

Simelane, Hamilton Sipho (2008) 'Security for All? Politics, Economy and the Growth of Private Security in Swaziland', *Review of African Political Economy*, 35 (118): 599–612.

Simon, Jonathan (2006) *Governing through Crime*, Oxford: Oxford University Press.

Simpson, Graeme (2004) '"A Snake Gives Birth to a Snake": Politics and Crime in the Transition to Democracy in South Africa', in Bill Dixon and Elrena van der Spuy (eds.), *Justice Gained? Crime and Crime Control in South Africa's Transition*, Cape Town: University of Cape Town Press, pp. 1–28.

Singer, Peter W. (2003) *Corporate Warriors: The Rise of the Privatized Military*, Ithaca, NY: Cornell University Press.

Slansky, David (2006) 'Private Police and Democracy', *American Criminal Law Review*, 43 (89): 89–105.

Slaughter, Anne-Marie (2004) *A New World Order*, Princeton, NJ: Princeton University Press.

Small Arms Survey (2007) *Guns and the City*, Cambridge: Cambridge University Press.

Small, Michelle (2006) *Privatisation of Security and Military Functions and the Demise of the Modern Nation-State in Africa*, London: ACCORD.

Smillie, Ian, Lansana Gberie and Ralph Hazleton (2000) *The Heart of the Matter: Sierra Leone, Diamonds and Human Security*, Ottawa: Partnership Africa Canada.

Smith, Anna-Marie (2007) 'South Africa: Mother City a Role Model', *Business Day* (Johannesburg), 9 November.

Smith, Michael P. (2001) *Transnational Urbanism: Locating Globalization*, Oxford: Blackwell.

Soares de Oliveira, Ricardo (2007) *Oil and Politics in the Gulf of Guinea*, London: Hurst.

South, Nigel (1984) 'Private Security, the Division of Policing Labor and the Commercial Compromise of the State', *Research in Law, Deviance and Social Control*, 6: 171–98.

(1988) *Policing for Profit*, London: Sage.

Sparks, Richard (1992) *Television and the Drama of Crime: Moral Tales and the Place of Crime in Public Life*, Milton Keynes: Open University Press.

Spitzer, Steven and Andrew Scull (1977) 'Privatization and Capitalist Development: The Case of the Private Police', *Social Problems*, 25 (1): 18–29.

Standing, André (2004) 'Out of the Mainstream: Critical Reflections on Organized Crime in the Western Cape', in Bill Dixon and Elrena Van Der Spuy (eds.), *Justice Gained? Crime and Crime Control in South Africa's Transition*, Cape Town: University of Cape Town Press, pp. 29–57.

Stavrou, Aki (2002) *Crime in Nairobi: Results of a Citywide Victim Survey*, Nairobi: UN-HABITAT.

Stees, John (1998) *Outsourcing Security: A Guide for Contracting Services*, Woburn, Mass.: Butterworth-Heinemann.

Steinberg, Jonny (2001) *Crime Wave: The South African Underworld and Its Foes*, Johannesburg: Witswaterand University Press.

Stoddard, Abby, Adele Harmer, and Victoria Didomenico (2009) *Private Security Contracting in Humanitarian Operations*, London: Overseas Development Institute.

Stoler, Laura Ann and Fredrick Cooper (1997) 'Between Metropole and Colony: Rethinking a Research Agenda', in Fredrick Cooper and Laura Ann Stoler (eds.), *Tensions of Empire: Colonial Cultures in a Bourgeois World*, Berkeley, Calif.: University of California Press, pp. 1–57.

Stone, Diane (2008) 'Global Public Policy, Transnational Policy Communities, and Their Networks', *Policy Studies Journal*, 36 (1): 19–38.

Strange, Susan (1996) *The Retreat of the State*, Cambridge: Cambridge University Press.

Strathern, Marilyn (1995) *Shifting Contexts: Transformations in Anthropological Knowledge*, London and New York: Routledge.

Sylvester, Sylvester E. (2002) 'It's Official: Cape Town Is Clean and Safe', *Cape Argus*, 6 March.

Taljaard, Raenette (2007) 'Implementing South Africa's Regulation of Foreign Military Assistance Act', in Alan Bryden and Marina Caparini (eds.), *Private Actors and Security Governance*, Berlin: Lit Verlag, pp. 167–86.

Tangri, Roger (1999) *The Politics of Patronage in Africa: Parastatals, Privatization and Private Enterprise*, Oxford: James Currey.

Thompson, John (1991) 'Introduction', in Pierre Bourdieu, *Language and Symbolic Power*, edited by John Thompson, Cambridge, Mass.: Harvard University Press, pp. 1–31.

Thomson, Brian (2007) *Sierra Leone: Reform or Relapse? Conflict and Governance Reform*, London: Chatham House, July.

Thomson, Janice (1994) *Mercenaries, Pirates and Sovereigns: State Building and Extraterritorial Violence in Early Modern Europe*, Princeton, NJ: Princeton University Press.

Throup, David (1992) 'Crime, Politics and the Police in Colonial Kenya, 1939–63', in David M. Anderson and David Killingray (eds.), *Policing and Decolonisation: Politics, Nationalism and the Police, 1917–65*, Manchester: Manchester University Press, pp. 127–57.

Tilly, Charles (1985) 'War Making and State Making as Organized Crime', in Peter B. Evans, Dietrich Reuschemeyer and Theda Skocpol (eds.), *Bringing the State Back In*, Cambridge: Cambridge University Press, pp. 169–91.

(1990) *Coercion, Capital, and European States, A.D. 990–1990*, Oxford: Blackwell.

Timmons, Heather (2009) 'Security Guards Become the Front Lines in India', *New York Times*, 3 March, p. A1.

Titeca, Kristof (2009) 'The "Masai" and Miraa: Public Authority, Vigilance and Criminality in a Ugandan Border Town', *Journal of Modern African Studies*, 47 (2): 291–317.

Tomlinson, Richard (1999) 'From Exclusion to Inclusion: Rethinking Johannesburg's Central City', *Environment and Planning A* 31: 1665–78.

Tonkiss, Fran (2001) *Space, the City and Social Theory*, Cambridge: Polity Press.

Toye, John (1987) *Dilemmas of Development*, Oxford: Blackwell.

Transparency International Kenya (2008) *Kenya Bribery Index 2008*. Available online at www.tikenya.org.

Travers, Tony and Jeroen Weimar (1996) *Business Improvement Districts: New York and London,* London: Corporation of London.

Trouillot, Michel-Rolph (2001) 'The Anthropology of the State in the Age of Globalization: Close Encounters of the Deceptive Kind', *Current Anthropology*, 42 (1): 125–38.

Truth and Reconciliation Commission of Sierra Leone (2004) *Final Report*, Freetown.

Turrell, Rob (2004) 'Murder and Capital Punishment after Apartheid', in Bill Dixon and Elrena van der Spuy (eds.), *Justice Gained? Crime and Crime Control in South Africa's Transition*, Cape Town: University of Cape Town Press, pp. 88–113.

Ukiwo, Ukoha (2007) 'From "Pirates" to Militants: A Historical Perspective on Anti-State and Anti-Oil Company Mobilization among the Ijaw of Warri, Western Niger Delta', *African Affairs*, 106 (425): 587–610.

Ungar, Mark (2007) 'The Privatization of Citizen Security in Latin America: From Elite Guards to Neighbourhood Vigilantes', *Social Justice*, 34 (3/4): 20–39.

United Nations (2006) *Third Report of the Secretary General of the UN Integrated Office for Sierra Leone*, 28 November, New York: United Nations.

(2007) *State of the World's Cities, 2006/07*, New York: Earthscan/ UN-HABITAT.

United Nations Office of Nairobi (2005) 'Karibu Kenya: An Orientation Guide for United Nations Staff Working in Kenya'. Available online at www.unon.org/karibukenya (accessed 24 June 2010).

UN Population Fund (2007) *Unleashing the Potential of Urban Growth: State of the World Population 2007*, New York: UN Population Fund.

Van der spuy, Elrena (2000) 'Foreign Donor Assistance and Policing Reform in South Africa', *Policing and Society*, (10): 343–66.

Van de walle, Nicolas (2001) *African Economies and the Politics of Permanent Crisis, 1979–1999*, Cambridge: Cambridge University Press.

Venter, A. J. (1995) 'Executive Outcomes: Mixing Business with Bullets', *Jane's Intelligence Review*, November, pp. 65–8.

Verkuil, Paul (2006) *Outsourcing Sovereignty*, Cambridge: Cambridge University Press.

Vines, Alex (1999) 'Ghurkas and the Private Security Business in Africa', in Jackie Cilliers and Peggy Mason (eds.), *Peace, Profit or Plunder?* Pretoria: Institute of Security Studies, pp. 123–40.

Volkov, Vadim (2002) *Violent Entrepreneurs: The Use of Force in the Making of Russian Capitalism*, Ithaca, NY: Cornell University Press.

Wacquant, Loic (2004) 'Penal Truth Comes to Europe: Think Tanks and the "Washington Consensus" on Crime and Punishment', in George Gilligan and John Pratt (eds.), *Crime, Truth and Justice: Official Inquiry, Discourse, Knowledge*, London: Willan Publishing, pp. 161–80.

(2005) 'The Great Penal Leap Backward: Incarceration in America from Nixon to Clinton', in John Pratt, David Brown, Mark Brown, Simon Hallsworth and Wayne Morrison (eds.) *The New Punitiveness: Current Trends, Theories, Perspectives*, London: Willan, pp. 3–26.

Wairagu, Francis, Jan Kamenju and Mwachofi Singo (2004) *Private Security in Kenya*, Nairobi: Security Research and Information Centre.

Wakefield, Alison (2003) *Selling Security: The Private Policing of Public Space*, London: Willan.

Walker, Andrew (2008) '"Blood Oil" Dripping from Nigeria', *BBC News Africa*, 27 July.

(2008) 'Elusive Peace in Nigeria's Oil Delta', *BBC News*, 18 July.

Walker, R. B. J. (1992) *Inside/Outside: International Relations as Political Theory*, Cambridge: Cambridge University Press.

Wallis, William and Matthew Green (2008) 'UK and Nigeria Aim to Stop Oil Theft', *Financial Times*, 15 July, p. 12.

Wallpaper (2007) 'Nice to CCTV You!' May, pp. 200–5.

Warutere, Peter (2005) *The Goldberg Conspiracy: The Game of Paper Gold, Money and Power*, Pretoria: Institute for Security Studies.

Watts, Michael (2003) 'Development and Governmentality', *Singapore Journal of Tropical Geography*, 24 (1): 6–34.

(2004) 'Resource Curse? Governmentality, Oil and Power in the Niger Delta, Nigeria', *Geopolitics*, 9 (1): 50–80.

Weiss, Linda (1998) *The Myth of the Powerless State*, Ithaca, NY: Cornell University Press.

(ed.) (2003) *States in the Global Economy*: Bringing Democratic Institutions Back In. Cambridge: Cambridge University Press.

Williams, Michael C. (2007) *Culture and Security: Symbolic Power and the Politics of International Security*, London and New York: Routledge.

Wilson, James Q. and George L. Kelling (2004) 'Broken Windows: The Police and Neighbourhood Safety', in Irwin Stelzer (ed.), *Neoconservatism*, New York: Atlantic Books, pp. 151–66.

Wood, Ellen Meikins (1981) 'The Separation of the Economic and the Political in Capitalism', *New Left Review*, 127 (1): 66–95.

Wood, Jennifer and Nancy Cardia (2006) 'Brazil', in Trevor Jones and Tim Newburn (eds.), *Plural Policing: A Comparative Perspective*, London and New York: Routledge, pp. 139–68.

Wood, Jennifer and Benoît Dupont (eds.) (2006) *Democracy, Society and the Governance of Security*, Cambridge: Cambridge University Press.

Wood, Jennifer and Clifford Shearing (2006) *Imagining Security*, London: Willan.

Wrong, Michela (2009) *It's Our Time to Eat: The Story of a Kenyan Whistleblower*, London: Harper Collins.

Yates, Douglas A. (1996) *The Rentier State in Africa: Oil Rent Dependency and Neo-Colonialism in the Republic of Gabon*, Trention, NJ: Africa World Press.

Yoshida, Naoko and Frank Leishman (2006) 'Japan', in Trevor Jones and Tim Newburn (eds.), *Plural Policing: A Comparative Perspective*, London and New York: Routledge, pp. 222–38.

Zedner, Lucia (2006) 'Policing before and after the Police: The Historical Antecedents of Contemporary Crime Control', *British Journal of Criminology*, 46 (1): 78–96.

Zureik, Elia and Mark B. Salter (eds.) (2005) *Global Surveillance and Policing: Borders, Security, Identity*, Cullompton: Willan.

Government documents

Government of Australia (2007) 'Fact Sheet 82: Immigration and Detention', Sydney: Department of Immigration and Citizenship.

(2009) 'Immigration Detention Statistic Summary', Sydney: Department of Immigration and Citizenship, 17 April.

Government of Israel (2004) *Economic Review of India: India Security Market*. Available online at www.moital.gov.il/NR/exeres/DE1DDFE9–4B91–46AD-A20E-18C642166454.htm (accessed 24 June 2010).

Government of Kenya (2003) *Economic Recovery Strategy for Wealth and Employment Creation, 2003–2007*, Nairobi: Government Printer.

(2003) Legal Notice No. 53: The Regulation of Wages (Protective Security Services) (Amendment) Order, Nairobi: Government Printer.

Government of Nigeria (1986) Private Guard Companies Act (1986), Cap 367. Laws of the Federal Republic of Nigeria, Abuja: Government Printing Office.

Government of Sierra Leone (2002) National Security and Central Intelligence Act, 2002. Supplement to the *Sierra Leone Gazette*, 132 (42), 4 July.

(2002) Sierra Rutile Agreement (Ratification) Act, 2002. Supplement to the *Sierra Leone Gazette*, 133 (5), 31 January.

Government of South Africa (1996) *National Crime Prevention Strategy*, Pretoria: Department of Safety and Security.

(1998) *White Paper on Safety and Security: In the Service of Safety, 1999–2004*, Pretoria: Department of Safety and Security.

(2001) *Private Security Industry Regulation Bill*, Cape Town: Government Printing Office.

(2002) *Provincial Government Western Cape: Strategic Plan 2003/04 to 2005/06*, Pretoria: Department of Community Safety.

Index

Printed in Great
Britain
by Amazon

31567985R00160